AUTOMATED TOOLS FOR
INFORMATION SYSTEMS DESIGN

IFIP WG 8.1 Working Conference on
Automated Tools for
Information Systems Design and Development
New Orleans, U.S.A., 26-28 January, 1982

organized by
IFIP WG 8.1, Design and Evaluation
of Information Systems

Programme Comittee
A. I. Wasserman *(Chairman)*, G. Bracchi, J. Bubenko Jr.,
S. Gutz, M. A. Jackson, W. Riddle,
H.-J. Schneider, D. C. P. Smith, A. Solvberg

NORTH-HOLLAND PUBLISHING COMPANY
AMSTERDAM ● NEW YORK ● OXFORD

AUTOMATED TOOLS FOR
INFORMATION SYSTEMS DESIGN

Proceedings of the IFIP WG 8.1 Working Conference on
Automated Tools for Information Systems Design and Development
New Orleans, U.S.A., 26-28 January, 1982

edited by

Hans-Jochen SCHNEIDER
Technical University of Berlin
Berlin, F.R.G.

and

Anthony I. WASSERMAN
University of California
San Francisco, U.S.A.

1982

NORTH-HOLLAND PUBLISHING COMPANY
AMSTERDAM • NEW YORK • OXFORD

ISBN: 0 444 86338 9

Published by:
NORTH-HOLLAND PUBLISHING COMPANY-AMSTERDAM ● NEW YORK ● OXFORD

Sole distributors for the U.S.A. and Canada:
ELSEVIER NORTH-HOLLAND, INC.
52 Vanderbilt Avenue
New York, N.Y. 10017

PRINTED IN THE NETHERLANDS

PREFACE

In 1975, the general assembly of IFIP (International Federation of Information Processing) initiated a new Technical Committee TC 8 with the name "Information Systems". In 1976, the Working Group WG 8.1 on "Design and Evaluation of Information Systems" started work and established the following scope and aims

Scope

The Scope of the Working Group is the development of approaches for the analysis, specification and evaluation of computer-assisted information systems.

Aims

The Aims of the Working Group are:

1) to identify concepts and to develop theories relevant to the design of information systems;

2) to develop methods and tools for applying these theories to the design process;

3) to develop methods for the specification of information needs within an enterprise, with emphasis on interface aspects;

4) to develop methodologies for evaluating proposals for information systems;

5) to develop methodologies for evaluating the operational effectiveness of information systems.

In Oxford in April 1979, WG 8.1 held his first working conference. The title of this conference was "Formal Models and Practical Tools for Information Systems Design".

In Budapest in September 1981, WG 8.1 organized together with WG 8.2 a joint working conference with the title "Evolutionary Information Systems".

In New Orleans in January 1982, WG 8.1 has organized its third working conference, titled "Automated Tools for Information System Design and Development". The aim was to address special research and development problems within the scope and aims of the Working Group WG 8.1.

The conference is concerned specifically with that branch of information systems which deals with the development of tools for analysis, system design and data design. Two further subject areas are addressed application development systems

integrated development environments.

These two subfields are especially of interest because users are now recognizing a need for tools which support the complete problem definition, solution and evaluation process.

The presented papers represent a significant contribution to the scope and aims of WG 8.1 as listed above. More than a hundred top-ranking professionals from more than 15 countries and from various groups such as industry, computer manufactures, research institutes and universities participated in the conference. Presentations were given by well-known experts from main organizations and universities in Europe and North-America.

The 3o paper submitted were reviewed by the Program Committee members

Chairman	A.I. Wasserman	U.S.A.
Members	G. Bracchi	Italy
	J. Bubenko, jr.	Sweden
	S. Gutz	U.S.A.
	M. Jackson	U.K.
	W. Riddle	U.S.A.
	H.-J. Schneider	FRG
	D.C.P. Smith	U.S.A.
	A. Sølvberg	Norway

who together, with the Organizing Committee Chairman S.B. Navathe, prepared the conference with the general chairmanchip of Peter Lockemann.

We are very indebted to the extensive and competent work of the referees, whose names are listed elsewhere in this volume. The help of a number of very well-known specialists provided the basis for the success of this conference. We would like to thank all of them very much for their contributions.

We hope that this book provides a challenge to the information system community and a stimulus to researchers, implementers and users.

January 1982

Hans-Jochen Schneider   Anthony Wasserman
Technische Universität Berlin   University of California,
                                      San Francisco

TABLE OF CONTENTS

* *not received in time to be included.*

The Programme Comittee gratefully acknowledges the assistance of the following referees:

P. Aanstad	B. Nagell
A. Albano	E.J. Neuhold
M.L. Brodie	B. Nilsson
J. Buxton	K. Rekdal
C.G. Davis	H.-J. Schek
E. Denert	D.T. Shewmake
A. DiLeva	R.A. Snowdon
R. Durchholz	B. Steinholtz
B. Dwyer	G. Stubel
R.S. Fenchel	D. Teichroew
J. Griese	H. Trauboth
S. Hagglund	L.L. Tripp
T. Halvorsen	G. Skylstad
A. Hansson	H. Wedekind
R.C. Houghton, Jr.	M. Weiser
W.E. Howden	J.R. White
C. Hulten	G. Wiederhold
R.B. Hunter	J. Wilander
F.F. Land	J. Wileden
E. Lindencrona-Ohlin	P. Zave
A.D. McGettrick	S. Zeldin
N. Martin	M. Zelkowitz
B.E. Meyer	S. Zilles
U. Montanari	

PROGRAMME COMMITTEE

A.I. Wasserman, Chairman

G. Bracchi	W. Riddle
J. Bubenko, Jr.	H.-J. Schneider
S. Gutz	D.C.P. Smith
M.A. Jackson	A. Sølvberg

Automated Tools for Information Systems Design
H.-J. Schneider and A.I. Wasserman (eds.)
North-Holland Publishing Company
© IFIP, 1982

AUTOMATED TOOLS IN THE INFORMATION
SYSTEM DEVELOPMENT ENVIRONMENT

Anthony I. Wasserman

Medical Information Science
University of California, San Francisco
San Francisco, CA 94143 USA

This paper describes the role of automated tools in an
information system development environment. Tools are seen
to be important in supporting system development
methodologies. However, it is also observed that present
tools capabilities are quite primitive and that a new
generation of software tools must be built to take advantage
of advances in hardware and database technology. The paper
concludes with a description of the characteristics that this
new generation of tools should exhibit, and identifies some
specific tools that are useful in the interactive information
system development environment.

An important consideration in the development of information systems is the
entire development environment. In its most general sense, the development
environment includes the technical methods, the management procedures, the
computing equipment, the mode of computer use (batch or interactive, centralized
or distributed), the automated tools to support development, and the physical
workspace. An ideal development environment should enhance the productivity of
the information system developers and provide a set of tools (both manual and
automated) that simplifies the process of software production. The environment
should contain facilities both for the individual member of a development group
and for the overall management of the project.

At the heart of the environment is a software development methodology, a
process for software production. Many organizations are presently working to
create their own methodologies that they can follow from the original concept of a
system through its specification, design, development, operation, and evolution
[1,2,3,4,5]. A methodology typically consists of a sequence of steps combining
management procedures, technical methods, and automated support to produce
information systems, as shown in Figure 1. For some organizations, the
methodology is well defined and well structured, with review procedures and
intermediate products prior to completion of the system; in other organizations,
the methodology is ill-defined and poorly structured.

In any event, though, it can be seen that technical methods, management
procedures, and automated support form the cornerstones of the information system
development methodology. Such a methodology includes technical methods to assist
in the critical tasks of problem solving, documentation, hierarchical
decomposition, design representation, coding, systematic testing, and software
configuration management. Such a methodology also includes management procedures
to control the process of development and the deployment of these technical
methods. The management and technical aspects of the methodology have a
synergistic relationship in that the technical methods provide the intermediate
results that are needed for effective managerial control, while the management
procedures serve to allocate technical resources and support the development

1

organization.

Finally, automated support exists for the purpose of enhancing the effectiveness of the developer, with technical needs serving to drive the development of new automated tools and the acquisition of new computer systems. Management procedures determine the nature of the automated support that is provided, both in terms of the computer system to be used and the languages and tools that comprise the software to be used in support of the system development effort.

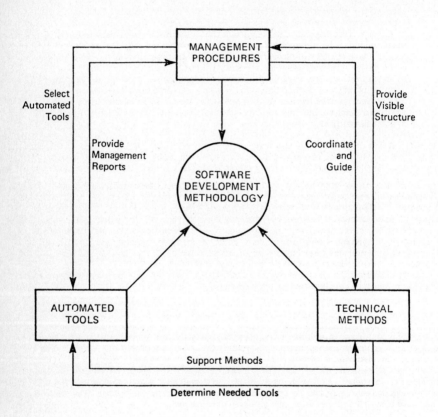

Figure 1 -- Components of a Software Development Methodology

Regardless of the item being produced or the details of the methodology, it is nevertheless possible to identify a number of desirable characteristics for an information system development methodology. These desirable characteristics include the following:

1) The methodology should cover the entire software development cycle. It does relatively little good to have a methodology for software design if there is no systematic procedure to produce the specification used for the design and/or the executable program that must be created from the design. Thus, a methodology must assist the developer at each of the stages of the development cycle.

2) The methodology should facilitate transitions between phases of the development cycle. When a developer is working on a particular phase of a project (other than requirements analysis), it is important to be able to refer to the previous phase and to trace one's work. At the design stage, for example, one must make certain that the architecture of the software system provides for all of the specified functions; one should be able to identify the software module(s) that fulfill each system requirement. During implementation, it should be easy to establish a correspondence between modules in the system design and program units, and between the logical data objects from the design stage and the physical data objects in the program. It is important to note that one must be able to proceed not only forward to the next phase of the life cycle, but also backward to a previous phase so that work can be checked and any necessary corrections can be made. This phased approach to software development makes it clear that information lost at a particular phase is generally lost forever, with an impact on the resulting system. For example, if an analyst fails to document a requirement, it will not appear in the specification. Eventually, during acceptance testing (or perhaps during system operation), that failure will be recognized and it will be necessary to make modifications to the system.

3) The methodology must support determination of system correctness throughout the development cycle. System correctness encompasses many issues, including not only the correspondence between the system and its specifications, but also the extent to which the system meets user needs. Accordingly, the methodology must not only be concerned with techniques for validation of the complete system, but also must give attention to obtaining the most complete and consistent description of user needs during the early stages of the project. For example, the methods used for analysis and specification of the system should aid problem understanding by the developers, the users, and other concerned parties, and make it possible to trace later system development back to the requirements and specification.

4) The methodology must support the software development organization. It must be possible to manage the developers and the developers must be able to work together. This requirement implies the need for effective communication among analysts, developers, and managers, with well-defined steps for making progress visible throughout the development activity. The intermediate products generated by the methods and tools, such as a detailed design or an acceptance test plan, can be reviewed by the organization so that progress can be effectively measured and so that quality can be assured.

5) The methodology must be repeatable for a large class of software projects. While it is clear that different methodologies will be needed for different classes of systems and for different organizational structures, an organization should be able to adopt a methodology that will be useful for a sizeable number of programs that they will build. Certainly, it makes little sense to develop a methodology for each new system to be built.

6) The methodology must be teachable. Even within a single organization, there will be a sizeable number of people who must use the methodology. These people include not only those who are there when the methodology is first adopted, but also those who join the organization at a later time. Each of these people must understand specific techniques that comprise the technical

aspects of the methodology, the organizational and managerial procedures that make it effective, automated tools that support the methodology, and the underlying motivations for the methodology. Since software engineering education is not yet very well advanced, much of the responsibility for teaching a methodology lies with the individual organization.

7) The methodology must be supported by automated tools that improve the productivity of both the individual developer and the development team. This collection of tools, and the way in which they are used, constitute what has been called a "programming environment," since most automated tools are aimed at the coding and implementation phases of software development. In considering the future nature of such tools, it is perhaps better to use the term "automated program development environment" or "automated development support system" (ADSS).

8) The methodology should support the eventual evolution of the system. Systems typically go through many versions during their lifetimes, which may last eight to ten years or more. New requirements arise from changes in technology, usage patterns, or user needs, and these changed or additional requirements must be reflected in a modified system. The development methodology can assist this evolutionary activity by providing accurate external and internal system documentation, and a well structured software system that is easily comprehended and modified by those making the system changes.

The information system development environment, then, which provides a framework for describing the way that software developers make use of a software development methodology, can be seen to be different for every organization, as it is dependent upon the individuals who comprise that organization. More importantly, it can be seen that the environment is affected by every change, no matter how minor, ranging from the use of new computer equipment to new hirings.

AUTOMATED DEVELOPMENT ENVIRONMENTS

The notion of an automated development environment, an integrated collection of computer-based tools that support software development, is subsumed within the notions of a software development methodology and a software development environment. This situation is as it should be, since automated tools do not normally exist as an end in themselves, but rather as a means to an end.

Even though much effort has been put into the design, development, enhancement, and evolution of tools, it should be remembered that the purpose of a tool is to support or facilitate some other activity. In some cases, the availability of a tool makes an activity practical where it might not have been in the absence of that tool. Hence, it is often the case that tools are developed in response to some perceived problem; it is rarely the case that one invents a tool and then searches for a practical application of the tool.

The inventor and developer of new and/or improved tools must have a solid understanding of the activities carried out by developers and must be able to produce tools that fit into these activities. While there has been considerable interest in concepts of "software development environments," it should be recalled that this automated support is merely part of a larger set of issues.

CHARACTERISTICS OF SOFTWARE TOOLS

With this understanding, it is possible to discuss automated support systems and to describe the features that tools within such an environment should possess. One key objective is to provide programmers with tools and techniques that can both improve the process of software production and the quality of the resulting software. Among the most common examples of such tools are text editors and compilers; file copying and printing routines are among the most common utilities.

At present, though, the state of the art of software tools leaves much to be desired. This is not to say that there are no good tools. Indeed, there are a number of sophisticated and effective tools [6,7] and there are several programming environments, notably Unix [8], INTERLISP [9], and Multics [10], that include a substantial number of such tools. Our point, though, is that there are few settings in which the tools actually work effectively in harmony with one another and in support of a software development methodology.

There are two extremely serious problems with most of these tools. First, they fail to support a software development methodology or to capture any data that assists in control of the software development process. There is a need for a qualitative improvement in tools to provide this critical missing dimension and to augment the power of the tools.

Second, present tools fail to support the software development life cycle in its entirety, primarily supporting coding activities. There is a need for more tools to assist with software specification, design, and testing, as well as with management of software projects. For example, there are tools that assist with problem specification, such as PSL/PSA [11], or detailed design, such as a program design language, but they address only a portion of the development process and must be incorporated into methodologies for software development. These points are discussed at greater length in [12].

In addition to these primary problems, there are a number of secondary problems with present tools, including the following:

(1) Lack of compatibility -- tools are difficult to combine with one another, both at the direct interface level and at the user level; some tools cannot even use the same data or file formats.

(2) Lack of uniformity -- the available set of tools differs among different machines, operating systems, and languages, making it difficulty for a programmer to move easily from one development environment to another.

(3) Lack of tailorability -- most tools are designed to be used in predetermined ways and cannot easily be customized to support different patterns of use by different developers.

Recently, there has been widespread recognition of these problems, with a resulting effort to develop better software tools [13,14]. One example of such an effort is the effort by the U.S. Department of Defense to specify needed tool capabilities to support the development of programs written in Ada [15]. Preliminary efforts are underway to develop tools that overcome some of these deficiencies, and to gather some evaluative data on the use of tools.

NEEDED TOOL CAPABILITIES AND PROPERTIES

In considering automated support for information system development methodologies, we must first consider the framework in which tools will operate, specifying their general properties, then proceed to identify tools that can be of assistance in the development process.

A future ADSS framework may be based on the introduction and unification of three new concepts within the development environment:

(1) The use of data bases in conjunction with tools to provide a "knowledge base" about programmers and their use of specific tools.

(2) The ability to capture information about program structures, design decisions, and the software process itself in real time.

(3) The utilization of sophisticated human interfaces for software development, perhaps based on "personal development systems" [12].

As the methodology for software development evolves, new tools will be introduced to support that methodology so that use of the associated tools will facilitate adoption of improved methods. The outcome of this process will be a whole spectrum of new software tools, based on the three concepts outlined above. While these tools will incorporate the essential properties of current tools, their character will change so that they will be compatible with each other in an integrated ADSS.

In particular, it will be necessary to make certain that new tools and the encompassing ADSS possess the following characteristics:

Singularity of Purpose. Each tool should carry out one and only one well defined function, or a small number of closely related functions.

Ease of Use. The user must not need elaborate knowledge in order to be able to use a tool. The features of a tool should be independent of one another, so that a user need not be aware of other features in order to use a specific feature.

Self-documenting. The user must not need to have voluminous hard-copy documentation within arm's reach in order to be able to use a tool. Although some compact hard-copy documentation should be available, most assistance would be provided to the user through structured HELP operations available interactively or through facilities that permit the user to make queries of an on-line reference document. Ideally, though, the tool should be human engineered so that its user interface is intuitive and it operates in such a way as to provide intelligent guidance through the use of the tool.

Consistency With Other Tools. Tools should interact with one another in a consistent way, typically by maintaining standard interfaces and communication protocols. Furthermore, tools within an environment should conform to a set of well-understood conventions so that a user familiar with tool x in that environment can easily become accustomed to another tool y. One of the maxims in the creation of the Unix environment is to "(e)xpect the output of every program to become the input to another, as yet unknown, program." [16].

Adaptability. Tools should be adaptable to specific user requirements. For example, they should operate in a variety of modes to support user classes such as "novice", "regular", and "expert". Different command formats, different capabilities, and different system messages may be associated with each user class. There should be an intuitive, smooth transition between these classes.

Similarly, tools should provide for a meaningful set of defaults that can be altered to satisfy the needs of individual users. In that way, each user can start with a generic tool, and can then adjust parameters and options to tailor it to his own mode of use.

Local Intelligence. Intelligence can be provided in the tool by designing it to collect useful information to be stored in a private database, perhaps using a general purpose database management system as a tool in that process. Such data may be captured automatically from the user and can be gained from a community of tool users to provide profiles of usage that could assist in the evolution of that tool and the development of new tools.

The database for an individual tool is private to that tool and under both the user's and the tool's control. In this way, it will be possible to provide powerful, useful, and personalized services, and to permit query requests for information stored in the database.

Support For The Software Life Cycle. Tools must be developed to provide support to cover the entire life cycle, from requirements analysis through testing and evolution over time. Tools must therefore provide not only technical support for a specific phase of the life cycle, but should also provide management assistance and should facilitate the transition from one phase of the life cycle to another (both forward and backward!).

Support For Management Of Software Development. Two kinds of management are essential: software configuration management and management of software development personnel. Software configuration management involves keeping track of the emerging product, possibly in multiple versions. An effective configuration management facility can be distributed across a set of tools to capture program structure, interface requirements, problem reports, and updates to source and object versions of programs.

Similarly, information about individual productivity and the amount of effort associated with various parts of a software project, organized either by project phase or by module, can be easily collected, usually in a manner that is largely invisible to the developer. Such information is particularly valuable in gaining a better understanding of the software development process itself, which can lead both to better techniques for estimating the effort required for new projects and to identification and development of improved software tools.

TOOLS FOR INFORMATION SYSTEM DEVELOPMENT

Examination of a number of tools, development environments, and proposed environments is useful in enumerating some specific tools that should be part of an information system development environment. These tools include the following:

Operating system level support. An operating system that provides access to shared resources, standard interfaces to I/O devices, and program linkage and loading facilities is basic to any information system development environment.

Data Base Management System. The data base management system can be used both by the tools in the development environment and by the information systems developed in the environment.

Language Processors. Compilers and/or interpreters, along with runtime support are needed for all of the programming languages that are to be used in the information system development environment.

Text editor. A text editor is essential for all of the documentation associated with the system development, as well as for the program code. Some programming environments may provide syntax-directed editors that are able to check program input for conformity to the syntax rules of the language.

Formatters. Formatting programs are useful both for documentation and for programs. Formatting programs support processing of tables, equations, and text, providing a means to produce documents for reproduction and/or phototypesetting. A "pretty printer" accepts program text as input and produces a reformatted program text as output, performing any needed indenting or line splitting to enhance the readability of the program text.

Static analyzer. A static analyzer is able to examine program text to determine whether there are any program variables that are used before they are assigned a value, any program variables that are assigned a value and never used, or any segments of "dead code," that cannot be reached through the program's control flow. Such a tool is valuable in uncovering errors and in improving program structures.

Dynamic analyzer. A dynamic analyzer is able to provide information about a program during its execution. One can obtain a snapshot giving the values of program variables, a trace that shows the program units that have been invoked, an analysis of the execution time spent in each program unit, or a count of the number of times that specific lines in the program have been executed. With a suitable graphics-based tool, one could observe the dynamic execution of a program seeing accesses to program units or data objects. All of this information is useful for uncovering errors and for tuning the system to enhance performance.

Similar dynamic analysis tools exist for database management systems, making it possible to count the number of I/O operations, the number of pages fetched, or the elapsed time for various database operations.

<u>Configuration management</u>. A configuration management tool may be used to keep track of the myriad documentation associated with an information system development project, including one or more versions of the source and object code. Such configuration management, as noted above, is an important aspect in controlling changes to the emerging information system.

<u>Logging tools</u>. Logging aids may be used for system auditing and as a way of determining the use of various programs in the information system environment. Logs may keep track of user access to the system and can assist in uncovering any security violations of the system.

This list is far from complete, since one could provide useful tools for specification, architectural design, detailed design, database design, program verification, project management, and library maintenance, but it is intended to be suggestive of the types of tools that can aid the developer in the effective production of high quality information systems. If such a collection of tools can be designed in a harmonious way, following the general framework for tools outlined above, then the automated development support system should have a signficant favorable impact on the development process.

CONCLUSION

Throughout history, we have seen that advances in tools have led to higher quality products, improved productivity of workers, and occasionally to social and cultural changes. We may expect the same thing to happen with tools for information system development, as newer, more sophisticated tools are built and as they are integrated into methodologies and environments for information system design and development.

The challenge of system development for the near future is to draw effectively upon the experience of the past and to develop more tools that embody the characteristics described in this paper. These tools must then be integrated with technical methods and management practices to create methodologies that can improve both the quality of information systems and the process of information system development.

These overall needs may be summarized in four goals:

(1) unify technical procedures with management practices covering the entire life cycle (development <u>and</u> evolution) to create an organized, engineering-like approach to information system construction and evolution;

(2) control the costs of development and evolution by enhancing developer productivity through improved automated tools integrated into ADSS's, improved management controls, and hardware support for individual developers;

(3) establish guidelines for measuring software quality from its original concepts through the entire life cycle;

(4) strike a balance between rigorous, phase-oriented development and the construction of prototype systems.

In these ways, it will become possible to achieve the goal of integrated software development environments.

ACKNOWLEDGEMENTS

Computing support for text preparation was provided by National Institutes of Health grant RR-1081 to the UCSF Computer Graphics Laboratory, Principal Investigator: Robert Langridge. The author gratefully acknowledges discussions with Peter Freeman of University of California, Irvine, and with Steven Gutz of Digital Equipment Corporation, that have helped to sharpen the ideas presented here.

REFERENCES

[1] M. Lundeberg, G. Goldkuhl, and A. Nilsson. Information Systems Development -- a Systematic Approach. Englewood Cliffs, NJ: Prentice-Hall, 1981.

[2] D. O'Neill, "The Management of Software Engineering -- Part II: Software Engineering Program," IBM Systems Journal, vol. 19, no. 4 (1980), pp. 421-431.

[3] A.I. Wasserman, "Information System Development Methodology," Journal of the American Society for Information Science, vol. 31, no. 1 (January, 1980), pp. 5-24.

[4] A.I. Wasserman, "Toward Integrated Software Development Environments," Scientia, vol. 115 (1980), pp. 663-684.

[5] E. Yourdon. Software Development Methodology. New York: Yourdon Press, 1982.

[6] E.F. Miller, Jr. (ed.). Tutorial: Automated Tools for Software Engineering. Los Alamitos, CA: IEEE Computer Society, 1979.

[7] B. Kernighan and P.J. Plauger. Software Tools in Pascal. Reading, MA: Addison-Wesley, 1981.

[8] B.W. Kernighan and J.R. Mashey, "The Unix Programming Environment," Computer, vol. 14, no. 4 (April, 1981), pp. 12-24.

[9] W. Teitelman and L. Masinter, "The INTERLISP Programming Environment," Computer, vol. 14, no. 4 (April, 1981), pp. 25-33.

[10] F.J. Corbato and C.T. Clingen, "A Managerial View of the Multics System Development," in Research Directions in Software Technology, ed. P. Wegner. Cambirdge, MA: The MIT Press, 1979, pp. 139-158.

[11] D. Teichroew and E.A. Hershey III, "PSL/PSA: a Computer-Aided Technique for Structured Documentation and Analysis of Information Processing Systems," IEEE Transactions on Software Engineering, vol. SE-3, no. 1 (January, 1977), pp. 41-48.

[12] S. Gutz, A.I. Wasserman, and M.J. Spier, "Personal Development Systems for the Professional Programmer," Computer, vol. 14, no. 4 (April, 1981), pp. 45-53.

[13] W.E. Riddle and R.E. Fairley (eds.). Software Development Tools. Heidelberg: Springer Verlag, 1980.

[14] H. Hünke (ed.). Software Engineering Environments. Amsterdam: North Holland, 1981.

[15] Advanced Research Projects Agency, "Requirements for Ada Programming Support Environments -- 'STONEMAN'", U.S. Department of Defense, Arlington, VA, 1980.

Automated Tools for Information Systems Design
H.-J. Schneider and A.I. Wasserman (eds.)
North-Holland Publishing Company
© IFIP, 1982

TOOLS FOR SUPPORTING STRUCTURED ANALYSIS

Norman M. Delisle
David E. Moniooay
Norman L. Kerth

Computer Research Laboratory
Tektronix, Inc.
Beaverton, Oregon

This paper describes a set of tools developed to support Structured Analysis (SA), a popular specification methodology used
during engineering and information systems development. It gives
a brief tutorial on SA, summarizes our analysis of how SA can be
automated, and describes the support tools that have been built.
These graphics-based tools are flexible, extendible and intelligent.
The paper closes with some observations of the impact that the
tools have on productivity at Tektronix.

1. INTRODUCTION

Today's rapid growth in the application of computers has put programmers in high demand.
In fact, the demand is much greater than the supply. When confronted with such a situation,
industry becomes interested in increasing the worker's productivity. One common technique
to increase productivity is to provide the worker with better tools.

This paper describes a set of software tools that aid programmers during the specification
phase of the software life cycle. These tools support the Structured Analysis methodology.
The objective of these tools is to increase productivity within Tektronix. The tools are
graphics-based and have a significant amount of intelligence, offering a distinct advantage
to the user over traditional pencil and paper approaches.

Structured Analysis (SA) has been used successfully at Tektronix for several years. Education for the methodology is available from a number of sources and the documentation is
very good [2] [3] [9]. Furthermore, SA uses graphics, which means that tools supporting it
can take advantage of the expertise Tektronix has in high-resolution graphics technology.

The most important advantage of SA is improved communications. SA provides a notation
for communication that is concise and easy to use. Therefore, as early as an idea can be
identified, it can be jotted down and communicated among the members of a group. In this
way, an analyst can get feedback early in the development of an idea. Because of improved
communication and early feedback, the number and severity of costly software specification
errors will be reduced.

Although the SA methodology is valuable, it has some inherent problems. When SA is
maintained with pencil and paper, changes to drawings become tedious and error-prone.
Checking for consistency and completeness between SA documents is not simple and gets
worse as the system being modeled gets bigger or the model becomes more detailed. These
difficulties reduce the productivity of software engineers and decrease the quality of their
work. Yet, software tools can solve many of these difficulties.

SA can be loosely described as a specification language that helps the analyst control redundancy, eliminate ambiguity, and assure completeness and consistency in a specification.

11

It offers a distinct advantage over English prose, but some automated support is still needed. Designers of other modern specification languages [8] [1] have recognized the need for automated tools to help detect inconsistencies, but until now, users of SA have not had such automated tools to address their needs.

Not only can inconsistencies be detected between SA documents, but for certain types of changes, it is possible for SA support tools to determine exactly what changes must be made to other parts of the SA to maintain consistency. We feel that this aspect of our work gives a significant advantage to the users of our SA tools.

The next section uses a simple example to introduce the basic concepts of Structured Analysis. Section 3 summarizes an analysis of what functions should be automated to support SA. Section 4 describes the SA support tools, and Section 5 gives some preliminary indications of the tool's effect on productivity.

2. AN OVERVIEW OF STRUCTURED ANALYSIS

SA is best used to clarify an understanding of a problem that is not well-defined. When using SA, the first step is to examine what information flows into and out of the system; the second is to determine what transformations are made on this information to change as it flows from input to output. As the inputs, outputs and transforms are studied, a model of the system is constructed. An important aspect of SA is that it is hierarchical in nature; as portions of the system that is being modeled are identified, they themselves can be modeled as distinct systems. This division of a single, large system into a hierarchy of smaller, more precisely defined systems, gets right to the heart of what analysis is all about: understanding a complex problem in terms of its components, eventually reaching components that are simple enough to be well understood.

SA uses three types of documents. First, there is a hierarchy of Data Flow Diagrams (DFDs), where each DFD describes a system that has distinct data flowing in and transformations on that data that eventually change it into the output data. Each transformation is detailed either with another DFD or with a Mini-spec. A Mini-spec, the second type of document, is a description of a problem that is simple enough to be stated in a restricted form of English called Structured English. The third type of document, the Data Dictionary (DD), is a collection of definitions of the data items used in the DFDs and Mini-specs. More information about SA can be found in DeMarco's book, "Structured Analysis and System Specifications" [2].

An Example Of SA

To illustrate the major aspects of SA, a portion of the specification of an automatic teller machine is presented. Figure 1 shows the top level DFD for the system. The circle represents a process, the arrow represents a data-flow and a file is represented by either a double or single horizontal bar. The process transforms the DFD's input data-flows into output data-flows. The file provides temporary storage for data.

Figure 2 lists the Data Dictionary for the system. Each data-flow and file name used in the specification of the Automatic Teller is defined in the Data Dictionary. The definition describes the components of the data item in terms of more primitive data items. The syntax used to define data is similar to BNF in that it uses iterations, '{ }', alternations, '[ ]', and lists of components joined by ' + '.

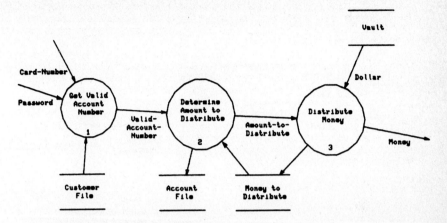

DFD 0 - Withdraw Money from Automatic Teller

Figure 1. Top Level DFD for the Automatic Teller Example

Account-File = {Account-Number + Balance-in-Account}
Account-Number = ID-number
Amount-to-Distribute = number-of-dollars
Amount-to-Withdraw = number-of-dollars
Balance-in-Account = number-of-dollars
Card-Number = ID-number
Customer-File = {Card-Number + Password + Account-Number}
Money = {dollar}
Money-to-Distribute = number-of-dollars
Password = ID-number
Valid-Account-Number = ID-number
Valid-Amount-to-Withdraw = number-of-dollars
Vault = {dollars}

Figure 2. Data Dictionary for Automatic Teller Example

Each of the processes on a DFD must be defined with either a Mini-spec or another DFD. Figure 3 describes the transformation of the second process in the Automatic Teller example. Two important points about the relation of these two DFDs should be made. First, the data that flows into and out of DFD 2 is the same data that flows into and out of the process that it describes. The second point concerns diagram numbering conventions. The second process on DFD 0 is labeled '2'. The descendant DFD retains this identification number and each process on it has the prefix '2.' added to its number.

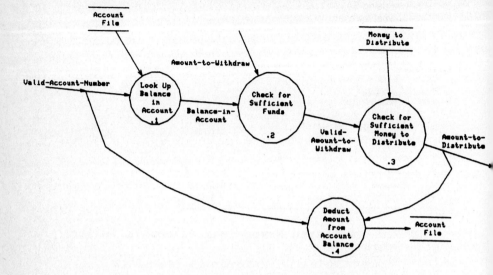

DFD 2 – Determine Amount to Distribute

Figure 3. Second Level DFD for the Automatic Teller Example

Figure 4 shows a Mini-spec for process 2.2. The Mini-spec is used to define a process when the process has been decomposed into primitive terms. There are no strict syntax rules for writing Mini-specs, but indentation is usually used to highlight logical constructions.

2.2 Policy To Check For Sufficient Funds

> *Check to see if the Amount-to-Withdraw is less than or equal to the Balance-in-Account.*
> *If Amount-to-Withdraw is less than or equal to the Balance-in-Account then:*
> > *Valid-Amount-to-Withdraw becomes the Amount-to-Withdraw otherwise:*
> > *Report an error.*

Figure 4. Sample Mini-spec for Automatic Teller Example

As SA is used, concentration is on what the data is and how it is transformed, not on why it flows. Questions about how the data flows and what triggers the flow of the data are control issues that are postponed until the design phase. This separation of concerns, understanding what the problem is before deciding how it will be solved, is another important aspect of SA.

3. AUTOMATING SA

Use of Structured Analysis in the Tektronix engineering environment was analyzed to determine what functions should be automated. SA itself was used to perform this analysis. The various benefits of using SA, and the experience and expertise gained provided a good understanding of what software tools are needed to support the SA methodology.

During the analysis of the use of SA, three functional areas were selected as candidates for automation. First, graphics and text editors could reduce the effort required to modify an SA document. Second, several types of errors that a computer could detect on an SA document were identified. Third, the possibility of automating the translation from SA to Structured Design was considered [7]. The following paragraphs describe this analysis of what tools can be effectively automated to support these three functional areas.

A DFD graphics editor can be effectively automated if careful consideration is given to graphics support. Automatic positioning of graphics elements in a DFD is not feasible because the positioning of these elements is critical to make the DFD easy to read and because there are no heuristics to determine what the relative positions of the DFD elements should be. Therefore, the user must manually position each element. Manual positioning is awkward if the user is required to type in graphics coordinates. So, some type of graphics pointing device should be used. The Data Dictionary and Mini-specs can be created and modified using any available text editor.

The DFD editor requires an interactive display such as a graphics terminal. Hard copy devices are also needed to review and mark up DFDs. Therefore, a support tool was needed that could produce graphics on both graphics terminals and hard copy devices.

When the evaluation functions were analyzed, it was decided that some functions should be automated and some should not. The computer can effectively check for errors that can be described with hard and fast rules, however, a human is more effective at detecting errors that require understanding the semantics of the SA document. For example, a computer can detect inconsistent use of a data flow among several hierarchically related DFDs. Humans are much better at determining whether or not a data flow is well named.

Since SA documents can be represented in a computer, an evaluate tool can detect inconsistencies among SA documents. However, detecting errors is not the most satisfying way to maintain consistency. Once a consistent set of SA documents is constructed, consistency will be violated only when one of the SA documents is modified. If the changes that are made to a DFD are monitored, some types of consistency errors can be avoided by automatically deriving changes to other SA documents effected by the changes to the DFD. Such a support tool works closely with the DFD editor to help a user maintain consistency rather than simply detecting inconsistency.

When the analysts have finished the specification, the next step is to design the system. Structured Design [10] is often used following Structured Analysis. The set of DFDs can be translated into preliminary structure charts[1]. An automated tool that performs this translation could interface with support tools for Structured Design. Since translating from SA to Structured Design requires human interaction, this process cannot be fully automated. The development of an effective, semi-automated translator is technically challenging, but considering the potential return on investment, it was decided to apply available resources to the other SA tools.

Summarizing, this analysis of the use of SA in an engineering environment determined that the SA tools should include the following capabilities: 1) modify and display SA documents, 2) check for errors in SA documents, and 3) help maintain the consistency of the SA documents.

4. THE SA SUPPORT TOOLS

The SA support tools are written in Modula-2 [11] and run under UNIX[2]V7. A Tektronix 4014

Terminal is used for interactive graphics. These simple tools can be used individually or in combinations. Users can tailor the SA support tools to accommodate their needs by using them in combinations with existing utility functions[3]. The guidelines listed below were followed to ensure that the tools could be tailored.

[1] Each tool performs a single, well defined function.

[2] All tool interfaces are simple.

[3] Tools make no assumptions about the source or origin of the data that is passed to them.

[4] The tools are organized in families, that is, the function of the tool is repeated for each SA document.

[5] All interfaces for a family of tools are consistent.

Besides being able to tailor these support tools, users are able to extend them by adding tools of their own. To simplify the definition of new support tools, abstract data types [4] have been defined for a DFD, a Mini-spec, and an entry in the Data Dictionary. The SA support tools use encapsulated functions to change information in or extract information from these abstract data types. Users do not have to be familiar with the details of data structures. Rather, they can use these encapsulated functions to build new tools.

The functions performed by each family of support tools are described as follows:

The **Edit** tool modifies an SA document interactively and derives change requests that help maintain the consistency of the SA documents.

The **Evaluate** tool detects errors in an SA document.

The **Format** tool converts the internal representation of an SA document into a form that is suitable for viewing.

The **Clean-up** tool helps maintain the consistency of the SA documents by validating and performing changes that were derived by the edit tools.

There are two edit tools: Edit DFD and Edit SA. Edit DFD is an interactive graphics editor that is used to create and modify a data flow diagram. A graphics pointing device, such as a mouse or thumbwheels, is used to specify the position of each item in the DFD. The second edit tool, Edit SA, is used to make modifications to the structure of the SA or to make changes whose effects are felt throughout the SA. Using Edit SA, a descendant DFD or Mini-spec can be connected to or disconnected from a parent process. This tool is also used to make changes throughout a portion of the SA, for example, when a data name is changed.

Each command that changes the SA or a DFD is analyzed by the Edit tool to derive changes that will help the user maintain consistency in the entire set of SA documents. Derived Change Requests are validated and performed by the Clean-up tool. Note that the Data Dictionary and Mini-specs are created and modified using any available text editor.

The Evaluate tools check for errors. There are four evaluate tools, one for each of the SA documents and one to evaluate the SA as a whole. These tools look for two types of errors. First, hard errors such as undefined data names or read-only files are detected. This type of error indicates a violation of the methodology rules. Second, soft errors are detected. These errors reflect the rules of thumb of the SA methodology such as the maximum number of processes that are allowed on a DFD. Usually, soft errors indicate that the problem the analyst is using SA to solve is not well understood.

Format tools transform the DFD, Mini-spec or Data Dictionary into a form that is suitable for viewing. The output of these tools is typically displayed on a graphics terminal. The DFD Format tool associates a graphics element with each item on the DFD; a circle for each process, an arrow for each data flow. This tool does not automatically position graphics elements. Rather, the user specifies the position of each graphics element via the Edit DFD tool. The DFD Format tool automatically positions text inside or next to its associated graphics element. For example, a process name and number are centered within the circle representing that process. The Mini-spec and Data Dictionary Format tools "pretty-print" the Mini-spec or Data Dictionary. The Data Dictionary Format tool also orders the data definitions, both alphabetically and hierarchically. Data names that are used within a definition can be listed in two or more places. First, the data definition appears in alphabetical order. Additional copies of the data definition are indented and placed immediately following the definitions where the data name has been referenced.

The Clean-up tool is used to maintain the consistency of the set of SA documents with respect to each other. Due to the relationships between SA documents, a change in one may affect another. For example, if a process is deleted from a DFD, the Clean-up tool deletes any DFDs or Mini-specs that are descendants of that process and deletes from the Data Dictionary any data names that are unique to that DFD or its descendants. The Edit tools derive these changes, but the Clean-up tool verifies that the change is actually needed to maintain consistency.

The SA support tools can be linked together in a variety of ways. The following paragraphs describe how the SA tools interact to perform a combined edit/clean-up/evaluate function.

Combining SA Support Tools

The SA support tools are designed to work together. The Edit DFD tool, the Clean-up tool and the Evaluate DFD tool can be used in combination to provide a more powerful edit function. This combination of tools not only modifies a DFD, but it checks for errors and it helps keep the rest of the SA consistent with the modified DFD. Each of the tools assumes responsibility for dealing with particular types of errors. Some errors are disallowed by the Edit DFD tool, some are prevented by the Clean-up tool, and some are reported to the user by the Evaluate DFD tool.

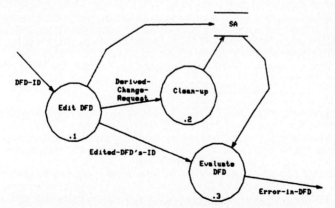

Edit/Clean-up/Evaluate Combination

The user edits a DFD interactively with the Edit DFD tool. As the editing session proceeds, the Edit DFD tool outputs Derived Change Requests, which are descriptions of changes made to this DFD that affect other parts of the SA. When the edit session is complete, the Clean-up tool reads through the Derived Change Requests and makes the changes to the SA that are needed to maintain its consistency. For example, if the label of a process is changed, the title of the descendant DFD or Mini-spec describing that process also must be changed. The Clean-up tool is responsible for making the change to the descendant's title.

Once the Clean-up tool has finished, the Evaluate DFD tool can begin. It evaluates the DFD and gives a report to the user about the errors it found. The Evaluate DFD tool looks for errors that the user must decide how to repair (since there is not enough information in the SA for the SA support tools to decide how to correct the error). For example, suppose there is a data flow shown going into a particular DFD, but there is no corresponding data flow going into the process that the DFD details. Since there are several possible ways to repair that data conservation error, the Evaluate DFD tool reports the error to the user.

The Clean-up tool works with another class of errors; those that can be repaired without question. For example, when a process number is changed, the numbers of the descendant DFDs and Mini-specs also must be changed. Changes made by the Clean-up tool correct inconsistencies in the SA that were caused when a DFD was edited. The Derived Change Requests describe changes that caused errors, and the Clean-up tool reads and processes these requests.

The Edit DFD tool maintains the validity of certain rules about DFDs. For example, each data flow must have an origin and a destination. A data flow cannot be entered unless both origin and destination are given, and if either should be deleted, the data flow is also deleted. These deletions and other changes affect the DFD that is being edited. Changes that affect the DFD that is being edited are made immediately; they are not passed to the Clean-up tool.

Extending The SA Tools

Suppose the SA Tools are being used on a large project, and a particular DFD is being reviewed. It would save time if the reviewers did not have to look through the many-page-long Data Dictionary for the whole system. They would prefer a Data Dictionary listing only the terms needed to review that particular DFD. A tool that would provide this specific information could be called "Extract DD".

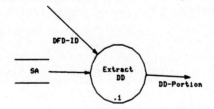

Extract DD

This Extract tool would retrieve the DFD of interest, get a list of terms that are used in it, extract those terms from the Data Dictionary (DD) and place the extracted definitions in DD-Portion. It might be included with other SA support tools as shown below.

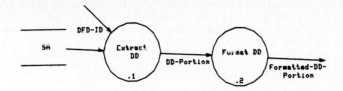

Extract/Format Combination

The simple interface to the Format DD tool makes it possible to determine what the Extract tool must output. The abstract data types for a DFD and for the Data Dictionary make it a straightforward task to extract the desired information. Adaptability of the SA tools has been an important consideration in their design and implementation.

5. MEASURING THE EFFECTIVENESS OF SA SUPPORT TOOLS

The purpose of the SA support tools is to increase the software engineer's productivity. But, measuring how well the use of these tools has achieved this purpose is quite difficult. The impact of using the SA methodology must be separated from the impact of using the support tools.

Since SA support tools are new to Tektronix, not enough data is available to develop a convincing argument about their effectiveness. One informal observation suggests an increase in productivity. Before the SA support tools were available, the major bottleneck of a project using SA was the drawing and redrawing of DFDs. When SA support tools were used, the bottleneck became the time it takes to review the documents.

Other observations, also quite informal, suggest that SA support tools could be counterproductive. When the drawings are given to a reviewer, there is a tendency to think that since they look nice, they must be correct, so not enough attention is given to details that might otherwise be addressed. This tendency is compounded by knowing that the tools do some evaluations themselves. "The computer has already checked these diagrams," a reviewer might say. "What errors are left for me to find?" The answer is an implied, "of course there are none," which is far from correct.

Despite these potential short comings the SA support tools should have a positive impact on software development at Tektronix.

6. CONCLUSION

Structured Analysis has been used successfully at Tektronix for several years. But, analysts using SA have been hampered by tedious and error-prone tasks that could be automated. The SA support tools address this problem by automating some of the SA process. In particular they assist in the creation and modification of SA documents, the evaluation of these documents and help the analyst keep the documents consistent.

The basic functions for supporting SA have been realized in a set of simple tools. Users can extend the capabilities of these support tools by using them in combination with existing utility functions or by building new tools.

Four types of tools have been developed: Edit and Clean-up tools are used to modify SA documents; Evaluate tools are used to check for errors; and Format tools are used to display SA documents. Since Evaluate tools know about the rules of SA, they can detect errors in the use of the SA methodology. The Clean-up tool knows the relationships among the SA documents, so it can help maintain the consistency of the entire set of SA documents.

We believe that these tools will significantly increase productivity in a wide variety of engineering and information systems developmental environments.

FOOTNOTES

[1] See Chapters 9 and 10 of The Practical Guide to Structured Systems Design [5] for a discussion of the manual methods for translating from SA to Structured Design.

[2] UNIX is a Trademark of Bell Laboratories

[3] The UNIX [6] environment provides many utilities that have been found useful. Shell scripts provide an easy way to specify the connections between tools.

REFERENCES

[1] Davis, C. G. and Vick, C. R., The Software Development System, IEEE Trans. on Software Engineering SE-3 (Jan. 1977) 69-84.

[2] DeMarco, T., Structured Analysis and System Specification (Yourdon Inc., New York, 1978).

[3] Gane, C. and Sarson, T., Structured Systems Analysis: tools and techniques (Improved Systems Technology Inc., New York, 1977).

[4] Liskov, B. H. and Zilles, S. N., Programming with Abstract Data Types, Proc. ACM SIGPLAN Symp. on Very High Level Languages, SIGPLAN Notices (ACM) 9, 4 (April 1974) 50-59.

[5] Page-Jones, M., The Practical Guide to Structured Systems Design (Yourdon Press, New York, 1980).

[6] Ritchie, D. M. and Thompson, K., The UNIX Time-Sharing System, Comm. ACM 17, No. 7 (July 1974) 365-375.

[7] Stevens, W. P., Meyers, G. J. and Constantine, L. L., Structured Design, IBM Systems Journal Vol. 13, No. 2 (May 1974) 115-139.

[8] Teichroew, D. and Hershey, E. A., PSL/PSA: A Computer Aided Technique for Structured Documentation and Analysis of Information Processing, IEEE Trans, on Software Engineering SE-3 (Jan. 1977) 41-48.

[9] Weinberg, V., Structured Analysis, (Yourdon Press, New York, 1978).

[10] Willis, P. R. and Jensen, E. P., Computer Aided Design of Software Systems, Proc. of the Fourth International Conference on Software Engineering, Sept. 1979, 116-125.

[11] Wirth, N., Modula-2, Institut fur Informatik, ETH Report 36 (1980).

Automated Tools for Information Systems Design
H.-J. Schneider and A.I. Wasserman (eds.)
North-Holland Publishing Company

IMT - AN INFORMATION MODELLING TOOL

Bengt Lundberg

SYSLAB[*]
Chalmers University of Technology
S-41296, Göteborg, Sweden

An information modelling tool (IMT) is presented. IMT is a tool
for development of information models, which are expressed in the
language of first-order predicate logic. IMT includes such facilities as a consistency tester of theories (informations models) and
satisfiability tester of a theory in the model- theoretical approach for semantics of theories. Besides the IMT also a framework
for information modelling with IMT is presented, including examples and discussion of the principles in using IMT

INTRODUCTION

Problems concerning representation of knowledge about some area of interest, e g
an organization, have been the object of research in artificial intelligence, information modelling and symbolic logic. Though the problems are similar, the three
research areas have focused on different issues. In artificial intelligence, a major area of interest has been deductive support in knowledge representation systems; in symbolic logic, researchers have mainly focused on the properties and semantics of languages for knowledge representation; and in information modelling, a
lot of work has been reported on the development of concepts and constructs for the
representation of, primarily, abstract knowledge. The aim of our current research
is to obtain a synthesis of results in these three areas.

In this paper we will present a framework for information modelling (representation
of abstract knowledge) and a computer based tool (IMT) for design of information
models within that framework. In our approach, an information model constitutes a
first-order theory, which is interpreted according to the model-theoretical approach [3]. From artificial intelligence we have employed the resolution principle,
e g [1], in order to check the consistency of an obtained information model (in
fact, a weaker result is obtained). Further, a technique is employed to check that
an information model is satisfied in a defined model, which is assumed to be a model of the area of interest. This approach has the advantage that an information
model not only can be shown to be consistent, i e it has a model, but also that the
information model is satisfied in the defined model.

The concepts which are employed in our approach conform, in principle, to the concepts of several information modelling approaches e g [2, 4]. However, we have restricted the set of concepts to a minimum, e g in the area of interest (the object
system) we only identify objects and associations between objects. Thus, aggregate
concepts such as generalizations and aggregations are not employed.

---

* This work is supported by the National Swedish Board for Technical Development.

2. A FRAMEWORK FOR INFORMATION MODELLING

In this section a framework for information modelling is presented, which is appropriate in using IMT for information modelling. Assume somebody, here called the observer, is going to create a model of some part of the "real world". The part of "real world" considered is called the object system. The observer is then assumed to make a classification of perceived phenomena of the object system. The perceived phenomena are called objects and associations.

An object, of the object system, is an abstract or physical phenomenon that the observer considers has an existence of its own. An association, of the object system, is constituted by objects that the observer considers be associated in some way.

In describing the object system the observer creates a model world that contains a set of assertions, each representing an association. The objects of the object system in the model world are referred to by names. This can be described as follows:

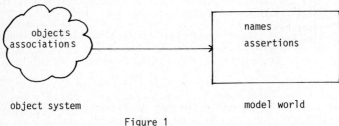

object system   model world

Figure 1

Examples of names are "John" and "Mary" which refer to objects, of the object system, which are usually called "John" and "Mary". These are examples of names refering to physical phenomena. An abstract phenomena may be referred to by "10" and "AC123" which are here intended to refer to the number "10" and "the marriage with registration number AC123".

Examples of assertions are:
     "John is a person"
     "John is married to Mary"
     "John is husband and Mary is wife of marriage AC123"

In the last example the observer has considered the marriage to be an object, which is associated with the persons involved.
Assertions will be represented as follows:

     P<John>   M<John,Mary>   N<John,Mary,AC123>

Thus, the assertions are represented as labelled tuples in which the names constitute the values and the label gives the semantics of the tuple.

The set of names will be referred to as the universe (of the model world). Depending on the object system the universe may include an infinite set of names, e g if real numbers are considered, and thus may even be uncountable. The same condition holds for assertions.

Having obtained a model world it is possible to make generalized assertions about it. An exemple of a generalized assertion is:

"A marriage is constituted by two persons" or, with a direct correspondence to the
model world above, "the names of an N-assertion are names that refer to two person
and a marriage, respectively".

An example:
Consider the following model world:

        E<John>   S<10>   SAL<John,10>
         <Jim>   <20>   <Jim,20>
         <Mary>   <Mary,10>

Here we assume that the meaning of the labels are (cf section 3):

        E = <x>;   x is an employee
        S = <x>;   x is a salary
        SAL = <x,y>; y is the salary of x

The generalized assertions are then, e g :

        "every employee has a salary"
        "a salary assertion is defined over an employee and a salary"
        "every employee who has a salary has only one salary"

The set of generalized assertions about a model world (and thus indirectly about
an object system) is called an information model. Thus, the generalized assertions
state the conditions holding in the model world (and in the object system). An
other point of view may be taken: one may consider the object system to be "controlled" by a set of rules, which are explicitly or implicitly stated. Having made
the rules explicit these can be considered to constitute an information model,when
expressed in the language of the information model.

The principles of the ideas presented so far can be illustrated as follows:

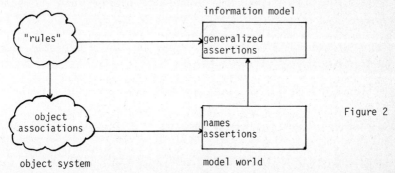

Figure 2

It is not a trivial task to create a model world, in particular if the universe is
infinite. However, in most cases a finite representative model world can be created and this will be useful in the construction of the corresponding information
model. This will be further elaborated in a later section.

In this section we have used a natural language as the language for information
models. This is not appropriate as, primarily, the semantics of such expression
is usually not well established and further we usually want to make operations on
information models, such as transformations. So, the next problem is to choose an
appropriate language for information models. Our approach is to use the language
of first-order predicate logic. Such an approach has several advantages, namely:

        - great expressive power
        - well-defined semantics
        - proof theory
        - criteria for consistency and completeness
        - established relationship between proof theory and semantics
          (soundness theorem).

3. SOME RESULTS FROM PREDICATE LOGIC

In this section we will introduce some concepts of predicate logic in order to have a theoretical basis for the presentation of IMT. The presentation is quite short and in particular the language of first order predicate logic is assumed to be well-known to the reader. A complete introduction to predicate logic can be found in any basic text book on symbolic logic, e g [3].

A first-order language is defined on a set of non-logical symbols, i e predicate symbols and individual constants, besides the logical symbols, e g $\forall$ ("for all"), - ("not"), -> ("implies"), and variables. (Note that we have omitted function symbols from the language; this will be explained later).

The permitted expressions in a first-order language (well-formed formulae) are of the type:

$\forall x(A(x) \rightarrow \exists y(S(x,y)))$

An expression such as this is called a sentence if every variable is associated with a quantifier ($\forall$ or $\exists$). Sentences are the only type of formula we will employ in this paper.

Given a first-order language a (first-order) theory is defined as:

- a set of logical axioms
- a set of inference rules
- a set of non-logical axioms

A specific language is characterized by the set of non-logical symbols employed and a specific theory is characterized by the set of non-logical axioms. The logical symbols, the logical axioms and the inference rules are invariant between theories.

Given a language, in which a theory is expressed, its semantics is given by a structure (U), which is a function whose domain is a set of parameters such that:

1. The structure assigns to the quantifiers
a non-empty set of objects (over which the quantifiers vary).

2. The structure assigns to the n-ary predicate symbols a relation $R \subseteq |U|^n$

3. The structure assigns to the individual constants an object of U .

We will here not formally define the semantics of a language, merely present an example which explain the principles and gives a basis for what follows.

Assume we have a first-order language with the predicate symbol LT. Let the following formula be the only non-logical axiom of a theory in that language:

$\exists x \forall y (- LT(y,x))$

For this language we define a structure:

U = the set of natural numbers
LT = $\langle x,y \rangle$; x is less than y

The structure is here given intensionally. An extensional representation is, e g:

$U = \{0,1,2,3,4,5,6,,,,\}$

LT $= \{\langle 0,1 \rangle, \langle 0,2 \rangle,,,\langle 1,2 \rangle, \langle 1,3 \rangle,,,, \}$

We can now translate the sentence, at the intensional level, to:

"There exists a natural number such that no natural number is smaller than it". As this statement is true according to the ordinary usage of natural numbers, we say that the sentence is true in the structure, or that the structure is a model of the theory, or that the sentence is satisfied in the structure.

In principle we can also formally check the satisfiability of the sentence in the structure (disregarding the infinite universe). This can be done by substituting for x and y, in $-LT(y,x)$, the components x_i and y_i of every binary tuple $\langle x_i,y_i \rangle$ in U i e $U = \{\langle 0,0 \rangle, \langle 0,1 \rangle, \langle 1,1 \rangle ,,,,, \}$. If we then find that there exists at least one x_i such that for every y_i, y_i is not smaller than x_i, then the sentence is true in the structure. (This holds for $x = 0$).

In a practical case, e g by the use of a computer, this satisfiability check can only be performed when the universe is finite. For the example above, consider a finite subset of the natural numbers, say $0,1,2$ and 3, as the universe. Then we have to explicitly represent the relation LT in such a way that we consider it representative, over the finite universe, for the (intended) structure.

In the following we will shortly review some definition and results from predicate logic which are of importance to this paper.

Consider a first-order theory defined over the set E of non-logical axioms. For E there then exist several models. A sentence e is said to be a logical consequence of E if e is true in every model of E. This is usually written

$$E \models e$$

Given the set E of non-logical axioms a sentence e may be deducible by the application of the inference rules to E, this is written

$$E \vdash e$$

If e is deducible from E then e is also logical consequence of E (the soundness theorem), i e

$$E \vdash e \Rightarrow E \models e$$

The reverse does not, however, hold in general.

A set E of sentences is said to be consistent if it does not hold that

$$E \vdash e \quad \text{and} \quad E \vdash -e$$

for any e.

A set E of sentences is said to be complete if it is consistent and for every sentence e of the actual language either

$$E \vdash e \quad \text{or} \quad E \vdash -e \quad \text{hold.}$$

This is the same as to say that a set of sentences is complete for a model if every sentence that is true in the model, is in that set, or is deducible from it.

Assume a set E of formulae which is consistent. If it does not hold that $E \vdash -e$ then $E \cup e$ is consistent.

A set E of sentences is consistent if and only if it has a model.

An important class of theories are theories with equality, i e which include the predicate symbol "EQ". This implies that a binary relation is assumed in their structures, the identity relation, which is defined as:

$$EQ = \langle x,y \rangle; \quad x \text{ is identical with } y.$$

For a theory with equality function symbols (and individual constants) may be omitted. This is the reason for us not to include function symbols in our languages.

In the presentation above of the concept of structure, we have defined a structure for a language, and a theory. The reverse process is, however, more interesting from an information modelling point of view.

Consider an area of interest and describe it by a structure, i e define its universe and its relations. Then a language is defined for the structure, i e a predicate symbol is assigned to each of the relations and, possibly, a set of individual constants are employed. Sentences in the obtained language that are true in the structure, then constitute the non-logical axioms of a theory for the structure.

In order to conclude this section, let us relate the concepts introduced in this section of section 2.

```
Concepts of              Concepts of
predicate logic          section 2
----------------         ----------------------
structure                model world
object                   name
relation                 assertions (with the same label)
tuple                    assertion
predicate symbol         label (approx)
non-logical axiom        generalized assertion
set of non-logical       information model
axioms
```

4. DESCRIPTION OF IMT

In this section we will present the IMT. The presentation will include the principles of IMT, with reference to section 3, and the users facilities. Implementational aspects will not be covered, except that we want to inform the reader that IMT is implemented in SIMULA. Strategies in using IMT will be described in section 5. The structure of IMT is as follows:

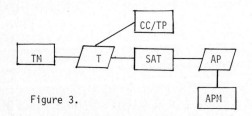

Figure 3.

```
TM          (stored) theory manager
T           (stored) theory
CC/TP       consistency checker/theorem prover
SAT         satisfiability checker
AP          assertion pool
APM         assertion pool manager
```

The TM is primarily a function for insertion/deletion of sentences to/from the stored theory. Other facilities are: list of sentences, dump/load of stored theory.

The T is the storage area of formulae, i e the non-logical axioms of a (first-order) theory. Thus, the logical axioms, including equality axioms, are not explicitly stored.

The CC/TP is a module for checking the consistency of a stored theory (CC), or to check if a formula is deducible from the stored theory (TP). In principle the two functions are reduced to one as the checking of the consistency of E ∪ e of sentences is the same as showing that E ⊢ -e does not hold. The principle of CC/TP is linear resolution with paramodulation [1]. In making the resolutions the inconsistency of a set F of sentences is looked for. If E is inconsistent, this will eventually be found, possibly after a finite set of resolutions. As we can not let a computer go for ever, then we might not find an inconsistency even if the set of sentences is inconsistent. Thus, the results of the consistency checking are:

- the set E is inconsistent
- the set E is not found to be inconsistent

This is a rather week result, but it is better than not knowing anything at all about a stored theory.

The AP is in principle a relational data base. The relations of AP contain assertions (labelled tuples) with the same label and they correspond to the predicate symbols of the stored theory.

The APM corresponds to a relational data base management system and include functions as: insertion/deletion of assertions (tuples) to/from relations, list of relations and dump/load of AP to/from an external device.

The SAT can be invoked to check the satisfiability of a stored theory in the actual AP. The SAT operates under the assumption that every predicate symbol has a corresponding relation in AP and that the universe of the structure (i e AP) is constituted by the names appearing in AP. Thus, only finite universes are considered. This is not very restrictive as we assume that an actual AP is a representative finite instance of the intended structure.

5. STRATEGIES IN USING IMT.

5.1 Introduction

In section 2 we have presented a framework for information modelling, which was illustrated as follows:

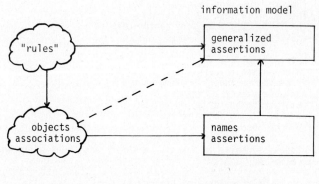

Figure 4.

We have assumed that an object system is considered and a model world is created and then from the latter the generalized assertions of the information model are intuitively deduced.

Most reports on information modelling do not make the model world explicit, nor even introduce a concept similar to that of model world; i e the information model is created directly from observations of the object system. Even if this approach is assumed the IMT can be used in designing information models in the language of first-order predicate logic. This approach is illustrated by the dotted line in the figure above.

In the following subsections we present strategies for information modelling with IMT. In section 5.2 the "direct" approach is considered and then in section 5.3 the "two step" procedure of section 2 is considered with reference to section 3.

5.2 The "direct"approach

In observing the object system the observer is assumed to intuitively deduce sentences in a first-order language. These sentences are then considered by the observer to be satisfied in the object system, and thus in an imagined model world. We say "intuitively deduce" as there is no explicit object system, i e a model world, in which the satisfiability can be checked. The usage of IMT in designing information models may be a support to detect errors to some extent, e g due to mistakes or erroneous perception of the object system that make the information model inconsistent.

After having arrived at a set E of sentences, which are stored in T, the consistency checker may be invoked. Let us assume that E is consistent in a strict sense.

In adding a sentence e to the stored theory, E, three cases may appear:

1. $E \models e$ As e can be deduced this sentence
               is redundant and it is not necessary
               to add it to the stored theory.
               This test is made by the TP-function
               of CC/TP in IMT.

2. $E \models \neg e$ If the sentence e is added to the
               theory this will become inconsistent.
               Thus, e must not be added to the
               theory. This test is performed with
               the TP-function, or more easily with
               the CC-function on $E \cup e$.

3. Neither $E \models e$ nor $E \models \neg e$.
               In this case the sentence e has to be
               added to the theory, giving $E \cup e$.
               As the sentence is assumed by the
               observer to be satisfied in the
               object system, it is relevant
               for the theory.

This process of adding formulae to the stored theory has to be performed iteratively. Then some problems may appear:

A.   Subsequent extended theories are obtained as formulae and added, e g. E_i is
     obtained after e_i is added. As we said before, we can only show that $^1 E_i$
     is not found to be inconsistent. Then after having added e_j ,
     $j > i$; E_j may be found to be inconsistent. This, however, does not imply that

e_j is an erroneous formula it, maybe, only works as a catalyst making it possible to find an inconsistency within the allocated number of resolutions. The problem is then to find the formula which is not satisfied by the object system. A trivial solution is to isolate subsets of the theory in order to check them for inconsistency and then intuitively inspect them for non-satis-fiability.

B. From symbolic logic we know that a theory has a model if, and only if, it is consistent, but it is not possible to point out the model as such. Assume that we have arrived at a consistent theory E, i e consistent in the strict sense, then E also has a model, say O_1 , and the object system under con- sideration is O_2. This does not imply that O_2 is a model of E. Such a problem may appear as the sentences of E are difficult to interpret intui- tively. This problem can easily be overcome if an explicit model is availab- le and a satisfiability check is performed on the theory.

C. As information models usually are intended as a basis for derivation of data base schemas, another problem may appear, which is similar to the one above.

A stored theory usually has several models, e g models with different univer- ses. Such models are said to be "elementary equivalent" as the difference between the models can not be concluded from the non-logical axioms of the theory. Further, an information model which is intended for data base appli- cations must also be satisfied by models which have principal differences, e g a relation may be empty. Consider the following example:

Assume the following sentences constitute a stored theory

$\forall x \; \exists y \; (EMP(x) \rightarrow SAL(x,y))$

$\forall x \; \forall y \; (SAL(x,y) \rightarrow SHAREHOLDER \; (x))$

$\forall x \;\;\; (EMP(x) \rightarrow SHAREHOLDER \; (x))$

with the semantics:

$EMP = \langle x \rangle;$ x is an employee
$SAL = \langle x,y \rangle;$ x earns y
$SHAREHOLDER = \langle x \rangle;$ x is shareholder

From knowledge about an imagined application one should intuitively conclude that this theory is inconsistent. This, is not the case as the theory has a model, e g the model in which the EMP-relation is empty. If we add the sen- tence $\exists x(EMP(x))$ then the "new" theory will be inconsistent and some of the sentences have to be changed. However, if the added sentence is included in the theory the information model is not directly appropriate as a data base schema as the EMP-relation is not allowed to be empty, which it certainly will be when the data base is initialized.

Thus, in the example we detected an error as the "existential" sentence was added. This principle may be helpful in detecting inconsistencies, but on the other hand, it decreases the set of models for a theory.

5.3 The "two step" (model world) approach.

The idea behind the model world approach is that the observer creates an explicit model world in AP, and then inserts formulae into the stored theory. For every ad- ded formula the SAT-function is executed. If the theory is not satisfied this imp- lies that the last formula is not satisfied and thus has to be changed. Having obtained a satisfiable theory this is also consistent in the strict sense, and further the information model is satisfied by the model world, which is a model of the intended object system. This scheme, however, will allow a redundant stored theory, a case which is easily circumvented by the following procedure:

```
- add a sentence  e  to the theory  E
- if  e  is satisfiable (see above) then
     check if  E |- e,  if so then  e  is
                    certainly redundant
  if  e  is not satisfiable then
          e  has to be excluded from
          the theory
```

The problems of this approach are mainly outside the formalized part of the design of an information model.

A.   The first problem is due to the construction of the model world. The model world must be finite and representative. This has to do with the perception of the object system by the observer and the inclusion of all relevant aspects of the object system in the model world, e g variations of assertions, will be difficult.

B.   The obtained theory of a model world should be as complete as possible, i e include as many as possible true sentences. The incompleteness of a theory is due to the difficulty of identifying formulae for the model world. In some cases this can be done more or less automatically, e g by generating sentences that correspond to the concept of functional dependency of the relational data model.

C.   We pointed out in section 5.2 that a theory usually has to be satisfied by several models, among them the empty model world (possibly with a (dummy) individual, as the universe must be a non-empty set). Thus, during the design of an information model this has to be checked for satisfiability in several model worlds each being representative of the (unrestricted) model.

6.   CONCLUSIONS.

This paper has presented an approach for information modelling, which has a firm theoretical basis as it employs results from predicate logic. A tool for information modelling within the presented framework, IMT, is presented together with strategies for its use in information modelling.

The advantages of the approach besides the theoretical framework are:

-    the expressive power of the language used
-    a consistency criterion can be introduced to information modelling
-    the semantics of the information models developed has a formal definition
-    an information model can be shown to be consistent and also to be satisfied by the intended object system, i e the model world.

REFERENCES:

[1] Chang, C.L., Lee, R.C., Symbolic logic and mechanical theorem proving, Academic Press, 1973.

[2] Pirotte, A., The entity-property-association model: An information oriented data base model, ACM Int Comp Symp, 1977.

[3] Schoenfield, J.R., Mathematical logic, Addison-Wesley, 1967.

[4] Smith, D., Smith, J.M., Conceptual Data Base Design, Infotech, 1979.

Automated Tools for Information Systems Design
H.-J. Schneider and A.I. Wasserman (eds.)
North-Holland Publishing Company
© IFIP, 1982

A Data Model for Programming Support Environments

and its Application

Walter Γ. Tichy

Department of Computer Sciences
Purdue University
West Lafayette, Indiana 47907

A critical issue in programming support environments is the data base that stores
all project information. This paper presents a model that can be used for analyzing and designing such data bases. The model represents systems as families
consisting of multiple versions and configurations. It is based on AND/OR graphs
and has the *hierarchical model*, the *relational model*, and the *sequential release
model* as subclasses.

A refinement of the model yields the concept of the *well-formed configuration*.
This concept establishes the basic rules for interface control and system composition. A generalization of the model leads to a data base structure that is a
directed, attributed graph. This idea is illustrated by presenting design and
implementation of a data base for the sequential release model.

1. Introduction

Programming support environments (PSE's) have recently been stressed as an approach to
improve programmer productivity and software quality [1, 2, 3, 4, 5]. A PSE provides a rich set of
sophisticated tools that support or automate various tasks during software development and
maintenance. The tools operate on a common data structure, namely the data base that stores
all information associated with a project. As in all software designs, the selection of an adequate data structure is crucial for a successful PSE. The design of that data structure is the
subject of this paper.

An important observation for PSE data bases is that all large software products evolve into
families of related versions and configurations. The existence of system families has long been
acknowledged by Parnas and others [6, 7, 8, 9], yet all current programming language designs
and most existing PSE's still ignore or skirt the issue. A few examples of system families are in
order.

The most common situation when multiple versions arise is during program maintenance. In
order to correct or enhance a software system, a subset of the modules must be modified. Normally this takes more than one iteration, resulting in several revisions per affected module. Some
sequences of modifications turn out to lead into the wrong direction, making it necessary to back
up to an earlier point. If one did not store the intermediate revisions, programmers have to
"undo" the changes they made since the backup point, or "redo" some changes to regain the
backup point from the initial revision. Both processes can be extremely difficult and time consuming.

Now suppose that the maintenance project is finished, resulting in a new system version. At this point one can usually discard the intermediate revisions that lead from the initial to the new revision. The initial revision, however, can often not be thrown away if a large user community depends on it. Thus, a system's administrator is forced to maintain "obsolete" versions [10].

The porting of programs to different environments is another cause for multiple versions. Compilers are typically ported to different environments, resulting in large families. Consider, for instance, Pascal [11] and C [12], which are available on a wide range of architectures. The same is now possible with some operating systems: Versions of UNIX [1] and Thoth [13] run on significantly different machines. The portability of programs is also a major goal of the Ada language and support efforts [3]. However, it is naive to assume that a program will execute correctly in every environment as long as it is written in a portable language. In reality, all kinds of minor and major changes are necessary, causing a single system to branch out into many parallel versions.

Enhancement and customization are additional, powerful forces that cause new versions to arise almost spontaneously. Users always apply a successful system in unexpected ways or unforeseen situations. Invariably, this requires improvements, bells and whistles to be added. Soon the system starts evolving away from its original characteristics, new errors creep in, and so the modification cycle goes on.

The naive approach to the problems of multiple versions is to eliminate them altogether. Unfortunately, this is not a viable approach. System families arise in response to widely differing demands. We shall never be able to write the all-encompassing compiler, operating system, telecommunications system, etc., that will adequately serve all user communities. On the other hand, the ad hoc approach of constructing a new, unique program for every user group is too costly. *We need to economize by building system families whose members share common parts.* In other words, we need to learn how to deal effectively with system families.

In Section 2 we present a model that has been designed specifically for multi-version programmed systems. This model leads to the concept of the well-formed configuration. Subclasses of the model are discussed in Section 3. Section 4 describes design and implementation of a small, multi-version PSE data base.

2. The AND/OR Graph Model for Families of Programmed Systems

Our model is based on AND/OR graphs [14]. An AND/OR graph is a directed, acyclic graph in which each node is either a leaf (without successors), an AND node, or an OR node. AND nodes and OR nodes must have at least one successor. When a node has a single successor, it can be viewed either as an OR node or an AND node.

Leaf nodes

The leave nodes are primitive objects in our model and represent program modules, intermediate code, documentation fragments, test data, etc.

OR nodes

OR nodes represent *version groups*. Successors of an OR node are considered equivalent according to some criterion. Thus, an OR node implies a choice -- one may choose one (or several) of its successors.

AND nodes

AND nodes represent *configurations*. All successors of an AND node must be combined to form a complete configuration. Thus, an AND node implies an integration process; this corresponds to a link-editing process for pure software configurations, a loading process for hardware/software configurations, and an assembly process for pure hardware configurations.

As an example, suppose we have a system *S* with three configurations *C1*, *C2*, and *E*. Suppose furthermore that configuration *C1* consists of components *A* and *B*, configuration *C2* of components *C* and *D*, and configuration *E* is primitive (i.e., a single component). This situation can be diagrammed in the following way (see Figure 1).

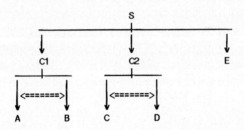

Fig. 1: An AND/OR graph with one OR node and two AND nodes.

The node with the label *S* is an OR node since it allows a choice of three alternatives. The nodes *C1* and *C2* are AND nodes, since their successors need to be combined. In the diagram, the AND nodes are marked with the symbol "<====>" linking their successors.

Note that we are dealing with a directed graph, not merely a tree or a forest. In a directed graph, a single node may have several predecessors. This permits the modeling of *component sharing*. For example, a situation like in Figure 2 is impossible to realize in a tree (except by copying whole subtrees).

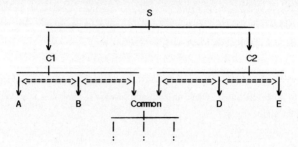

Fig. 2: Configurations C1 and C2 share node Common.

AND and OR nodes may be intermixed freely. Thus, one can form version groups out of primitive nodes, configurations, and even other version groups. Likewise, configurations may consist of primitive nodes, configurations and version groups. This reflects the *orthogonality* of the concepts of version group and configuration.

We shall now demonstrate with a few more examples how AND/OR graphs can be used to represent various types of hardware/software systems, including their documentation and test data. This will be accomplished by attaching special significance to the branches emanating from AND nodes and OR nodes.

In our model, a program module cannot be subdivided. However, each module normally evolves in a sequence of revisions that are incremental changes to some initial version. The revisions are ordered by their creation date. This situation is diagrammed with an OR node (see Figure 3).

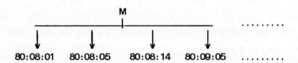

Fig. 3: Revisions of a software module.

Suppose furthermore that our compiler is capable of generating code for the PDP-11, the VAX-11, and the Intel 8086 from any of the revisions. Assume that in each case the compiler may generate optimized or non-optimized code. This is represented with two more levels of OR nodes (see Figure 4).

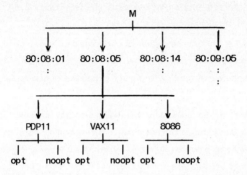

Fig. 4: Revisions, target versions, and optimized versions.

Now suppose that we would like to add documentation to our module, for example a general description and some implementation decisions. That is quite easily done by adding yet another OR node, this time on top. Note that the documentation may go through several revisions, just like source code. It may even be compiled for several output devices, for example for the terminal, the line printer, the photo typesetter, etc. Thus, the structure for documentation is similar to the one for implementation (see Figure 5).

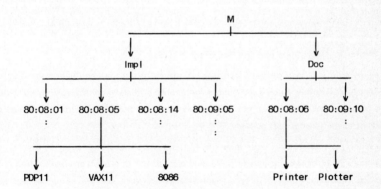

Fig. 5: M has two alternatives, implementation and documentation.

Note that OR nodes with documentation and implementation branches are different from the OR nodes we have seen so far. Up to now, OR nodes only combined equivalent implementations. Documentation and implementation are also equivalent, but in a different sense: they describe the same object, one giving the specification, the other the implementation. Recall that we defined OR nodes as representing an inclusive-or relation. Thus, we can even model the view that documentation and implementation form an entity.

Clearly, an OR branch for documentation can be added wherever desirable. For example, one may add documentation to the revisions in the form of a "change log." One can also associate documentation with higher-level nodes to supply a general overview, a user's manual, or the requirements specification.

The AND/OR graph can be applied to hardware as well. However, the decomposition into subgraphs may have a somewhat different shape. For example, there may be components that have no revisions, like bolts or other standard parts. There may be additional document types, like circuit schematics or instructions for the assembly of certain configurations. Hybrid configurations consisting of both hardware and software are best represented with AND nodes. For instance, if a particular program is to be stored in a specific PROM, then both components should be successors of the same AND node. A combination of hardware and software is permissible anywhere in the graph. For instance, we may want to indicate that a certain operating system can run on several machine models, or that some software components have to be distributed over specific nodes in a network.

All these different interpretations are actually overloading our simple AND/OR graph model. The three basic node types are no longer sufficient. For building intelligent software tools, we need additional node types. The types indicate the semantics associated with a given node. Software tools can then take advantage of that information. We shall come back to this idea in Section 4.

2.1. Generic Configurations and the Selection Problem

A single AND node may actually represent a number of possible configurations if some of its successors are OR nodes. Such an AND node represents a *generic configuration* and is therefore called a *generic AND node*. Generic AND nodes are important for avoiding the combinatorial explosion of the number of AND nodes.

Consider Figure 6, which describes the I/O subsystem of some larger family. It has two major versions, one for the line printer (*LPT*), and one for the terminal (*Terminal*). The *LPT* version is a configuration consisting of three components: *open*, *close*, and *put*. The modules *open* and *close* exist as a sequence of revisions, labeled with release numbers. The node *put* has two machine specific versions, one for the *VAX* and one for the *PDP11*. Each of those has again several revisions.

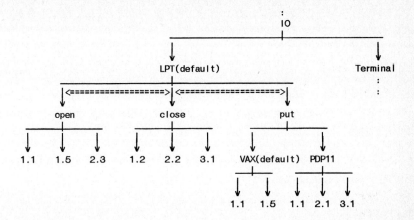

Fig. 6: Several versions of an I/O subsystem.

This diagram compactly represents 3*3*(2+3)=45 configurations. Without the generic node *LPT*, we would need 45 structurally identical AND nodes. If we add just one more revision to module *open*, the number of configurations increases to 60, and we would need 15 more AND nodes. By contrast, with generic nodes we have to add only a single offspring to module *open*. This example should demonstrate that the lack of generic configurations may lead to serious bookkeeping problems as the number of modules and revisions increases[1].

In large families, there are easily thousands of configurations that can be created by arbitrary selection of offsprings at OR nodes. Relatively few of them will actually work together. The problem is how to select the proper ones. One possibility is to use "cutoff" release numbers, "cutoff" dates, and defaults. A cutoff release number (date) selects at each node the revision with the number (date) that is less than or equal, but closest to the cutoff. In the above example, *IO:2.3* would select the configuration {*open:2.3, close:2.2, put:VAX:1.5*}. This is consistent with the practice of defining releases to be the newest revisions of all components at a given date. Note also the application of two user-specified defaults (*LPT* and *VAX*). The default for release numbers and dates should correspond to the newest one for each component. We also need a mechanism to specify "symbolic" release numbers like *current, experimental, stable*, etc. Of course, it must be possible to override the defaults to express something like: "I want the default for everything, except that I need the *Terminal*-version of *IO*." This is specified with *IO.Terminal*. Notations for cascading those selections are easily included.

---

[1] The *cardinality* of a node, i.e., the number of versions represented by it, is computed as follows. (1) The cardinality of a leaf node is 1; (2) the cardinality of an AND node is the product of the cardinalities of its offsprings; (3) the cardinality of an OR node is the sum of the cardinalities of its offsprings (assuming that exactly one alternative must be chosen).

An additional selection mechanism involves the labeling of OR branches. The labels serve as criteria for global selection. For example, suppose that some of the branches emanating from OR nodes are labeled *basic*, *intermediate*, or *advanced*, indicating the obvious qualities about the three choices. Assume that these labels are spread through a large graph. Then one can select a desired configuration by simply requesting, for instance, the *basic* branch wherever there is a choice. (Note that this is similar to the global selection by cutoff date.) This technique is also convenient for specifying the target machine or optimized/unoptimized versions. An example is *IO:PDP11:nonopt*.

2.2. Well-Formed Configurations

An extremely important issue in multi-person projects is interface control: to establish and maintain consistent interfaces between the numerous components. The concept of the *well-formed configuration*, defined in this section, forms the basis for interface control. Our concept is a generalization of the conditions on system structure presented in [15] and [16].

We start by associating an interface with every node in our graph. An interface consists of two sets: the provided facilities and the required facilities. The provided facilities are the data types, operations, data structures, etc. exported from a node. An example of provided facilities are the visible interfaces of Ada packages [17]. The required facilities are the types, operations, data structures, etc. that must be imported into the node.

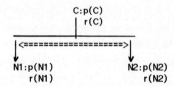

Fig. 8: A configuration with two components; interfaces attached.

The set of facilities provided by a node N is denoted as $p(N)$, the set of required facilities as $r(N)^2$. We have to make sure that a facility mentioned in the provided set of a node does not also occur in the required set. This leads to the following definition.

A node N is *free of contradictions* if and only if
$$p(N) \cap r(N) = \phi$$

---

2 We could link the interfaces into our diagram with some extra OR nodes, but it is more convenient to think of them as node attributes. Compare Section 4.

We define node M to be upward compatible with node N if M provides at least what N provides, and requires not more than what N does. That means that M can be used instead of N, but not vice versa.

Node M is *upward compatible* with node N if and only if
$$p(M) \supseteq p(N) \text{ and } r(M) \subseteq r(N)$$

Similarly, two nodes are compatible if they have the same interface. Thus, compatible nodes are interchangeable.

The nodes M and N are *compatible* if and only if
$$p(M) = p(N) \text{ and } r(M) = r(N)$$

The last two definitions apply to arbitrary pairs of nodes. They will be especially interesting for OR nodes.

We can now define *well-formed nodes*. There are different, recursive definitions for each node class (leaf, AND, and OR nodes).

A. A leaf node is well-formed if and only if it is free of contradictions.

(Since a leaf node usually corresponds to a given source module, we have to make sure that the source actually satisfies the interface. Techniques for implementing that have been presented in [18].)

B. An OR node R with direct successors $K_1, \ldots, K_n$ ($n \geq 1$) is well-formed if and only if

i. R is free of contradictions;

ii. There exists at least one direct successor $K_i (1 \leq i \leq n)$ of R which is well-formed and upward compatible with R.

(Since only one K_i needs to satisfy condition ii, we can add documentation to OR nodes without problem, or make configurations versions of each other although they have different interfaces.)

C. An AND node S with direct successors $K_1, \ldots, K_n$ ($n \geq 1$) is well-formed if and only if

i. S is free of contradictions;

ii. All K_i ($1 \leq i \leq n$) are well-formed;

iii. $p(K_i) \cap p(K_j) = \phi$ if $i \neq j$ (freeness of conflicts)

iv. $p(S) \subseteq \bigcup_{i=1}^{n} p(K_i)$

v. $r(S) \supseteq (\bigcup_{i=1}^{n} r(K_i) - \bigcup_{i=1}^{n} p(K_i))$

Since configurations correspond to AND nodes, we say that a configuration is well-formed if its AND node is well-formed. The basic conditions given above are precisely those which must be checked when a configuration is built from a set of components. The conditions can also be used to construct the interfaces of newly created AND nodes and OR nodes if a system designer is composing new system versions interactively. They are applied in search algorithms that compose well-formed configurations automatically, as discussed by [16]. The interfaces can also be used to assess proposed interface changes by analyzing the effects for each node. Finally, interface changes can be carried out by propagating the modifications to all affected nodes, as described in [18]. The required algorithms and their complexities are currently being explored.

3. Comparison of other Models for Representing System Families

In this section, we analyze the data models underlying some existing software tools. The comparison concentrates on what kind of AND/OR graph structures the tools permit. We shall see that most of them place severe restrictions on the shape of the graph. We distinguish the following 4 major submodels. (Example implementations or proposals are noted in parenthesis.) More detail can be found in [19].

a)   The Hierarchical Model (Ada [17], Simula67 [20], Mesa [21]),

b)   The Relational Model ([22] and [23]),

c)   The Sequential Release Model (SCCS/MAKE [24, 25]).

d)   The AND/OR graph model ([9, 15, 16]).

The hierarchical model imposes a partial ordering on the program modules, and multiple versions are not permitted. The result is an AND/OR graph without any OR nodes. In the relational model, configurations are specified as lists of components in rows of a single, large matrix or several, cascaded matrices. Again, no multiple versions are permitted. Because of the lack of OR nodes, both the hierarchical and relational models are essentially equivalent. Versions cannot be specified, which makes it impossible to build tools within these models that work on version groups rather than individual components. Generic configurations are also lacking, which leads to the combinatorial explosion of the number of configurations.

The sequential release model allows program modules to exist as a sequence of revisions. This leads to a graph where OR nodes are permitted only as predecessors of leaf nodes. Configurations that are structurally identical and whose modules differ only in the revision numbers can be represented with a single, generic configuration. However, it is not possible to indicate that two different configurations are actually versions of each other, no matter how slight the differences. This is due to the fact that the sequential release model permits no internal OR nodes.

The general AND/OR graph model has none of these restrictions. Any two configurations can be made versions of each other, and a single, generic description suffices for structurally identical configurations. Structurally similar configurations can be described without duplication of information. Hardware configurations, documentation, test configurations, and test data can be added without problem. (None of the examples listed under point d permits an AND/OR graph in its full generality.)

4. Application of the Model

We noted previously that three node classes (leaves, AND nodes, and OR nodes) are not sufficient for building an intelligent PSE. For example, software tools need to treat revisions of source modules differently from object code or configuration versions. Yet in our basic model, these are all offsprings of OR nodes. We suggested already that types associated with nodes would alleviate the problem, because then the tools can be programmed to treat each type properly. Besides the types, we also need to attach various attributes to the nodes, for recording creation dates, release numbers, selection labels, access lists, interfaces, etc.

A refinement of the AND/OR graph model that permits this information to be represented is the *directed, attributed graph*. Every node in an attributed graph has a type and a set of attributes. The type determines the attribute set associated with a node. In this section, we use attributed graphs to define a PSE data base for the *Revision Control System (RCS)*. RCS is a variant of the sequential release model.

4.1. Design of the RCS Data Base

As a first step, we specify the general structure of the attributed graph. We could use the data declaration facility of a general purpose programming language for that. However, this approach would dictate a large number of representational details which are either wrong or should not be fixed at this point. The same is true for the CODASYL data definition language. The latter also forces some awkward constructions for certain kinds of graphs. Instead, we use IDL (Interface Description Language) [26]. IDL is a language for declaring attributed graphs as abstract data types. It has been used for defining Diana, the intermediate form of Ada programs [27]. IDL satisfies three important requirements. First, IDL is programming language independent. Thus, IDL graphs may be manipulated by tools written in diverse languages. Second, IDL does not prescribe any particular realization -- the graphs are merely conceptual ones. Indeed, we chose a rather uncommon way of implementing IDL graphs, to be discussed in Section 4.2. Third, IDL defines a standard, externally visible ASCII representation for graphs. In this form, the graph can be read by the user, and communicated between arbitrary tools and even arbitrary PSEs on different computer systems. All that is needed are encoders and decoders for porting the contents of a PSE data base from one implementation to the next.

Below is the IDL specification of RCS. The reader need not be familiar with the IDL notation; those aspects of IDL that are used here are informally described as we go along.

```
mode Revision_Constrol_System root RCSnode is

    RCSnode      ::=   Delta | Module | Config;
    -- There are 3 basic node types.

    Delta       =>   RevisionNo      : string,
                     Date            : string,
                     Author          : string,
                     LogEntry        : string,
                     State           : string,
                     Text            : string,
                     Next            : Delta,
                     Branches        : seq of Delta;

    -- This specifies the attributes of nodes of type Delta.

    Module           AccessSet       : set of string,
                     Language        : string,
                     Locks           : set of Lock,
                     Head            : Delta;


    Lock        =>   RevisionNo      : string,
                     Locker          : string;

    -- A lock node indicates which branch is locked for expansions.


    Config      =>   AccessSet       : set of string,
                     ReleaseNo       : string,
                     State           : string,
                     Components      : set of RCSnode;

end
```

Fig. 9: IDL specification for the revision control system.

The first line of the specification indicates that a new data type with the name Revision_Control_System is defined. The root clause gives the starting symbol of the specification. There are 3 basic node types in the graph: *Delta*, *Module*, and *Config*. The delta nodes represent the revisions of a module and are organized in a tree with the initial revision as the root. The tree has a main branch, called the *trunk*, along which the main development occurs. The field *Next* links deltas on the same branch of the tree. A delta may sprout one or more parallel branches. The entries in the field *Branches* point to the first delta on each branch. Figure 10 illustrates an example tree with 3 branches (not counting the trunk). Deltas on the trunk are numbered 1.1, 1.2, ..., 2.1, 2.2, etc. Other branches are numbered *fork*.1, *fork*.2, ... etc, where *fork* is the number of the delta that sprouts the branch. Deltas on a branch are again numbered sequentially, using the branch number as a prefix.

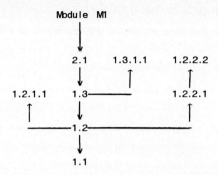

Fig. 10: A revision tree with 3 side branches.

Note that the links in the trunk point backwards from the latest delta rather than forwards from the root. This is an optimization to speed up access time. The latest delta on the main branch is the one that is most often used. We therefore store this version intact. All others are stored as a set of differences that will restore the revision given the previous one. To obtain, for instance, revision 1.3, the differences stored in delta 1.3 are applied to revision 2.1. The older the revision is, the more deltas need to be applied. This technique is called reverse deltas. Deltas conserve space, and reverse deltas minimize the average time needed to restore a revision[3].

Unfortunately, reverse deltas do not work so well for side branches. To avoid keeping a complete copy of the newest revision on each branch, we use forward deltas from the branch point. Thus, applying to delta 2.1 first delta 1.3 and then 1.3.1.1 will regenerate revision 1.3.1.1. This is still shorter than regenerating 1.3.1.1 from the root 1.1.

Let us now examine the definition of the *Delta* node more carefully. The text following the symbol "=>" is a record definition. Each field or attribute declaration is composed of an attribute name and a type. *RevisionNo* numbers the deltas as discussed above. The *Date* field records the creation date and time, and the *Author* field stores the identification of the person who created the new revision. The *LogEntry* attribute contains a short note describing the nature of the change that made the revision necessary. The author of the revision is prompted by the data base system to supply the log entry when the revision is deposited. *State* indicates the status of a revision, for example whether it is experimental, stable, or released. Finally, the attribute *Text* contains the actual program text.

The *Module* node contains attributes that are common to all deltas. The *AccessSet* attribute is a set of user names that have write-permission, i.e., those who may create deltas. (Read permission is given to all other users.) The *Language* field records the programming language or

---

[3] The use of reverse, non-intermixed deltas is one of the chief differences between RCS and SCCS.

document formatting language used. This is needed for automatic system or document generation. The locks make sure that there are no overlapping changes on a branch while somebody is preparing a new revision for it. A *Lock* node records the branch number and locker. The field *Head* points to the most recent revision on the main branch.

Nodes of type *Config* record configurations. The offsprings of this AND node are recorded in the attribute *Components*. Note that this is a set of *RCSnodes*. Thus, members of this set may be modules, configurations, and even deltas. The attribute *AccessSet* defines who may change the node. There are additional fields to record the release number and the state of the configuration. Figure 11 presents an example instantiation of RCS.

4.2. Implementation of RCS

A prototype of RCS has been successfully implemented on a VAX/UNIX system. It uses reverse deltas, but without branches. The purpose of the prototype was to investigate the feasibility of a PSE data base patterned after an attributed graph. A more ambitious project providing a full attributed graph structure (including reverse deltas and branches) is under way. Another project develops ADABASE, a PSE data base specifically designed for the Ada programming language [28]. We wish to report here on the important implementation decisions and the data base operations of the prototype.

An important problem is the representation of the attributed graph. The naive approach would be to place an encoding of the graph into a single file. Since the file is the unit of change, only one programmer at a time can modify the graph. This leads to unacceptable delays since there are usually several people modifying the data base simultaneously. For example, there may be several programmers checking modules in and out for modification, adding documentation and object modules, constructing test configurations, and accessing the data base for interfaces and various other data items.

The opposite approach of placing every node into a separate file may lead to another kind of inefficiency caused by frequent directory lookups. We therefore adopted the approach that one or several nodes may be stored in a single file. Pointers to nodes in the same file can be traversed quickly; pointers to "remote" nodes require a directory lookup or even a network transfer. In that manner one can optimize the data base bandwidth by rearranging the assignment of node groups to files (possibly spread over a computer network). In RCS, one should place each *Module* node together with all its descendants into a single file because these nodes are usually accessed together.

The encoding of the graph is the standard ASCII representation defined in the IDL manual. This simplifies the operations for browsing through the graph. Graphics support for pictorial

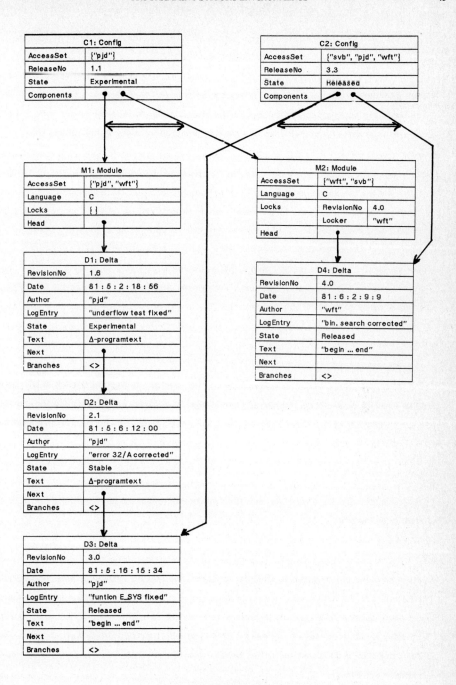

Fig. 11: Example data base for RCS.

rather than textual display is under investigation. The high-level operations for handling revisions are patterned after SCCS [24]. A synopsis of the commands is given below.

Rcs

> *Rcs* modifies or initializes a module or configuration node. There are parameters to expand or shrink the access set, and to specify the other attributes. Special options lock, unlock, or break the lock of a branch. *Rcs* may only be executed by users on the access set.

Co

> *Co* checks out a revision of a module node for update or inspection. If an update is desired, *Co* first locks the corresponding branch (if not already locked). This avoids that two people create overlapping updates to the same branch. (A lock can be released by performing an update with the *Ci* command, or by releasing it, without update, using *Rcs*.)

> *Co* places the retrieved revision into a file in the user's directory for editing or inspection, or sends it to the terminal for perusal. The desired revision may be selected by revision number, symbolic name, creation date, state, or author. The default is the most recent revision.

Ci

> *Ci* appends a new revision to a branch. Only the user who locked the branch in his name may execute it. Normally, the new revision number is obtained by incrementing the number of the latest revision, but the user can specify a higher number explicitly. After successful completion, *Ci* releases the lock.

Rlog

> *Rlog* displays the log messages and other information about module and delta nodes in a variety of formats.

Make

> *Make* compiles a configuration. Normally, it selects the latest revisions of all modules composing it, but the notation suggested in Section 2 can be used to specify other selections by state, symbolic name, cutoff date, or cutoff release number. It is also possible to select specific versions individually. *Make* uses the *Language* field to determine which processor (e.g., compiler or document formatter) to call. It does not attempt to avoid redundant compilations and linkings.

Make could be extended to save redundant compilations and linkings if our graph structure included derived versions. In that case we would need additional offsprings at *Delta* and *Config* nodes for recording object modules and the derivation history. We have omitted these details for clarity. It should also be noted that it is easy to add an OR node for representing versions of configurations.

5. Conclusions

We have introduced a simple and flexible model for representing families of programmed systems. The model allows the sharing of components among configurations, treats configurations and versions completely orthogonally, provides generic configurations, and yields the concept of the well-formed configuration. The model can also be used to compare the data base structures underlying other software tools.

A refinement of the model leads to a directed, attributed graph with several node types. We designed the graph structure for the revision control system and presented a data base implementing that structure. The design and implementation demonstrate that the directed, attributed graph is adequate for developing data bases for programming support environments.

Acknowledgments: Part of this work was done at the ITT Programming Technology Center in Stratford, Conn., and I am especially grateful for comments from Donn Combelic and Tom Love.

References

1. Kernighan, Brian W. and Mashey, John R., "The UNIX Programming Environment," *Software -- Practice and Experience* **9**(1) pp. 1-15 (Jan. 1979).
2. Habermann, A. Nico, "An Overview of the Gandalf Project," in *CMU Computer Science Research Review 1978-1979*, Carnegie-Mellon University (1979).
3. Buxton, John N. and Druffel, Larry E., "Requirements for an Ada Programming Support Environment: Rationale for Stoneman," pp. 66-72 in *Proceedings of COMPSAC 80*, IEEE Computer Society Press (Oct. 1980).
4. Osterweil, Leon J., "Software Environment Research: Directions for the Next Five Years," *IEEE Computer* **14**(4) pp. 35-43 (April 1981).
5. Teitelman, Warren and Masinter, Larry, "The Interlisp Programming Environment," *IEEE Computer* **14**(4) pp. 25-33 (April 1981).
6. Parnas, David L., "On the Design and Development of Program Families," *IEEE Transactions on Software Engineering* **SE-2**(1) pp. 1-8 (Mar. 1976).
7. Parnas, David L., "Designing Software for Ease of Extension and Contraction," *IEEE Transactions on Software Engineering* **SE-5**(2) pp. 128-138 (March 1979).
8. Habermann, A. Nico, Flon, Lawrence, and Cooprider, Lee W., "Modularization and Hierarchy in a Family of Operating Systems," *Communications of the ACM* **19**(5) pp. 266-272 (May 1976).
9. Cooprider, Lee W., *The Representation of Families of Programmed Systems*, PhD thesis, Carnegie-Mellon University, Department of Computer Science (1978).

10. Belady, L.A. and Lehman, M.M., "The Characteristics of Large Systems," pp. 106-138 in *Research Directions in Software Technology*, ed. Peter Wegner,M.I.T. Press (1979).

11. Wirth, Niklaus, "The Programming Language Pascal," *Acta Informatica* 1 pp. 35-63 (1971).

12. Kernighan, Brian W. and Ritchie, Dennis M., *The C Programming Language*, Prentice-Hall (1978).

13. Cheriton, David R., Malcom, Michael A., Melen, Lawrence S., and Sager, Garry R., "Thoth, a Portable Real-Time Operating System," *Communications of the ACM* **22**(2) pp. 105-115 (Feb. 1979).

14. Nilsson, Nils J., *Problem Solving Methods in Artificial Intelligence*, McGraw-Hill (1971).

15. Tichy, Walter F., *Software Development Control Based on System Structure Description*, PhD Thesis, Carnegie-Mellon University, Department of Computer Science (Jan. 1980).

16. Habermann, A. Nico and Perry, Dewayne E., "Well-Formed System Compositions," CMU-CS-80-117, Technical Report, Carnegie-Mellon University, Department of Computer Science (March 1980).

17. Ichbiah, Jean D., *Reference Manual for the Ada Programming Language*, United States Department of Defense (July 1980).

18. Tichy, Walter F., "Software Development Control Based on Module Interconnection," pp. 29-41 in *Proceedings of the 4th International Conference on Software Engineering*, ACM, IEEE, ERO, GI (Sept. 1979).

19. Tichy, Walter F., *A Model for Representing Families of Programmed Systems*, Technical Report, Purdue University, Computer Science Department (January 1981).

20. Birtwistle, G., Enderin, L., Ohlin, M., and Palme, J., "DECsystem-10 Simula Language Handbook Part 1," C8398, Swedish National Defense Research Institute (March 1976).

21. Mitchell, James G., Maybury, William, and Sweet, Richard, *Mesa Language Manual*, Technical Report, Xerox Palo Alto Research Center (Feb. 1978).

22. Belady, L.A. and Merlin, P.M., "Evolving Parts and Relations: A Model for System Families," RC-6677, Technical Report, IBM Thomas J. Watson Research Center (1977).

23. ITT,, *CMSS3 Users's Manual*, International Telephone and Telegraph (1980). Document No. 211ITT26366-PC

24. Rochkind, Marc J., "The Source Code Control System," *IEEE Transactions on Software Engineering* **SE-1**(4) pp. 364-370 (Dec. 1975).

25. Feldman, Stuart I., "Make - A Program for Maintaining Computer Programs," *Software -- Practice and Experience* **9**(3) pp. 255-265 (March 1979).

26. Nestor, John R., Wulf, William A., and Lamb, David A., *IDL - Interface Description Language, Formal Description*, Technical Report, Carnegie-Mellon University, Computer Science Department (Feb. 1981).

27. Goos, Gerhard and Wulf, William A., *Diana Reference Manual*, Technical Report, Carnegie-Mellon University, Computer Science Department (March 1981).

28. Tichy, Walter F., *ADABASE -- A Data Base for Ada Programs*, Technical Report, Purdue University, Computer Science Department, in preparation (November 1981).

Automated Tools for Information Systems Design
H.-J. Schneider and A.I. Wasserman (eds.)
North-Holland Publishing Company
© IFIP, 1982

A DECISION TOOL FOR ASSISTING WITH THE COMPREHENSION OF LARGE SOFTWARE SYSTEMS*

John R. White

Computer Science Division
Department of Electrical Engineering and Computer Science
The University of Connecticut
Storrs, Connecticut 06268
U.S.A.

To modify or extend a software system we must have a
clear understanding of how the system is structured,
the function or role each component performs, and
the   interrelationships that exist between components. Frequently, this comprehension process is
hampered by subtle interdependencies that exist
between components or between components and the environment. These interdependencies typically result
from assumptions made in order to reach certain
design decisions and are usually ignored in automatic and manual documentation. In this paper a tool
is described for tracking the decision process so
that assumptions surrounding a decision are recorded
and, thus, available for system comprehension. The
tool is based upon a model of decision making during
detailed design that treats a decision as a process
of selecting a refinement from a group of alternatives.   The model and associated tool allow a decision to be based upon almost any property considered
important and record the alternatives considered,
the criteria used, and any assumptions made.   In addition, the state of the decision making process is
tracked so that previous decisions can be recon-
sidered to explore alternative designs.

1   INTRODUCTION

Within the last few years there has been considerable interest
in the development of tools and environments (collections of tools)
to assist designers and programmers in the application of emerging
software engineering technology. By and large, the focus of these
efforts has been limited to software development tools.   Moreover,
most commercially available tools (see, for example, the recent
Tools Fair at the Fifth ICSE) only focus on the implementation phase
of development. Tools aimed at earlier phases such as design (e.g.,
SARA [3]) or specification (e.g., AFFIRM [13]) are still considered
experimental research efforts.

* This work was supported by the National Science Foundation through grants
MCS77-02484 and MCS80-05113

The general objectives of software development tools are to improve the quality of the system being constructed and to increase
the productivity of the individuals involved in system design and
construction. The key issue is clearly one of cost; yet, tools
oriented solely towards development ignore the maintenance portion
of the software life-cycle to which a majority of cost (typically
more than 60%) can be attributed. To bring software costs under
control and to insure quality throughout a system's lifetime, we
must develop tools that directly address issues related to maintenance and investigate how these tools can be integrated with traditional development aids.

A research project underway at the University of Connecticut is
exploring the issue of software maintenance with the objective of
developing tools to assist software engineers in the evolution [18]
of large, complex systems. The goal of the research is to support a
specific maintenance/evolution paradigm and, thereby, achieve a
reduction in actual maintenance costs and an improvement in a
system's maintainability throughout its lifetime. A key step in
this maintenance paradigm is the process of understanding an existing system's structural, functional, and performance properties in
preparation for actually making a change. For a large system this
can be an extremely difficult task and one susceptible to error. A
major problem is that knowledge about how a system is structured,
what function each component performs, and what the performance
characteristics of each component are is often insufficient to successfully carry out a desired change. Frequently, subtle assumptions exist about the way in which a component fits into a system or
about the manner in which related components function. These dependencies are typically not properties of any single system component
and, thus, are frequently missed in both manual and automatic documentation.

The subtle interdependencies and assumptions that must be known
for successful evolution of a system are typically the result of
making decisions. For example, the choice of a representation for a
data structure may be based on assumptions about the expected number
of times certain operations will be executed and, therefore, is tied
to assumptions about expected inputs. Or, for example, in selecting
a particular algorithm to carry out a function, assumptions may be
made about the performance of lower-level operations.

In this paper we present a model and associated automated tool
for tracking the decision process during development so that
relevant information (particularly assumptions) can be recorded and
later retrieved to assist with system comprehension prior to a
maintenance operation. The decision model and tool described are
part of an experimental software development and maintenance environment. In the next section, some background is provided to
place the decision model and tool in perspective. In Section 3 the
models upon which the tool is based are described. Finally, in Section 4, a brief overview of the decision tool itself and the system
into which it is being incorporated are presented.

2 PERSPECTIVE

2.1 Background

Research directed at the maintenance of software has often

focused on the problem of inadequate documentation. This focus reflects the fact that although current development methods can lead to well-structured, evolvable systems, to carry out an extension or contraction in a system's capability requires that we understand: 1) how the system is structured; 2) how the functions performed by various components interrelate; and 3) how the current structure impacts system performance. From a practical maintenance point of view, documentation is a record of what is known about a system and, thus, is fundamental in obtaining the understanding required to carry out a maintenance request. If documentation is incomplete, inadequate, and out-of-date (as it often is), maintenance costs increase and the useful life of a system is reduced.

Traditional approaches to amelioration of the "documentation problem" have centered heavily on automating documentation production. Early work [4, 11] focused on machine generated, low-level documentation of the actual code. More recent systems such as ISDOS [17] and various extensions (e.g., DAS [22]) allow one to describe initial (high level) architectural characteristics of a system in terms of a set of relations among fixed classes of objects. The relations are stored in a data base from which documentation (reports) can be generated.

These systems can provide a maintenance engineer with volumes of up-to-date documentation. The usefulness of this documentation, however, is limited by the sophistication of the knowledge-base from which it is generated. AUTOFLOW [4], for example, knows only about control flow within specific languages (e.g., FORTRAN, IBM/360 Assembly). Mills' system [11] extends this idea with knowledge about both the data flow and control flow in a particular language (PL/360). The ISDOS system, on the other hand, has knowledge about high level descriptions of systems, yet this knowledge is limited to what can be inferred from a fixed (small) number of relations.

Our approach to assisting with maintenance differs from previous work in two important ways. First, the focus is not on automatically generating a standard set of documents that _may_ be useful during maintenance. Instead, the concern is with collecting (a potentially large amount of) information from the development process and organizing this information in such a way that facts relevant to some future maintenance request can be retrieved in an "uncanned" manner. Second, the information collected from development and the way in which it is organized are based on a specific model of how systems are comprehended. Thus, the maintenance paradigm that we are working with is one in which: 1) a maintenance request is received; 2) the maintenance data base is used to support application of a learning model to understand the structural, functional, and performance properties of relevant system components; 3) the necessary changes are designed and implemented following a specific methodology; and 4) information is extracted from this new "development" effort so that the maintenance data base reflects up-to-date knowledge of the system.

The important step in this paradigm and the one for which we are developing tools is, of course, understanding relevant system components. This comprehension process involves acquisition of knowledge about: 1) the function or role a particular system component performs and how that role contributes to the overall function of the system; and 2) interdependencies that exist between components and between components and the environment in which the system is to execute. Our attention in this paper is directed towards acquisition of the latter type of knowledge. Our work in automated assistance for acquiring knowledge about the role various components play is based upon a learning model proposed by Brooks [1] and is described further in [21] and [5].

2.2 The Role of Decision Making

As discussed in Section 1, the decisions that are made during development are the primary source of information regarding inter- dependencies and assumptions between system components or between components and the environment. The entire development process can in fact be viewed as a continuum of decisions from choices about in- itial high-level system layout, to selection of algorithms and data representations, through implementation issues of which low-level data representations or control structures to use. Each decision involves the exploration and evaluation of alternative representa- tions and the eventual selection of a single representation. To adequately capture the impact of a decision we must record not just the resulting refinement, but the decision itself.

Initially, we are focusing our attention on decisions made dur- ing the detailed design phase of development. These decisions typi- cally involve selecting algorithms and data representations and are decisions that have a substantial impact on performance. To track these decisions we take a very specific view of what the software design process involves and how it can be modeled. Even with these constraints, the evolution of a design involves a myriad of deci- sions, not all of which can be accounted for in a single model.

2.3 Modeling Design

The view taken of detailed design is based on the work of numerous researchers [2, 7-10, 14-16, 19] and considers design to be a process of first identifying and then refining useful abstrac- tions. An abstraction can represent a procedural concept that ac- cepts inputs and produces output, or it can represent a data concept (i.e., an abstract data type) that characterizes the behavior of a set of objects (values) through the operations associated with the type. Each concept (data abstraction or procedural abstraction) can have one or more refinements. A refinement for a concept is re- ferred to as a design for that concept and in the case of procedural abstractions consists of an algorithm expressed as a procedural com- putation in DLN (DLN is a design/programming notation described briefly in Section 4 and in detail in [12]). The refinement of a data abstraction involves selecting a representation for objects of the type and then, based upon that representation, constructing al- gorithms for each operation. Refinements (or designs) for a data abstraction are represented in DLN as type definitions.

Each refinement or design for a concept is done at some level of abstraction and, therefore, uses other concepts. Thus, there is a hierarchical relationship between concepts as shown in Figure 1. In that figure circular nodes represent concepts and boxes represent designs. Data concepts are distinguished from procedural concepts in that the node for a data concept contains both the name of the type and the name of the operations. Figure 1.a illustrates a pro- cedural concept with three alternate (and functionally equivalent) refinements. With a data abstraction (see Figure 1.b) the initial level of refinement expresses the representation chosen for objects of the abstract type. The lower-level types from which this representation is constructed are shown as data concepts 'used' by

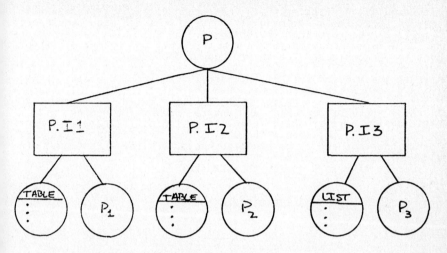

Figure 1.a   Procedural Concept

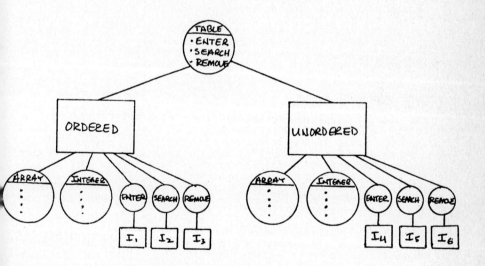

Figure 1.b   Data Concept

Figure 1   Hierarchical Relationship

the representation refinement box. Attached to each representation refinement box is a procedural concept node for each operation. This reflects the fact that the design of the operation is dependent on the data representation chosen for the type, but allows different designs to be considered for an individual operation.

If we identify an initial, highest-level (root) concept (typically a procedural abstraction), then the relationships illustrated in Figure 1 merge into a <u>design</u> <u>tree</u> as illustrated in Figure 2. The design tree represents an entire family of designs with a specific design corresponding to the selection of a refinement for each concept in the tree. The design tree explicitly illustrates the decisions that are to be made and the alternatives that must be considered, and it allows the refinement chosen for a concept to vary from one part of a design to another.

3   THE DECISION MODEL

The design tree illustrates each decision that must be made during the detailed design phase of development. The objectives of the decision model are to account for (and record): 1) each decision that has been (or needs to be) made; 2) the alternative refinements considered and the criteria used in reaching a decision; and 3) assumptions made (about expected inputs or the performance of lower level conepts) in the process or making a decision. The first of these objectives simply keeps track of the status of the decision process. The second records information about <u>why</u> a particular refinement was chosen, and the third records information about the interdependencies that exist as a result of a decision.

3.1 <u>Model</u> <u>Structure</u>

The overall structure of the decision model is identical to that of the design tree and is referred to as a <u>decision</u> <u>tree</u>. Circular concept nodes in the decision tree represent points in the design at which a decision must be made; square nodes emanating from a decision point represent the alternative designs that must be considered. In the decision tree, information associated with a decision point (i.e., a concept) relates to the decision as a whole, while design nodes record information specific to the associated refinement.

Selecting a refinement from a set of alternatives requires the establishment of criteria upon which alternatives will be compared. This process is modeled in a manner similar to classical decision theory; however, it should be remembered that our objective is not to automatically make an optimal decision, but to record the process by which a software engineer reaches (hopefully) an optimal decision.

3.2 <u>Properties</u>

At a decision node we can define a set of <u>properties</u> that represent important characteristics of the alternative refinements upon which a decision will be based. A property is simply a function that maps each refinement of a concept into a value of some type T. (At present T can be the type INTEGER, REAL, or an ENUMERATION of arbitrary constants). A property can represent a perfor-

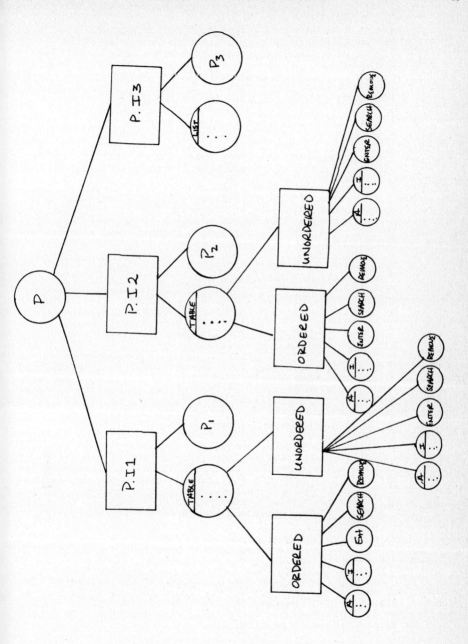

Figure 2   A Design Tree

mance measure such as expected execution time, a complexity measure,
or almost any characteristic of a refinement (e.g., verified or not
verified). Given the procedural concept of Figure 1.a, some possible properties are:

```
            Exp_Exec_Time        : REAL
            Verified             : {YES,NO}
```

With the data concept in Figure 1.b, we might have:

```
            Exp_Space            : REAL
            Exp_SEARCH_Time      : REAL
            Exp_ENTER_Time       : REAL
```

Once a property has been declared and associated with a decision node, the value of the property at each refinement can be defined. At present the value of a property for a refinement is
represented as either a single value, a set of ranges with associated probabilities, or a symbolic expression. Continuing with our example, we could state:

```
            Verified(P.I1) = YES
            Verified(P.I2) = YES
            Verified(P.I3) = NO
            Exp_Exec-Time(P.I1) = <.1[0,10], .8[11,80], .1[81,100]>
            Exp_Exec-Time(P.I2) = (A)*(Exp_SEARCH_Time(Table))+
                                  (B)*(Exp_ENTER_Time(Table))
                                  (C)*(Exp_Exec_Time(P₂))
            Exp_Exec-Time(P.I3) = <[20,100]>
```

In the case of a symbolic expression, the unknowns can be properties
associated with the subconcepts used or quantities (e.g., operator
frequency) obtained from analysis of the refinement itself. A formal treatment of the definition and combination of properties is
beyond the scope of this paper but can be found in [24].

Determining values for the properties upon which a decision
will be based requires careful analysis of the design. It has been
argued [20] that such analysis is essential to the engineering of
quality software. The objective of the decision model, however, is
to record the result of whatever analysis has been done, not to require that specific analyses be performed or that analysis proceed
in any particular manner (e.g., top-down vs bottom-up). In fact,
properties can be left undefined and important information still
gleaned from a decision.

3.3 Objective Function

Properties represent individual characteristics considered important in comparing alternatives. The actual criteria used to
select a refinement may involve a combination of properties. Such a
combination is referred to as an objective function. Objective
functions can be single properties:

```
                   OBF = Exp_Exec_Time
```

indicating that the decision will be based solely on the expected
execution time of alternative refinements, or they may involve a
combination of properties, for example

```
                   OBF = Exp_Exec_Time * Exp_Space
```

or

    OBF = (5)*(Exp_SEARCH_Time(Table)) + (1)*(Exp_ENTER_Time(Table))

The first of these indicates that a time-space performance measure will be used as the criterion to select a refinement. In the second example the criterion is once again execution time, yet the objective function reflects a relative weighting (5 to 1) of the expected number of SEARCH operations to the expected number of ENTER operations.

3.4 Making Decisions

Once an objective function has been defined the actual decision process can begin. A decision is made at a concept node by systematically rejecting alternatives until a single alternative is left. To track this process, we keep a record of the local state of a decision node with a five-tuple:

$$Q = <\{U\}, \{R\}, \{Props\}, OBF, \{Assumps\}>$$

where {U} is the set of currently undecided (i.e., unrejected) alternative refinements, {R} is the set of rejected refinements, {Props} is the set of properties that have been defined, OBF is the objective function, and {Assumps} is the set of explicit assumptions that have been made (assumptions are described later in this section). For example, the initial state for the decision regarding the procedural concept P in Figure 2 would be:

    Q0 = <{P.I1,P.I2,P.I3}>, {}, {...prop defs...}, Exp_Exec_Time, {}>

If the next step is to reject P.I3, the state changes to

    Q1 = <{P.I1,P.I2}, {P.I3}, {..prop defs..}, Exp_Exec_Time, {}>

Thus, the sequence of actions leading to a decision at a concept node can be tracked as a sequence of states Q0 to QF where in QF the set {U} contains a single refinement. With the automated tools of Section 4 it is possible to save any (or all) of the states in the sequence and to return to any previous state to back up the decision process at a node. It is also possible to explore alternative decisions at a specific node by establishing alternate decision paths (sequences of states) and then later make a decision by selecting one path that ends in a state Q with a single refinement in {U}.

3.5 Assumptions

In reaching a decision to select a particular refinement and to reject others, a designer is essentially optimizing the objective function across the alternatives. No attempt, however, is being made here to automate this process although symbolic manipulation tools could be used to provide assistance. Instead, the model records as an implicit assumption the fact that in any final state QF the value of the objective function at the selected refinement is less than its value at any of the rejected refinements. Thus, even if we have no idea of the exact value of a property, for example Exp_Exec_Time for the procedural concept P in Figure 2, a decision to reject P.I2 and P.I3 based on an objective function OBF = Exp_Exec_Time results in the assumption that

    Exp_Exec_Time(P.I1) < Exp_Exec_Time(P.I2)

and

$$Exp\_Exec\_Time(P.I1) < Exp\_Exec\_Time(P.I3)$$

being recorded for later use.

While there is no attempt to automate the selection of the optimal refinement, the model does allow a designer to make and record
additional assumptions for the purpose of simplifying relationships
to the point where a decision is clear. These _explicit_ assumptions
are currently restricted to boolean valued expressions in which
operands are either: 1) constants; 2) the value of a property at a
"used" concept; 3) an unknown in the symbolic expression for the
value of a property at a specific refinement; or 4) in the case of
a data concept, the expected number of times an operation will be
executed. For example, given the design in Figure 2, we might say

       ASSUME Exp_SEARCH_Time(Table) < Exp_ENTER_Time(Table)
       ASSUME Exp_No(SEARCH) < Exp_No(ENTER)
       REJECT P.I2, P.I3

If the final state for this decision is :

$<\{P.I1\}, \{P.I2,P.I3\}, \{..props..\}, OBF=Exp\_Exec\_Time,$
           $\{..above\ assumps..\}>$

then we have a retrievable record of the following assumptions:

Exp_Exec_Time(P.I1)	<	Exp_Exec_Time(P.I2)
Exp_Exec_Time(P.I1)	<	Exp_Exec_Time(P.I3)
Exp_SEARCH_Time(Table)	<	Exp_ENTER_Time(Table)
Exp_No(SEARCH)	<	No_of(ENTER)

3.6 Decision Sets

The preceding discussion deals with a decision at a single concept node. In developing a design we must, of course, make a decision for each concept node in the decision tree. A decision tree
has an overall state in terms of what decisions have and have not
been made (this state is simply the cummulative state of each decision node). Alternate designs can be constructed by having separate
decision trees (in different states) for each alternative. This
idea is realized in terms of a _decision set_ which is simply a decision tree (and all its associated information) in a particular
state. Decisions are always made with respect to the current decision set. When a decision set is created, it can initially be empty
(i.e., each node in its decision tree is in state Q0), or it can be
initialized to the state of an existing decision set (say DS_i). In
the first case, the new set being created (call it DS_j) is unrelated
to the existing set, while in the latter case DS_j is explicitly related to its _predecessor_ DS_i. In fact, in this case we have saved
the current state of the decision making process as DS_i.

A decision set such as DS_i can have many _successor_ decision
sets each of which represents an alternative design that is being
explored. Thus, there is a tree-like relationship between decision
sets as illustrated in Figure 3. In that figure DS_0 is the initial
decision set with no decisions having been made. DS_2, DS_3, and DS_6
share those decisions encapsulated in DS_1. The decision making process can be backed-up to a previous state by simply creating a new
decision set initialized to the decision set for that state. If DS_6
is created after DS_5, then DS_6 represents returning to state Q to
begin exploration of a third alternative. Whenever a decision set

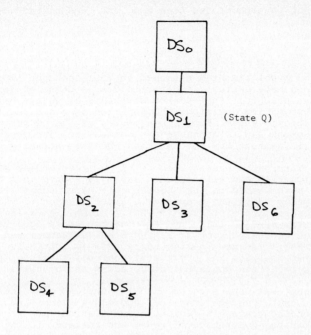

Figure 3   Decision Set Tree Structure

is destroyed, that portion of the tree and the associated designs
are lost.

4   DECISION TOOLS

The decision model has been designed to represent one important
class of decisions made during the detailed design phase of development. To explore practical application of the model we are building
a set of tools for making decisions and for recording and retrieving
decision information. These tools are part of an experimental
software development and maintenance environment and are overviewed
briefly here to illustrate how the decision model is actually used.

All of the information associated with a development effort
(i.e., the design tree and all decision sets) is stored in a design
data base. New concepts (data or procedural) are added to the
design data base by compiling a syntactic specification of the data
or procedural abstraction expressed in DLN. (DLN is a language
similar to CLU [9], ALPHARD [23], and Ada [6] but which ignores many
programming language issues such as nested block structure and complex scope rules). A new design data base is initialized with
specifications for the data and procedural concepts that are predefined in DLN; user-defined concepts can be added at any time.

Once a concept has been entered into the design data base, a
refinement for that concept can be added by compiling a DLN
representation of the concept's design. Compilation of a design
does not result in the generation of code, but instead, in the creation of new entries in the design data base to describe the internal
structure of the refinement (e.g., concepts used, data flow, control
flow) and to link this information to the parent concept. Refinements for a concept can be added at any time provided that specifications for all "used" concepts have been entered into the design
data base. The design tree comes into existence when its root is
made known to the system. Thus, if the concepts and refinements in
Figure 1 have been entered into the design data base, then execution
of the command

ROOT   P

will create the design tree of Figure 2.

To begin making design decisions, we must first create a new
decision set.

MKDS   DS$_{\emptyset}$

This brings a new decision tree into existence with each decision
point (concept node) in the initial state Q0 described in Section 3.
From this point, all decisions will be associated with DS$_{\emptyset}$ until
another MKDS or a CHNGDS (change to an existing decision set) command is executed. Once a decision set has been established, we can
make decisions about refinements in any order.

To make a decision we must first identify the desired concept
node in the decision tree. For example, with a decision tree based
on Figure 2, we could prepare to make a decision about the representation of the data concept Table in P.I2 with the command

POSITION /P/P.I2/TABLE

where UNIX-like pathname is used to identify the desired concept.
If the decision is to be based on execution time, we could then introduce relevant properties to be considered with

```
PROP   Exp_SEARCH_Time : REAL
PROP   Exp ENTER_Time  : REAL
PROP   Exp_REMOVE_Time : REAL
```

Assuming that we have analyzed the two refinements we might then define the value of these properties at each refinement with:

```
DEF   Exp_SEARCH_Time(ORDERED) : LOG(N) + 1
DEF   Exp_ENTER_Time(ORDERED)  : LOG(N) + N/2
DEF   Exp_REMOVE_Time(ORDERED) : LOG(N) + N/2

DEF   Exp_SEARCH_Time(UNORDERED) : N/2
DEF   Exp_ENTER_Time(UNORDERED)  : 1
DEF   Exp_REMOVE_Time(UNORDERED) : 1
```

To intelligently choose a refinement for the concept Table, something must be known about the way in which the concept is used.
This knowledge can be expressed through the objective function, assumptions, or a combination of the two. For example, if it is known
that Enter operations will dominate, we might state

```
OBF = Exp_ENTER_Time
REJECT   ORDERED
```

indicating that the decision is based soley on the expected execution time for Enter. Or we might enter

```
OBF = Exp_SEARCH_Time + Exp_ENTER_Time
```

indicating that both Search time and Enter time will be considered,
but then later add the assumption

```
ASSUME   Exp_No(SEARCH) > Exp_No(ENTER)
```

and finally reject the unordered representation

```
REJECT UNORDERED
```

Assuming this latter decision has been made, we can move on to consider the procedural concept P

```
POSITION  /P
```

Here assume we introduce two properties

```
PROP   Exp_Exec_Time : REAL
PROP   Verified : {YES,NO}
```

and define them as follows

```
Verified(P.I1) = YES
Verified(P.I2) = YES
Verified(P.I3) = NO

Exp_Exec_Time(P.I1) = (A)*(Exp_SEARCH_Time(Table)) +
                      (B)*(Exp_ENTER_Time(Table)) +
                      (C)*(Exp_Exec_Time(P₁)
Exp_Exec_Time(P.I2) = (A)*(Exp_SEARCH_Time(Table)) +
```

$$(B)*(Exp\_ENTER\_Time(Table)) +$$
$$(C)*(Exp\_Exec\_Time(P_2))$$

Now assume our decision will be to choose the refinement that has the lowest expected execution time and that has been verified. First, we define an objective function

$$OBF = Verified$$

and reject the unverified design

$$REJECT \quad P.I3$$

Now we save the current state of the decision at this node with

$$PUSHSTATE$$

and define a new objective function

$$OBJ = Exp\_Exec\_Time$$

In comparing the two remaining refinements for P, we note that a decision about a refinement for Table in P.I1 has not been made but should be identical to that made in P.I2 (since the decision was based on operator frequencies and these would be the same for either refinement of P). We indicate that a decision identical to a previous one should be made with

$$SET \; P.I1/Table \; TO \; P.I2/Table$$

Now the only difference between the two refinements is the expected execution time for P_1 and P_2. If these two procedural concepts have not yet been designed, we need to make an assumption to reach a decision.

$$ASSUME \quad Exp\_Exec\_Time \; (P_1) < Exp\_Exec\_Time(P_2)$$
$$REJECT \quad P.I2$$

Note that since the assumption about P_1 and P_2 was made prior to considering refinements for these concepts, the assumption is logged as a constraint on a future decision. Also note that since the state of the decision was saved after rejecting P.I3, if at some later point P.I3 is verified, we can return to this state (with a POPSTATE command), "unmake" the rejection of P.I3, and reconsider the whole decision.

The preceding is intended to give a glimpse of how the decision tool is used during development. All of the information associated with the design decision process is kept as a permanent record of the detailed design phase. Thus, at any point (during design or long after development is complete) we can inquire about alternatives considered and assumptions made. For example,

```
                ALTERNATIVES /P
response:       P.I1, P.I2, P.I3

                ASSUMPTIONS /P
response:       Verified(P.I3) = NO
                Exp_Exec_Time(P₁) < Exp_Exec_Time(P₂)

                ASSUMPTIONS /P/P.I1/Table
response:       Exp_No(SEARCH) < Exp_No(ENTER)
```

```
                  ASSUMPTIONS  /P/P.Il/P₁
response:             Exp_Exec_Time(P₁) < Exp_Exec_Time(P₂)
```

This tells us the constraints under which P_1 and P_2 were designed and the environmental assumptions under which an ORDERED representation was chosen for Table. Other commands allow one to inquire about the current or previous state of a decision as well as what properties and objective function were used to make a decision.

5 SUMMARY AND STATUS

We have presented a brief overview of a tool for tracking and recording information associated with an important class of design decisions. The tool is based upon a model that treats a decision as a process of choosing a refinement for a concept from a group of alternatives. The model and tool allow a decision to be based upon almost any property considered relevant and allow important states in the decision process to be saved and re-entered to remake a decision or to explore alternatives.

The experimental system described in Section 4 is being implemented on a VAX-11/780 running the UNIX operating system (UNIX is a registered trademark of Bell Laboratories). The design data base is implemented as an INGRES relational data base. Language processors have been completed for the DLN notation. The relations required to represent decision sets, decision trees, and all the information associated with a decision have been designed. The implementation of the operations used in Section 4 is complete and is currently being evaluated.

At present all symbolic expressions (i.e., the representation of properties at refinements or the boolean expressions that make up an assumption) are stored in a canonical form, but no automatic symbolic manipulation is done. This is an area of future work we wish to pursue with the objective of assisting in the verification of assumptions and constraints across an entire design. The more automated assistance we can provide a designer, the better the opportunity for extracting meaningful information for use during the comprehension of complex systems.

Acknowledgements

I am grateful to Ed Balkovich, Taylor Booth, Rich Hart, Lee Derbenwick, Reba Kraus, Mary Murtha, Mark Vogel, and Kokou Yetongnon for many interesting discussions on software design decisions and for their comments on an earlier draft of this paper. The system described in Section 4 was designed and implemented by Kokou Yetongnon as part of a Master's thesis at the University of Connecticut.

REFERENCES

[1] Brooks, R. E., "Using a Behavioral Theory of Program Comprehension in Software Engineering," *Proc. Third International Conference on Software Engineering*, Atlanta, Ga. 1978.

[2] Dijkstra, E. D., Notes on Structured Programming, in <u>Structured</u> <u>Programming</u>, Academic Press, 1972.

[3] Estrin, G., "A Methodology for Design of Digital Systems - Supported by SARA at the Age of One,", <u>AFIPS</u>, <u>Conference</u> <u>Proceedings</u>, Vol. 47 (1978).

[4] Goetz, M.A., "Automatic System for Constructing and Recording Display Charts, U.S. Patent Office, Patent 3,533,086, AUTOFLOW, Applied Data Research (ADR), October 6, 1970.

[5] Hart, R. O. "Intelligent Tools for Software Development and Maintenance," Ph.D. dissertation, The University of Connecticut (in preparation).

[6] Ichbiah, J., "Reference Manual for the Ada Programming Language," US Department of Defense, November 1980.

[7] Jackson, M. <u>Principles</u> <u>of</u> <u>Program</u> <u>Design</u>, Academic Press, 1975.

[8] Liskov, B. H., "A Design Methodology for Reliable Software," <u>Proc</u>. <u>AFIPS</u> <u>FJCC</u>, 1972.

[9] Liskov, B., Snyder, A., Atkinson, R., and Schaffert, C., "Abstraction Mechanisms in CLU," <u>CACM</u>, Vol. 20, No. 8, 1977.

[10] Liskov, B. H., "Modular Program Construction Using Abstraction," <u>MIT</u> <u>Technical</u> <u>Report</u>, <u>1981</u>.

[11] Mills, H. D., "Syntax Directed Documentation for PL/360," <u>CACM</u>, vol. 13, no. 4, 1970.

[12] Murtha, M. "Design and Implementation of DLN - A Language for Specifying Hierarchically Structured Designs," Technical Report CS-81-1, University of Connecticut.

[13] Musser, D. R. "Abstract Data Type Specification in the AFFIRM System," <u>Proc</u>. <u>Specification</u> <u>of</u> <u>Reliable</u> <u>Software</u>, Boston, 1979

[14] Myers, G. <u>Reliable</u> <u>Software</u> <u>Through</u> <u>Composite</u> <u>Design</u>, Petrocelli-Charter, 1975.

[15] Parnas, D. L., "A Technique for the Specification of Modules with Examples," <u>CACM</u>,. vol. 15, no. 5, 1972.

[16] Parnas, D. L., "On the Design and Development of Program Families," <u>IEEE</u>-<u>TSE</u>, vol. SE-2, no.1, 1976.

[17] Teichroew, D. and Hershey, E., "PSL/PSA: Computer Aided Documentation and Analysis of Information Processing Systems," <u>IEEE</u>-<u>TSE</u>, vol. SE-3, no. 1, 1977.

[18] VanHorn, E., "Software Must Evolve," Technical Report, Digital Equipment Corporation, Maynard, Mass. 1979.

[19] Warnier, J. D., <u>Logical</u> <u>Construction</u> <u>of</u> <u>Programs</u>, Van Nostrand Reinhold, New York, 1974.

[20] White, J. R. and Booth, T. L., "Towards an Engineering Approach to Software Design," <u>Proc</u>. <u>Second</u> <u>International</u> <u>Conference</u> <u>on</u>

Software Engineering, San Francisco, 1976.

[21] White, J. R., "Computer Assisted Software Evolution," Technical Report, CS-79-12, University of Connecticut.

[22] Willis, R. R., "DAD: An Automated System to Support Design Analysis," Proc. Third International Conference on Software Engineering, Atlanta, Ga. 1978.

[23] Wulf, W. A., Shaw, M., and London, R. L., "An Introduction to the Construction and Verification of ALPHARD Programs," IEEE-TSE, vol. SE-2, December 1976.

[24] Yetongnon, K., "A Model and Tool for Making and Recording Software Design Decisions," M.S. Thesis, University of Connecticut, in Preparation.

Automated Tools for Information Systems Design
H.-J. Schneider and A.I. Wasserman (eds.)
North-Holland Publishing Company
© IFIP, 1982

SYSTEM D - AN INTEGRATED TOOL FOR SYSTEMS DESIGN,
IMPLEMENTATION AND DATA BASE MANAGEMENT

Hannu Kangassalo, Hannu Jaakkola, Kalervo Järvelin,
Tapio Lehtonen, Timo Niemi

Department of Mathematical Sciences, Computer Science,
University of Tampere, P.O. BOX 607,
SF-33101 Tampere 10, Finland

System D is an experimental, integrated tool for information
systems design, implementation and database management. It
can be used as a relational database management system but
it can also be used as a tool for database design and data
processing systems design. It provides a user an external
view both on the conceptual level and on the relational
level. It provides also a spectrum of different query
languages. The database administrator (DBA) can see all
four schema levels: conceptual, relational, data structure
and storage structure levels. The DBA has at his disposal
a special language, called Data Administration Language
which can be used to design, define, and maintain the
database. System D has an adaptive query optimizer which
can use different sets of optimization rules in different
situations. If information requirements of a user are
formulated as a query, then System D can be used as an
automated design tool which produces a set of programs and
optimized intermediate files which corresponds to the
original query. Produced programs can be stored for later
use. System D Optimizer can also be used as a tool for
physical data base design.

1. INTRODUCTION

During the last few years considerable progress has been made in the fields of
data base management, programming methodology and information systems design
methodology. However, all these fields have been developed quite independently
of each other, in spite of the fact that they are all approaching the same or at
least very similar problems from different directions. Very little research has
been done in order to integrate the results achieved on all these separate
fields [4].

System D is an experimental, integrated tool under development at the University
of Tampere for information systems design, implementation and data base management.
Its development has originated from the study of relational data base management
systems, which has later evolved to embrace different aspects of data management
and data processing activities. The purpose of the development of System D is in
the first phase to build a flexible, experimental tool for the research and
education of the theory and methodology of data management problems. The long
term goal is to develop a practical and efficient system for systems design and
implementation work.

Because of the experimental nature of System D one of the main design criteria has
been a high degree of modularity and flexibility. At the current phase of
development the changeability has been regarded as a more important property than
fast response times. The obvious reason for that is the possibility to develop

and test different alternatives of the system architecture as well as methods for
solving some specific problems. The final version of the system will, of course,
be built as efficient as possible.

Other important design criteria are:

- It must be possible to use several different query languages for different
  purposes or in different environments,

- The system must be able to optimize a query written in any query languages
  of the system,

- It should be possible to manipulate the data base description with the same
  routines as the data base itself,

- It should be possible to use the system as a tool for data processing system
  development and implementation together with its use as an ordinary data base
  management system,

- The system should incorporate an efficient and flexible interface for the data
  base administrator. This interface should contain facilities for data base
  design and maintenance as well as for control of data base usage.

In this paper we will describe System D on the general level paying special
attention to some features we think are of high importance for the development of
a versatile tool. Some of these features are on a rather advanced level and much
more work is still needed before the complete implementation is running.

The general architecture of System D is described in section 2. The database and
the database description are illustrated in section 3. In section 4 the general
design principles of user interfaces are discussed. Section 5 contains the
description of the Data Administration Language which is intended to be a tool for
a database administrator (DBA). Section 6 gives an overview of the query optimizer
and the optimization process. In this section also the use of System D as a tool
for data processing systems design and implementation is discussed. Section 7
contains a short summary of System D as well as an account of the status of the
development work.

2. THE ENVIRONMENT AND THE ARCHITECTURE OF SYSTEM D

System D recognizes four classes of users in its environment: a non-experienced
end user, a professional user, a data base administrator and a computerized data
processing system.

Basically the system is based on the relational view of data [9]. A non-
experienced end user is given a relational external view. The user can formulate
information requirements with a query language by using relations defined in
his/her external schema. It is supposed that at least some query languages will
contain also features for updating the data base. The user has also to a certain
extent a possibility to define new relations in his external schema. New relations
may be either stored or virtual relations.

Because of the basic design principles it is possible to give a wide variety of
different interfaces to professional users. The minimum which can be offered is
the relational view of data. However, there is no reason why he couldn't be
given a CODASYL-type interface or a hierarchical interface as well in some later
phase of the development. The profits which can be achieved by the co-existence
of several data models within one data base management system in a research and
education environment are obvious.

The data base administrator (DBA) can "see" the implementation of relations and he can modify data structures without changing the relational view in any way. The DBA has at his disposal a Data Administration Language (DAL) which can be used for initial data base design, data base implementation as well as maintenance of the data base. The DBA can also define the data authorization rules.

The data base of System D must also be used and updated by computerized data processing systems. One of the tasks of the DBA is to develop specifications needed to translate data from the format used in System D to the format used in the data processing system and vice versa.

The system is using relational algebra as an intermediate language which is used as a standard interface between the translators of query languages and the query optimizer. The advantage of this arrangement is that the system can be developed and tested although the query languages have not yet beet implemented. The disadvantage is that in some cases the use of relational algebra may lead to an inefficient implementation of the query.

The general architecture of System D is illustrated in figure 1. The general description of components is given below. A more detailed description of each component is given in subsequent sections.

The database description and authorization subsystem is the kernel of System D. It is used by all other components of the system to transfer data descriptions between the description database and system components.

Data administration subsystem consists of facilities needed by the DBA to design and maintain the data base. Its components are the data description language, the data base maintenance facility and the data base design facility.

Query language translators translate queries into relational algebra expressions. The intermediate language used to express relational algebra expressions must be extended in such a way that it is capable of manipulating local functions, i.e. user defined application functions needed to perform simple calculations on data. Some query languages will be especially oriented to making simple queries from the data base. At least one language will be oriented to the definition of data processing systems.

The optimizer tries to modify the relational algebra expressions produced by the translators in order to improve the performance of the query program. A special feature of the optimizer in System D is that it is using an adaptive set of optimizing rules for different situations. The optimizer is using data base descriptions transferred by the database description and authorization subsystem.

The program constructor produces from the optimized query one or more programs which manipulate the data base. The algorithms corresponding to different data structure/relational operation -pairs are complemented from the data base description and composed together to a complete program.

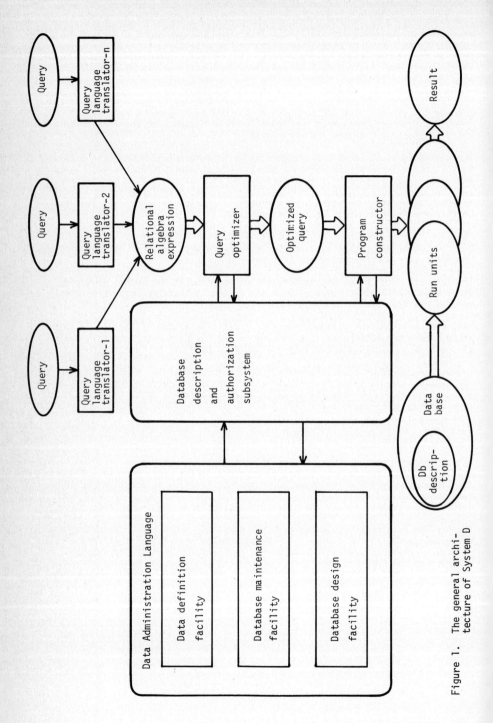

Figure 1. The general architecture of System D

3. THE DATABASE AND THE DATABASE DESCRIPTION

The database of System D is based on the relational view of data. The implementation of it will be based either on the use of sequential files, indexed files or inverted files. Although the design of System D is currently built on the use of these three types of data structures, the mechanism allows also the use of some other types of data structures, as hashing, multilists etc.

The description database will also be implemented as a relational data base so that in most situations same routines can be used to manipulate both the database and its description.

Conceptually the db-description is organized according to the principle of abstraction levels developed by H. Kangassalo [14, 15]. This principle is in some respects relatively close to the approach used by M. Senko [27]. However, it was developed independently and there are also some fundamental differencies. The basic idea of the principle of abstraction levels is that properties of units of data are different in their epistemological abstractness and these properties can be arranged into a hierarchy of abstraction levels according to the degree of their epistemological abstractness. The epistemological abstractness of a property is the higher the more knowledge is required for the recognition of that property [14]. A detailed description of the principle of abstraction levels is out of the scope of this paper and therefore it will not be described here in more detail.

The principle of abstraction levels allows the use of the three-schema architecture of ANSI/SPARC, although in a modified form [29]. Figure 2 shows an overview of the db-description.

On the left side of the figure are the common schemas of System D. They describe the whole data base and data processing systems produced by using System D. According to the principle of abstraction levels each schema describes the data base and the data processing system in terms specific to that level of abstraction. These schemas are the common conceptual schema, the common relational schema, the data structure schema and the storage structure schema.

On the right side of the figure are the schemas needed to specify the user interfaces or the external schemas. These schemas are: the user description, the user's conceptual schema and the user's relational schema.

The conceptual schema describes the conceptual content of the data base and data processing systems in relation to the object system, i.e. the slice of the real world which is supported by the data base and data processing system. This part of reality is called an object system. The conceptual schema consists: 1) of concept definitions describing concepts allowed to be used for the description of the object system, 2) of relationships and/or constraints recognized to exist in the conceptual description between concepts, 3) of concepts, relationships and/or constraints based on the existence rules of data in the data base. Thus the conceptual schema contains a specification of a system of concepts, called a concept system, and a conceptual model of the object system. By a concept system we mean here the consistent set of concepts which can be used to make up the conceptual model of the object system.

The structure made up of concepts and relationships between them is a kind of semantic network. The basic relationship between concepts is that of intensional containing [16, 17] which can be regarded as a generalization of well-known relationships of an IS-A-relationship, a component-relationship and an attribute-relationship [2]. The intensional containing between concepts determines the intensional structure of the concept system. Some other relationships and constraints are needed to determine how concepts are applied to make up the conceptual schema of the object system.

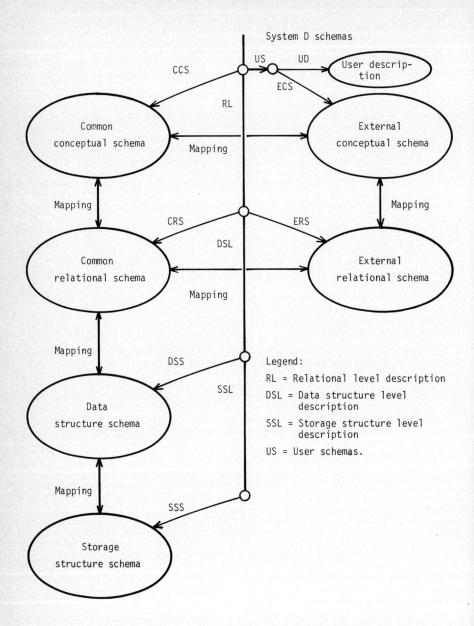

Figure 2. The overview of the database description

New concepts, new relationships and new constraints between concepts can be
inserted via data base administration subsystem. DAL contains facilities for
graphical and linear interface. Also the user has limited capabilities to insert
new concepts into his own conceptual schema.

The conceptual schema describes the content and dynamics of the object system.
Concepts related to dynamics of the object system, i.e. an event and a process are
defined as concepts and they are described by using a similar mechanism which has
been used for the description of static concepts. The definition of events
contains the notions of time and change as special constructs which facilitate the
description of changes in the object system. However, there is no exact boundary
between dynamical and static features of concepts in a conceptual schema because
an important part of the definition of a static concept are its rules of behavior.
The conceptual schema contains also a section which describes the conceptual
content of that portion of the database which does not have any direct corresponding counterpart in the object system, e.g. data concerning the past history
of the object system, derived data like averages, totals etc. The conceptual
schema is completely free of any technical details of the implementation of the
data base or the data processing system.

The relational schema represents concepts as relational schemas which in turn are
described as relations in third normal form. The schemas of these description
relations are:

RELATION-1 (<u>REL-NAME</u>, REL-TYPE, CONSISTENCY, VIRT-RULE, SEM-DEF)
RELATION-2 (<u>REL-NAME, DOM-NAME</u>, STATUS, ROLE-NAME)
VIRTUAL   (<u>REL-NAME, PREC-REL-NAME</u>)
SEMANTICS (<u>REL-NAME, DOM-NAME</u>, SEM-DEF)

In RELATION-1 the consistency rules are described in CONSISTENCY-domain and
VIRT-RULE contains the relational algebra expression for producing an instance of
a virtual relation if the type of the relation in REL-TYPE is virtual. In
RELATION-2 STATUS specifies whether the domain is a main key, a secondary key or
an attribute. In VIRTUAL the names of the relations are given from which the
virtual relation named in REL-NAME is to be produced. This relation is used e.g.
for the control of authorization rules if the authorization class of the relation
in REL-NAME has to be changed. The value SEM-DEF contains a reference to the
conceptual schema which gives the explanation of the meaning of the domain in this
relation as well as the meaning of the relation itself.

The data structure schema describes the implementation of relations as data
structures in terms of value sets and access paths. The data structure schema
contains only one relation which specifies the method used to implement the domains
of the relations.

The storage structure schema describes the implementation of each data structure
in terms of storage locations, storage sequences etc. It contains also some
technical information which is used by the optimizer, e.g. the actual cardinality
of a stored relation, its sort time, time required to read the whole relation and
an average access time.

The user description contains the identification of a user as well as his task
descriptions which are used to assist the DBA in his work. The user schema
consists of the external conceptual schema (and possibly of the external relational
schema). The external conceptual schema describes the concept system applied by
the user in his work as well as his view of the object system described with
the aid of concepts defined in his concept system. The external conceptual schema
allows a user to work only on the conceptual level without taking care of relations
or other structuring features of the system. This is quite different approach as
compared to ANSI/SPARC or CODASYL -78 approaches in which the user is in fact
working with external data structures [29, 7].

The user may also be allowed to work on the relational schema level on which he has
the external relational schema at his disposal. The external relational schema
corresponds to his external conceptual schema. Thus the user can choose the level
he wants to work on. On the conceptual level he has only to know the concepts and
the relationships between them which brings this level very close to semantic
networks like for example KLONE [3] or TAXIS [20].

4. USER INTERFACES TO SYSTEM-D

System D provides a variety of languages for different users. Some of those
languages are on the conceptual level, others are on the relational level. The
latter includes also possible languages for the network or hierarchical interfaces.
Because of this variety we will not describe any detailed languages. Instead we
want to describe some general aspects which must be taken into account in the
design of these languages [12].

1. Nature of a query process. Querying can be described as a communication
   process in which a query expressed in concepts based on the abstraction from
   reality is transformed into the form required by the query language. In general
   this transformation should be as minimal as possible, i.e. these two forms or
   structures should be as close to each other as possible. A query is said to be
   natural if this transformation is minimal. A language on the conceptual level
   meets this requirement of naturality better than a language on the relational
   level.

2. Heterogenity of users. Users of System D are supposed to be very different in
   their level of adp-education and experience as well as in their interest to
   learn new things. In System D this heterogenity is taken into account in two
   different ways. First, the languages are different in their level of
   abstraction. At least the conceptual level and the relational level should
   be used. Secondly, adaption into users' experience can be reached by having
   a layered language structure, i.e. an easy-to-learn kernel of the language
   provides a capability to express the most commonly used query types. This
   easy-to-learn kernel consists of the expressions for restriction, join and
   projection [10, 24, 25, 26]. Along experience users can learn to use new
   language features and increase their ability to make more complicated queries.
   The difficult features are the universal quantification, the use of functions
   and arithmetic, grouping etc.[10, 24, 25, 26].

3. A classification of query types is an important design aspect. Simple queries
   have the greatest frequence. Query languages must provide an easy way to
   express simple queries, i.e. those containing projection-restriction- and
   join-type of operations. According to several research results these features
   are the most commonly used and also easiest to learn (e.g. [25, 26]).

Users are disposed to make a sequence of queries having nearly the same form.
Query systems should support this kind of use so that users can formulate their
queries using a work space. Contents of this work space can be edited, executed
as a query, listed and removed using special commands. It must also be possible
to store it for later use.

Queries are modular. Users must have a possibility to divide their queries into
parts. This can be implemented by providing them the virtual relation concept.
Users can define in their external relational schema their queries, not only
results of queries, to be named relations in the database with the same properties
as the database relations have. This property also supports the possibility to
use continuing queries. System D contains this property as one basic design
principle.

The relational level language Query D of System D is planned to be a stand-alone system, which is extendable to a host-language system. It is based on keyword oriented SQL (SEQUEL) language [5, 6], which according to research results [10, 25, 26] has been proven to be easy to learn and easy to use. Because of its textual interface type it is also easy to implement. Differences between Query-D and SQL are quite small, mostly in the expressing forms. Query-D is a powerful language and it contains all the necessary components to express queries, and update and manage database. Final design and implementation of the language has not yet been done. The more detailed features of Query-D are introduced in the following.

Language Features of Query D

In addition to the principal aspects mentioned above, Query-D has the following features:

- the basic structure of a query is (as in SQL)
  virtual-relation-description ←
  SELECT attribute-list
  FROM target-relation-name
  WHERE conditional
  GROUP BY grouping-attributes
  HAVING conditional
- language is relationally complete [6] including the power of relational algebra, operations to manage data, and full updating features
- universal quantifying is based on set expression
- row-constants are included into the language
- user has the possibility to manage duplicates
- functions (like sum, avg, max, min, ...) are included into the language and can be used as a result and as a condition in queries, both in attribute list and in conditional
- arithmetic operations are included into the language and can be used as a result and as a condition in queries
- set operations are included into the language, i.e. query results can be handled as a set of rows
- ordering of relations is possible (ordered by ...)
- facilities to communicate with some operating system features are allowed
- all operation types (quering, updating, maintenance of data) have identical format

The detailed specification and implementation of the language is at its starting point. In the first phase only a subset of the query properties are implemented. In the second phase the language is extended to contain all of the query facilities. The final phase will add data management and updating facilities to the language.

The conceptual level language Concept D of System D allows a user to define, manipulate and analyze conceptual constructs based on the concepts defined in the external conceptual schema. This feature makes it possible for a user to study and develop the semantics of data stored in the database and in the data processing system. By using Concept D a user can define the semantics of the whole data processing system on the conceptual level without any consideration of technical details of the underlaying data processing system. The conceptual constructs defined with the aid of Concept D do not only describe "data structures" and operations applied on them, they also give a user all the interpretation functions needed to understand the meaning of data, all the relations and constraints between concepts within the conceptual system of a user as well as all the rules needed to derive the data required by the user.

The basic research for Concept D is now almost completed and the detailed

specification of the language can be started. We believe that the use of
Concept D offers to users a possibility to improve the quality of systems design.

5. DATABASE ADMINISTRATOR'S INTERFACE TO SYSTEM D

The data base administration subsystem of System D consists of three different
layers (see fig. 2):

1. Data definition layer contains language features for constructing data
   descriptions on all schema levels (i.e. conceptual, relational, data structure
   and storage structure).

2. Database maintenance layer contains language features for reorganizing and
   restructuring the database on all schema levels.

3. Database design layer contains language features for assisting the database
   design in all phases of the process.

The data administration language (DAL) has features on each schema level to
define, to analyze and to modify the corresponding schema. The data definition
component of DAL contains features for the specification of conceptual content of
data, the format of data, the structure of data and some storage oriented
parameters of data. The conceptual content of data is defined by using Concept D
augmented with some features allowed only for use of the DBA. These additional
features are for example the definition of a mapping between the common conceptual
schema and an external conceptual schema, the definition of authorization rules,
etc.

The format definition features of DAL are quite similar to corresponding features
of other data definition language, e.g. [7]. The structuring features are divided
on the relational schema level and on the data structure schema level.

The features contained on the database design layer and on the database maintenance
layer are intended to make DAL an integrated and useful tool for a DBA for
designing, maintaining and controlling the content and use of a database.

The definition of the database description can be done level by level in several
phases by using the DEFINE-command. An example of the use of DEFINE for concept
definition is the following:

```
DEFINE CONCEPT employee WHICH
       REFERS TO person CONTAINING ADDITIONAL CONCEPTS job-agreement,
       starting-date, salary-class
       WITH INTERNAL CONSTRAINTS
       1. At any period of time, an employee can have at most one job-agreement,
          starting-date and salary-class.
       AND WITH EXTERNAL CONSTRAINTS
       1. An employee works for one department only,
       2. An employee cannot earn more than his manager.
```

In the example, the constraints are here written in a simplified form. The
lower-case words are user-defined terms whereas the upper-case words are reserved
DAL words.

On the relational schema the corresponding definition might look as follows.

```
DEFINE RELATION emp-rel FOR employee:
       RELATION    person
       ADD         job-agreement-no, DOMAIN IS integer
```

```
ADD          starting-date, DOMAIN IS date
ADD          salary-class-code, DOMAIN IS s-code
MAINKEY      IS person-id
RELTYPE      IS VIRTUAL
EXISTENCE RULE IS
             FOR person-id
                 THERE IS job-agreement-no  (1:1) AND
                 THERE IS starting-date     (1:1) AND
                 THERE IS salary-class-code (1:1)
```

This definition states that the concept employee will be represented in the database as a virtual relation the tuples of which are constructed from tuples of the person-relation together with values from the given domains added to it. The existence rule specifies which are the valid tuples of the employee relation.

An alternative way of defining an employee relation might be:

```
DEFINE FOR employee:
      NEW RELATION emp-2: person-id, DOMAIN IS integer;
                          job-agreement-no, DOMAIN IS integer;
                          starting-date, DOMAIN IS date;
                          salary-class-code, DOMAIN IS s-code;
      MAINKEY IS         person-id
      CONSTRAINTS        person-id → job-agreement-no,
                                     starting-date,
                                     salary-class-code,
                          job-agreement-no → person-id.
      RELATION emp-rel FOR employee:
      RELTYPE IS VIRTUAL, JOIN (person.person-id = emp-2. person-id)
      MAINKEY IS person.person-id
```

In this case an auxiliary relation emp-2 is defined which is then used to construct a virtual relation employee. The construction rule of empoyee is given in RELTYPE paragraph. The constraints for emp-2 must be given explicitly because if the auxiliary relations are used, it is not always possible to derive constraints for them directly from the concept definition (from internal constraints).

On the data structure schema the DBA has to select and describe data structures which are used to implement the corresponding relation. System D is using three different data structures: sequential, indexed sequential or inverted structure.

```
DEFINE DATA STRUCTURE FOR emp-2:
      DATA-STRUCTURE IS I-S, person-id, LEVELS = 2,
                     INV starting-date,
                         salary-class-code
```

This specification states that the relation emp-2 is to be implemented as an indexed sequential structure. The main key is person-id and the index contains two levels. The relation has an inverted structure for domains starting-date and salary-class-code.

On the storage structure schema the DBA can define the storage structure of data structures, give the estimated sort times, read times, etc. These details will not be described here more in detail.

The database administrator can use the DISPLAY-command to print out the descriptions specified by the parameters of the command. Some examples are:

```
DISPLAY user y CONCEPTS department,
                        sales-order and
                        weekly-wage.
```

This command will print out concept descriptions from the external conceptual
schema of the user y. It shows how these concepts have been defined for this
user.

The command

```
DISPLAY RELATIONAL SCHEMA
```

will print out all the relation schemas defined in the common relational schema.
The data structures of relations emp-2 and person can be printed out by

```
DISPLAY DATA STRUCTURE emp-2, person.
```

The DBA can also define, change and delete authorization rules for the data base.
These commands will not be described here more in detail.

On the database maintenance layer the DBA can change database descriptions and
order the changes to be performed in the actual database. For security reasons
the system has to make a feasibility check before any actual change can take
place in order to find all the consequences or possible sources of errors. The
system has to find all programs stored in the system library and which will be
affected by the change. It has also to find out if the required change is
impossible because of some inconsistencies between the old and new data structures.
If an inconsistency is found, the system gives a warning and rejects the command.
If no inconsistencies or other possible sources of errors are found, the system
gives a message and waits for the command from DBA which triggers the actual data
translation process.

The DBA can use the CHANGE-command to change either the names used in the description, the description itself or the authorization rules. The issuing of a
CHANGE-command will cause copying of the source data description on the internal
working space, creation of the target description, checking of the change for
inconsistencies, a message written to the DBA and finally waiting for a reply from
the DBA.

If the DBA wants the translation of stored data to be performed, he can issue a
command which causes the data translation program be generated and run and finally
the new data description will be stored into the description database. If no
actual data translation is involved, the description database will be updated.

For the exact and detailed definition of the semantics of the data conversion
tasks an abstract syntax has been created. The abstract syntax has been formed
in such a way that synthesized and inherited attributes of data structures can be
applied in it in the same manner as with context-free grammars [18, 21, 22, 23].
The abstract syntax specifies abstract objects which correspond to objects on the
schema level and on the instance level. It also generates as abstract objects all
essential elements needed in transforming data structures. Thus the definition of
semantics of data conversion reflects the phases of a conversion process. In fact,
the analysis and transformation functions of data structures describe those tasks
which the restructurer implements at run time.

So far, data structures for which the exact semantics for transformation has been
defined are based either on the flat file data model or on the hierarchical data
model [22]. The set of possible data structures must still be extended to contain
all types of data structures used in System D.

On the database design level the DBA can feed in information produced in the information analysis phase, manipulate it in order to produce a conceptual schema and then proceed "downwards" level by level until the complete definition of a database has been created. The design level consists of commands for analyzing design alternatives, for generating new alternatives and for storing specifications of accepted alternatives into the description database.

The input to the design system consists of concept definition hierarchies, called concept structures, which correspond to the initial information requirements of users. Concept structures are expressed in Concept D. Concept structures are analyzed for consistency, broken down into smallest semantically meaningful components and stored into the description database. The conceptual schema and external conceptual schemas are composed of these concept definitions.

The relational schema design component accepts names of domains and dependencies between them, checks the consistency of dependencies and generates a relational schema. The schemas of relations are stored in the description database and their implementation is designed. The generation of the relational schema is based on the synthesis of irreducible relations [1], which correspond to the smallest semantically meaningful components of concept structures. Therefore every dependency in input is meaningful and has a counterpart in the semantic description of the database. The resulting relational schemas are guaranteed to be in third normal form but not necessarily in optimal third normal form. The gain of our approach is that the resulting relational schema corresponds structurally very closely to the semantics of the conceptual schema.

The schema design component is highly interactive and makes fast iteration possible. The design process consists of several subphases. In every phase it is possible to take one or more steps backwards and to redefine the input on the bases of output diagnostics. The first version of the relational schema generation component has been implemented.

The relational schema generation component is using an algorithm which has been developed from the method described by Mijares and Peebles [19].

DAL can be easily extended by adding new commands to it. Data definition level contains all the features needes to create and maintain data descriptions in the description database. The maintenance level and the design level can be enhanced almost without any limits. The large set of useful analysis and design functions as well as the flexibility of DAL make it a very efficient tool for a database administrator.

6. QUERY OPTIMIZER AND PHYSICAL DATA BASE DESIGN TOOLS

The relational data interface allows the users to concentrate on expressing what kind of data they want without having to indicate how it should be retrieved. The task of query optimizers is to solve the "how" problem - to select efficient access strategies for query implementation. The optimizer seeks to minimize query response time i.e. the total time for query program construction and one execution. The low break-even point between increasing optimization costs and diminishing improvements in the resulting query program allows only very crude optimization methods in an on-line query environment. On the other hand, in the data base design environment certain queries or types of them are known, in advance, to occur repeatedly. This information can be used in two ways. Firstly, the data base may be designed to support these queries (types) with suitable access paths. Secondly, more sophisticated and time consuming methods of optimization are reasonable. Recurring queries can be pre-optimized and stored for later use.

The System D Optimizer is designed to adapt itself to both types of optimization tasks. For an on-line query, expressed in relational algebra (RA), heuristic

rules are used in choosing efficient access strategies. The rules are used to
reorganize the algebraic expression and to coordinate the access path selections
for the operations. The rules being heuristic the access strategies are not
always optimal. However, the optimizer itself may still be optimal in minimizing
the total response time. Expressions for repeated evaluations are optimized using
functions to estimate intermediate file sizes, numbers of block accesses and the
access times for different design altenatives. In both cases the optimizer output
consists of a coordinated set of procedure calls to be converted into a query
program by the program constructor subsystem.

The general outline of optimization resembles that by Smith and Chang [28].
Several features are incorporated from the PRTV system [30]. The database
description subsystem of System D is used for retrieving data and storage structure descriptions for the stored data. There are in total some twenty data
structure dependent procedures available for implementing the relational operations
in different situations. The procedure codes are augmented with access method
codes according to the storage structure of the files to be accessed. Among the
new features used is a method for join optimization which selects among alternative
join predicates the one likely to lead to most efficient file access. Predicates
leading to an one-to-one join, an one-to-many join and a many-to-many join are
searched for in this order of preference. Queries of virtually any complexity may
be processed by the optimizer. The data sublanguage supported by the optimizer is
relationally complete.

The System D Optimizer is as such a useful tool for system design. The users'
information requirements are interpreted as a set of possibly complex queries
formulated using - as the optimizer sees it - RA. Now, given a set of files and
their descriptions, the queries are optimized and corresponding programs generated.
All necessary intermediate files, their data structures, sorting and index construction operations are specified by the optimizer. The use of the intermediate
files shared by the queries is coordinated. Complex or otherwise memory consuming
queries have to be divided into several run units by the program constructor.
Here the stored intermediate files are natural points of decomposition. A
stratified description of the system so designed is easily produced using
System D's data base description subsystem.

More generally, the optimizer is a tool for evaluating physical data base or file
design alternatives during data base (or system) design and maintenance phases.
Given a set of design alternatives and a set of queries weighted by the expected
number of runs per time period the optimizer estimates for each alternative query
response times and the total number of block accesses resulting from it's adoption.

A physical data base design facility, into which the optizer is embedded, is under
development for System D. This facility uses heuristic methods to generate data
base (file) design alternatives based on the relational schema, the RA expressions
and their frequencies, and the response time requirements per expression (or type)
[11]. The technique first separates the expressions into subsets of 'core' and
'marginal' expressions. Query optimization techniques are then utilized to find
interesting access paths, which should be created, for the core expressions.
Based on this, data structures for schema relations are chosen. An in-depth
treatment of the steps involved here is beyond the scope of this paper and will be
covered in later publications. There are still open problems in solving
conflicting design issues - for ex. in selecting permanent indices. Unrecon-
cilable inter-expression conflicts form the basis for the generation of design
alternatives. The query optimizer is then used to select access strategies for
both the core and the marginal queries in each of the design altenatives.[1]
Finally the optimizer evaluates the design altenatives as stated above. The
results are then summarized to allow iterative design cycles under human control.

At the present state of development the design facility is still too query
oriented. To some extent, the updates can be treated in the same way as queries.

However, further work is required to incorporate index maintenance or overflows caused by updates into the facility. An important advantage of embedding the optimizer into the design facility is that the data base (files) will be designed particularly for the optimizer used for transaction implementation with all it's possible weaknesses. Now a possibly excellent design will not be paralyzed by an optimizer not able to take the advantage of it.

One difficulty which still must be overcome is the use of application functions in query expressions. The application functions are user defined functions for calculations and other data manipulation tasks. At the current stage of development there are no rules for passing these functions from query expressions through the optimizer into the database programs. One possible approach for solving this problem has been analyzed on a preliminary level. In this approach application functions are isolated into blocks which are local within some relational subexpression. The relationship between the subexpression and application function block is recognized and used as an additional constraint during the optimization phase.

7. SUMMARY OF SYSTEM D AND THE CURRENT PHASE OF DEVELOPMENT WORK

System D is an integrated tool for information systems development, database management and system implementation. One of the main design principles is modularity which allows the system be developed in several phases and extended in a stepwise fashion without influencing very much the other components of the system.

The core of System D is the database description subsystem. According to the principle of abstraction levels it consists of four schema levels: conceptual, relational, data structure and storage structure schemas. It contains also external schemas on two levels: external conceptual schema and external relational schema.

Closely associated with the database description subsystem is the Data Administration Language (DAL), which is a database administrator's tool for database design, definition and maintenance. DAL can be used to check the correctness of proposed changes in the database description, to define data translation tasks, to aid the database design and definition process as well as to print out the database descriptions. The detailed specification of DAL has begun. It is expected to be completed by the end of this year.

The relational schema generation component has been developed by Tapio Lehtonen. The rules for some data translation situations have been developed by Timo Niemi. The study of the semantics of data translation problems is still in progress. The general architecture of System D as well as the architecture of the database description subsystem has been developed by Hannu Kangassalo. He has also designed the first drafts of DAL and is working with Concept D -language.

System D is able to support several different query languages. All languages are using relational algebra as an intermediate language which makes it possible to use the same underlaying system components in each case. Theoretical research for the development of query languages is in progress. The work is being done by Hannu Jaakkola.

The query optimizer of System D is able to adapt in different requirements. It can be used without any detailed cost functions for optimizing on-line queries. It can also be used to optimize extensive and complicated queries which represent the information requirements of data processing systems. In the latter case the optimizer can use detailed cost functions to evaluate the performance. The specification of optimization rules for on-line queries is completed and the·

specification of cost functions is in progress. The work is being done by
Kalervo Järvelin.

---

†
It is assumed that each of the schema relations is used at least in one of the
core expressions. Otherwise some marginal expressions migth miss data structures of some of their operands.

REFERENCES

[1]   Biller, H.: On the Notion of Irreducible Relations. In Bracchi, G., Nijssen,
      G.M., (Eds.), Data Base Architecture. North-Holland, 1979.

[2]   Brachman, R.: On the Epistemological Status of Semantic Networks. In
      Findler, N., (Ed.), Associative Networks. Academic Press, 1979.

[3]   Brachman, R., Ciccarelli, E., Greanfeld, N., Yonke, M.: KLONE Reference
      Manual. BBN Report No. 3848 July 1978.

[4]   Brodie, M., Zilles, S. (Eds.): Proceedings of Workshop on Data Abstraction,
      Databases and Conceptual Modelling. Pingree Park, Colorado, June 23-26,
      1980. ACM SIGMOD Record, Vol. 11, No. 2, February 1981.

[5]   Chamberlin, D.D., Boyce, F.: A Structured English Query Language. IBM San
      Jose Research Laboratory, Report RJ1394, 1974.

[6]   Chamberlin, D., et al.: SEQUEL2: A Unified Approach to Data Definition,
      Manipulation and Control. IBM Journal of Research and Development 20,6
      (Nov. 1976).

[7]   CODASYL Data Description Language Committee: Journal of Development,
      January 1978.

[8]   Codd, E.F.: Extending the Database Relational Model to Capture More Meaning
      ACM TODS, Vol. 4, No. 4, December 1979.

[9]   Date, C.J.: An Introduction to Database Systems. Second Edition. Addison-
      Wesley Publishing Company 1977.

[10] Greenblatt, P., Waxman, I.: A Study of Three Database Query Languages.
      In Shneiderman, B., (Ed.), Databases: Improving Usability and Responsiveness.
      Academic Press, London, 1978.

[11] Housel, B.C.,   Waddle, V., Yao, S.B.: The Functional Dependency Model for
      Logical Database Design. In: Proc. 5th int.nat. conf. on VLDB, Rio de
      Janeiro, Brazil, Oct. 3-5, 1979.

[12] Jaakkola, H.: Making Queries in Relational Data Base Management Systems.
      University of Tampere. Department of Mathematical Sciences. Report C-12.
      May 1980. (In Finnish).

[13] Jaakkola, H.: A Survey of Query Languages for Relational Data Base
      Management Systems. University of Tampere. Department of Mathematical
      Sciences. Report C-13. May 1980. (In Finnish).

[14] Kangassalo, H.: Stratified Description as a Framework of the File
      Description. In DIFO-vuosikirja 2/1973. DIFO-tutkimus ry., Tampere 1973.
      (In Finnish).

[15] Kangassalo, H.: Conceptual Structure of the File Design Problem: a general view. Scandinavian Workshop on Data Base Schema Design and Evaluation. Røros, Norway, February 1975.

[16] Kangassalo, H.: On the Concept of a Concept, Conceptual Constructs and Conceptual Models. University of Tampere. February 1980 (Unpublished working paper, a new version is in preparation).

[17] Kauppi, R.: Einführung in die Theorie der Begriffssysteme. Acta Universitatis Tamperensis. Ser. A. Vol. 15. Tampereen yliopisto, Tampere 1967.

[18] Knuth, D.E.: Semantics of Context-free Languages. Mathematical Systems Theory, No. 2, 1968, 127-145.

[19] Mijares, I., Peebles, R.: A Methodology for the Design of Logical Data Base Structures. In Nijssen, G.M. (Ed.), Modelling in Data Base Management Systems. North-Holland, Amsterdam 1976.

[20] Mylopoulos, J., Bernstein, P.A., Wong, H.K.T.: A Language Facility for Designing Database-Intensive Applications. ACM TODS Vol. 5, No. 2, June 1980.

[21] Niemi, T.: Formal description of flat file and hierarchical data structures and the definition of analysis and transformation functions for them. University of Tampere, Department of Mathematical Sciences. Report A 56, July 1981. (In Finnish).

[22] Niemi, T.: The definition of semantics of data restructuring for flat files and hierarchical data models by using the attribute method. University of Tampere, Department of Mathematical Sciences. Report A 57, July 1981. (In Finnish).

[23] Niemi, T.: A comparison of two formal definition methods of semantics in a data base environment. University of Tampere, Department of Mathematical Sciences, Report A 58, July 1981. (In Finnish).

[24] Reisner, P.: Human Factors Studies of Database Query Languages: A Survey and Assesment. Computing Surveys, Vol. 13. No. 1. March 1981.

[25] Reisner, P.: Use of Psychological Experimentation as an Aid to Development of a Query Language. IEEE Transactions on Software Engineering SE-3,3 (May 1977).

[26] Reisner, P. et al.: Human Factors Evaluation of Two Database Query Languages: SQUARE and SEQUEL. IBM San Jose Research Laboratory, Report RJ1707, 1976.

[27] Senko, M.E., Altman, E.B., Astrahan, M.M., Fehder, P.L., Wang, C.P.: A data independent architecture model: four levels of description from logical structures to physical search structures. RJ982 IBM Research, Yorktown Heights, New York 1972.

[28] Smith, J., Chang, P.Y-T.: Optimizing the performance of a relational data base interface. Univ. of Utah, 1975.

[29] Tsichritzis, D., Klug, A.: The ANSI/X3/SPARC DBMS Framework. Report of the Study Group on Data Base Management Systems. Computer Systems Research Group. University of Toronto, July 1977.

[30] Verhofstad, J.S.M.: The PRTV optimizer: The current state. UKSC0083, IBM UK Scientific Centre, May 1976.

Automated Tools for Information Systems Design
H.-J. Schneider and A.I. Wasserman (eds.)
North-Holland Publishing Company
© IFIP, 1982

A COMPUTER AIDED TOOL FOR CONCEPTUAL DATA BASE DESIGN

Paolo Atzeni(**) Carlo Batini(*) Valeria De Antonellis(***)
Maurizio Lenzcrini(*) Fulvio Villanelli(**) Bruna Zonta(***)

(*) Istituto di Automatica. Università degli Studi di Roma
Via Eudossiana 18 - 00184 ROMA - ITALY
(**) ITALSIEL S.p.A. Via Isonzo 21B 00100 ROMA - ITALY
(***) Istituto di Cibernetica. Università degli Studi di Milano
Via Viotti 5 - 20133 MILANO - ITALY

We describe the general structure of INCOD-DTE, a computer aided system for INteractive COnceptual Design of Data, Transactions and Events in a data base application. INCOD-DTE is a
tool for the incremental definition of the conceptual schema
of a data base. Both the static and the dynamic aspects are ta
ken into account. An enriched Entity-Relationship model is used
for the representation of static aspects, a specific language
for the representation of transactions and Petri Nets for the
representation of events.

1. INTRODUCTION

A methodology for data base design may be seen as a set of tools, methods and
techniques to:
1. Collect user requirements.
2. Design a data base application that consistently and efficiently implement user
   needs.
3. Plan the development activity.
4. Produce a documentation that can be useful both during the design and during the
   production phase (e.g. in occurrence of possible restructurings) of the applica
   tion life cycle.
   Area 2 is seen [15] as dealing with three separate subareas:
2.1 Information analysis and definition (conceptual design).
2.2 Implementation design.
2.3 Physical design.
   This paper is concerned with the conceptual design phase, whose goal is "to ob
tain an integrated, formal, implementation-indepedent specification of application
specific enterprise information" [16]. This formal specification (often called *Con
ceptual Schema*) is based on a specific model that is usually chosen from the so cal
led semantic models (or second generation models). These models explicitly represent
the semantics of data, suitably describe dynamic properties of data and their evolution according to the occurrence of events.
Both modelling transactions and modelling events in the conceptual design phase is
useful for checking the presence in the data schema of all the constructs that are
needed to execute the operations expressed in the user requirements.

Furthermore, modelling transactions is useful for:

This research has been supported by the Computer Science Program of the Italian Na
tional Research Council: Project DATAID.

- Determining relative access frequencies along functional paths; this piece of in formation is useful for logical and physical design phase.
- Providing formal specification for the detailed design of application programs.

Modelling events is useful for:
- Identifying causal dependencies between transactions, i.e. sequences, parallelism and mutual exclusion; this information is useful for logical and physical design.
- Defining the conceptual schema evolution rules to describe dynamic integrity constraints.

  For such reasons, it is usually accepted that the conceptual schema be the formalized representation of both the static and the dynamic requirements of the application and that a methodology for conceptual data base design consider both.

  The process of formalization of user requirements into a conceptual schema is often ([15]) divided into two steps:
1. User schema design (view modelling).
2. User schema (user view) integration.

For a detailed description of this point see [7].

  The aim of this paper is to describe INCOD-DTE, a computer aided system for INteractive COnceptual Design of Data, Transactions and Events in data base applications, whose design and implementation are in progress. INCOD-DTE provides a set of tools that support the designer during the phase of conceptualization of the sta tic and dynamic requirements, automatically checking the consistency of the design process and simplifying the management of the corresponding documentation. Earlier versions of INCOD, in which only data and transactions are handled, appear in [7], [1].

  The paper is organized as follows.

  In section 2 the conceptual model is described: we use as data model an enriched Entity-Relationship model [8], [9]; as transaction model a specific language; as event model a modified version of Petri Nets ([17]). In section 3 the general struc ture of INCOD-DTE is described. In section 4 we present our conclusions.

2. THE CONCEPTUAL MODEL

  For the reasons discussed in the introduction, the conceptual model adopted in INCOD-DTE allows the formalization of both the static and the dynamic aspects of the application of interest at the same level of abstraction. The dynamic aspects involve transactions and events.

  As a consequence, the *conceptual schema* is defined as a triple S = <D,T,E>, where D, T and E are respectively the *data schema*, the *transactions schema* and the *events schema*, i.e. the formal descriptions of the sets of data, transactions and events of interest for the application in terms of the corresponding models.

  In the following of this section the *data model*, the *transaction model* and the *event model* are described.

2.1 *The Data Model*

  The data model used in INCOD-DTE is an extension of the E-R model proposed by Chen in [8].
Three different *classes* of objects exist in the E-R model: entities, relationships and attributes. Each object must have an *object name* and may moreover have associa

ted a set of synonyms, a set of related keywords and an explicative text in natural language. For each couple of different objects the sets of associated names (object name and synonyms) are disjoint.

We now extend the original model (see also [6]) defining two kinds of abstraction hierarchies between entities.

The first type of hierarchy is the *subset relationship* (inversely *superset relationship*); an entity εl is a subset of another entity ε2 if every instance of εl is also an instance of ε2.

The second type of hierarchy is *generalization* (inversely *specialization*); an entity ε is a generalization of the entities εl, ..., εn if each instance of ε is also an instance of one and only one of the entities εl,........, εn. The partition over the instances of ε established by generalization may be seen as induced by a property of ε. Such property is represented by an attribute of ε, referred to as *underlying attribute*.

Both in subset relationship and in generalization, attributes (and relationships) of the entity at the upper level of a hierarchy are also attributes of the entities at the lower level. Entities at the lower level will generally have additional attributes with respect to the entity at the upper level: in the model we explicitely represent only such attributes.

An E-R schema will be represented by means of the diagrammatic representation of table 1.

OBJECT	REPRESENTATION
Entity	▭
Relationship	◇
Attribute	——○
Key attribute	——●
Generalization relationship with underlying attribute	⬡
Subset relationship	⇑

Table 1: The Diagrammatic Representation

See in fig. 1 an example of data schema.

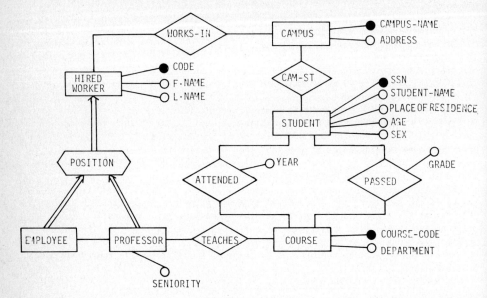

Fig. 1

A *consistent* data schema is a collection of objects (entities, relationships, attributes, subset relationships and generalizations) that satisfy the above definitions.
The following example shows an inconsistent schema.

Example 1

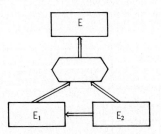

For the definition of generalization the sets of instances of E_1 and E_2 are disjoint and so E_2, being a subset of E_1, cannot have instances.

2.2 *The Transaction Model*

Some proposals of E-R oriented languages exist in the literature (see, for instance, [12],[18],[19]). Their goal was the high-level interaction between the user and the data base. On the contrary, the language adopted in INCOD-DTE has been conceived to be used in two situations:
- in the conceptual design phase as a means of implementation independent formalization of transactions;
- during the life of the data base, as a high-level DML.
The language is briefly described here. For a complete description see [3], [4].
The language allows the specification of both queries and manipulations, direc

tly referring to the data model described in section 2.1.

Since manipulations are usually performed on data to be previously retrieved, the structure of the language is based on queries and allows the specification of updates on their results. So we describe first the structure of the queries and then the manipulations.

Queries

The fundamental operation in a query is the selection of instances of an enti ty or of a relationship.

The selection of instances of an entity may be specified:
- indicating a condition on the attributes of the entity (here and in the following <> brackets and {} brackets have their usual meaning and [] brackets include op- tional clauses):

FIND <entity name>[DISPLAY(<attribute list>)]WITH(<condition>)
where the clause DISPLAY(<attribute list>) indicates the attributes whose values must appear in the result and <condition> is a boolean expression, whose operators are AND,OR,NOT and whose terms have the form <attribute name> θ <attribute name> or <attribute name> θ <constant> (with $\theta \in \{=, \neq, >, \geq, <, \leq\}$);
- requiring that they take part in instances of a given relationship, selected with a condition on attributes analogous to the one above described:

FIND <entity name>
THROUGH HAVING <relationship name> WITH (<condition>)

- requiring that they take part in instances of a given relationship that involve instances of another entity that satisfy a "WITH" clause:

FIND <entity name 1>
THROUGH <relationship name>
HAVING <entity name 2> WITH (<condition>)

- requiring that they correspond to instances of an entity that is the superset, the subset, the generalization or the specialization of the entity they belong to:

FIND <entity name 1>
$\left\{ \begin{array}{l} \text{ASCENDING} \\ \text{DESCENDING} \end{array} \right\}$ <hierarchy-id>
HAVING <entity name 2> WITH (<condition>)

For the semantics of the hierarchies (see section 2.1), the explicit specifi cation of steps of this type can be omitted in many queries, but it is useful, in the design phase, to compare transactions and data schemata.

The selection of instances of relationships may be specified in similar ways:
- indicating a condition on the attributes:

FIND <relationship name> WITH (<condition>)

- indicating that they involve instances of a given entity selected via a "WITH" clause:

FIND <relationship name>
HAVING <entity name> WITH (<condition>)

The constructs described above may be combined to form more complex queries with the following three rules:
- *merging:* several different conditions on a single object may be combined to form a boolean expression, with the operators AND,OR,NOT and parentheses;

- *chaining:* two queries such that the first one ends at the same object as that at which the second begins:
     ... HAVING <object name> (<condition>)
   and
       FIND <object name>...
   may be combined as follows
       HAVING FOUND <object name> WITH (<condition>)...
- *nesting:* among the terms of a selection predicate (WITH clause) there may appear terms referring to the results of other subqueries.

   In order to perform queries involving correlation between various references to the same object the language allows the definition of variables: a *variable* may appear several times in an expression (either always in the place of an entity name or always in the place of a relationship name) and once and only once it must appear toghether with the name of the object that constitutes its range.

   The introduction of variables allows us to specify another kind of nesting, with the following structure: among the terms of a WITH clause referring to an object X there is a term that compares two sets of instances of a given entity (or relationship) obtained by means of operations that involve X:
       FIND x:X WITH (...(FIND X_1...x...)η(FIND X_1...x...))
where η indicates one of the set comparison operators $(=,\neq,\supset,\subset,\supseteq,\subseteq)$.

Manipulations

   As we said at the beginning of this section, manipulations are usually performed on data retrieved by means of queries. They have the following structures:

1. Deletion of one or more instances of an entity or relationship:
   DELETE FOUND .....

2. Modification of values of attributes in one or more instances of an entity or relationship:
   MODIFY (<attribute name>:<value>,...) IN FOUND...

3. Insertion of an instance of an entity:
   INSERT <entity name> (<attribute name>:=<value>,...)

4. Creation of one or more instances of a relationship between instances of the related entities, already present in the data base:
   CREATE <relationship name> (<attribute name>:=<value>,...)
       BETWEEN FOUND <entity name 1> ...
                        .
                        .
                        .
       AND   FOUND <entity name 2> ...
                        .
                        .
                        .
       END

   The input values can be replaced by the keyword INPUT.
   For reasons to be explained later we call *executable* a transaction expressed in the language described in this section.
   We show now several examples of transactions, which refer to the schema shown in figure 1. For each of them we give the natural language text and the specification in the transaction language.

Example 1
"Find the students that have been enrolled to a certain course for more than one year and have not yet passed the corresponding exam".
    TRANSACTION bad students
    FIND student
        (THROUGH attended WITH (year ≤ 1979)
        HAVING course WITH (course-code='CS')
    AND   NOT THROUGH passed
        HAVING course WITH (course-code='CS'))

Example 2
"Insert a student and enroll him in a certain campus".

TRANSACTION enroll-student
INSERT student (ssn:='31487562'; place-of-residence:='LOS ANGELES'; age:='19';
          sex:='M')
CREATE cam-st
BETWEEN FOUND student WITH (ssn:='31487562')
AND   FOUND campus WITH (campus-name:='UCLA')
END

Example 3
"Check if a given course has been attended in the last year by at least one student".

TRANSACTION course-attendance
EXIST FOUND student
    THROUGH attended WITH (year='1980')
    HAVING course WITH (course-code='CS')

"Exist" is a boolean function whose value is true if the retrieved set of students is not empty.
Example 4
"Delete the logical links between a given course and its professors".

TRANSACTION delete-course-professor-link
DELETE FOUND teaches
    HAVING course WITH (course-code='CS')

Example 5
"Find the students that have passed the exams of all the courses they have attended"
    FIND s: student WITH ((FIND course
               THROUGH passed
               HAVING s) ⊇ (FIND course
                          THROUGH attended
                          HAVING s))

Before giving the definition of consistent transaction, we observe that, given a transaction t, it is straightforward to associate to it a *transaction view*, i.e. a data schema in which every object referred to in the transaction appears with the corresponding type. For instance, the transaction view corresponding to the transaction in example 5 is

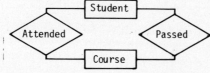

A transaction t is consistent with a conceptual schema S = <D,T,E> if:
1. no transaction in T has the same name of t;
2. the transaction view derived from it is consistent with D.

A transaction view is consistent with a data schema if:
1) each entity, attribute, relationship, subset and generalization hierarchy of the transaction view is also an entity, attribute, relationship, subset and generali zation hierarchy of the schema respectively
2) each property (attribute, relationship, subset or generalization hierarchy) of each entity of the transaction view is a property of the corresponding entity of the schema
3) each attribute of each relationship of the transaction view is an attribute of the corresponding relationship of the schema.

2.3 *The Event Model*

In the recent years several solutions have been proposed to embody, at the con ceptual level, the description of the changes that occur in the modelled systems (see [14], [5], [22], [10]).

In order to establish a framework to introduce explicitly the event notion in to a conceptual model, it is opportune to start giving a stable definition of event. Such a definition must fulfill two requirements: to reflect adequately the real world dynamics and to fit an efficient implementation.

To this end, we adopt ([10]) the following definition:
an event expresses a change of conditions, from the conditions which hold before (preconditions) to those which hold after (postconditions). An event is described in terms of its preconditions and of the actions making the change (postconditions just follow as a consequence of doing those actions).
According to this definition, a suitable formalism to represent events are Petri Nets (see [17]), i.e. two-color graphs with places and transitions connected by arcs to express conditions, actions, and their causal dependencies. In this paper, pla ces denote conditions and transitions denote actions. Graphically, places (condi tions) are expressed by circles, transitions (actions) by bars, connections between conditions and actions by arcs:

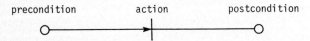

The holding of a condition is expressed by a dot (marker) in the corresponding cir cle. An action has concession, i.e. can occur, if all its preconditions hold (fi ring rule). After the execution of the firing rule, preconditions no longer hold and postconditions begin to hold.

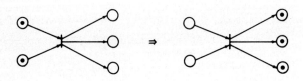

In Petri Nets, causal relationships are expressed by sequences

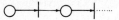

concurrency by parallelism,

conflicts by branching,

and cycles by rings.

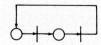

In the language we assume for the formalization of events, the "event-declaration"
has the following structure:

EVENT <event-name>
CONDITIONS: <conds>
ACTIONS: <acts>
ACTIVITY: <activity-name>
where
   — <conds>:= <sem-type> <cond> '['<pragc-type>']'/<cond-list>
      <sem-type>:= IF/WHEN classifies the event as regards logical and temporal
                aspects (semantic type)
      <cond>:= <predicate-expression> is exemplified in the following
      <pragc-type>:= EXT/CAL indicates the type of involved conditions (pragmatic ty
                pe of condition). Precisely,
                EXT are conditions holding as effects of transactions external
                to the activity referred to in the event-declaration.
                TRANS are conditions holding as effect of transactions belonging
                to the activity referred to in the event-declaration.
                CAL are conditions holding in correspondence of calendar states.
      <cond-list>:= '['<conds> <synt-type> <conds>']'
      <synt-type>:= AND/OR/OREX classifies the conditions/actions structure (synta-
                tic type)
      <acts>:= <act> '['<praga-type>']' <act-list>
   — <act>:= <transaction name>
      <praga-type>:= OBS/MOD classifies the nature of actions, that is observation
                or modification (pragmatic type of action)
      <act-list>:= '['<acts> <synt-type> <acts>']'
The term
      <activity-name> refers to an activity performed in the system, which has to be
      automatized.

Example 6
"On June 30th the list of bad students is requested".

EVENT bad-student-selection
CONDITIONS: WHEN CURRENT-TIME=June 30 [CAL]
ACTIONS: bad-students
ACTIVITY: student-statistics

Example 7
"When a student asks for enrollment, enroll him".

EVENT enrollment
CONDITIONS: WHEN MSG=student-request ARRIVES [EXT]
ACTIONS: enroll-student
ACTIVITY: enrollment-processing

In a predicate expression, terms can refer to results of a transaction, i.e. obj ects retrieved by the transaction or values computed by a function, as in the following example.

Example 8
"On September 1st, if no student attended a certain course, cancel the relationship between it and its professor".

EVENT course-check
CONDITIONS: (IF course-attendance.EXIST=FALSE [TRANS] AND WHEN CURRENT-TIME= Sept
                ember 1 [CAL])
ACTIONS: delete-course-professor-link
ACTIVITY: student-statistics

The representation of events by means of Petri nets is achieved using the association grammar (see [10] for a detailed description) whose basic graphs are shown in fig. 2.
For each event the corresponding graph is picked up in the grammar according to the syntactic type as it appears in its declaration. Graph labels are actualized with event's conditions and actions.

For example, in the event declaration of example 8 an AND of conditions and an elementary action appear. So we have to apply rule 5 and we obtain the following elementary graph.

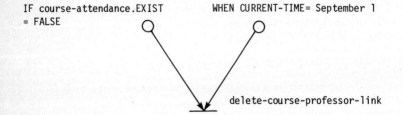

IF course-attendance.EXIST   WHEN CURRENT-TIME= September 1
= FALSE

delete-course-professor-link

1. EL(cond):EL(ac)

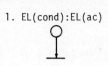

2. EL(cond):AND(ac)

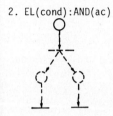

3. EL(cond):OREX(ac)

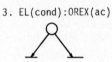

4. EL(cond):OR(ac)

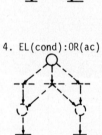

5. AND(cond):EL(ac)

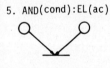

6. AND(cond):AND(ac)

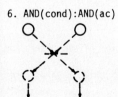

7. AND(cond):OREX(ac)

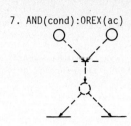

8. AND(cond):OR(ac)

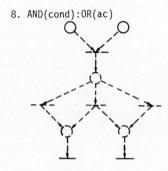

9. OREX(cond):EL(ac)

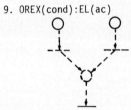

10. OREX(cond):AND(ac)

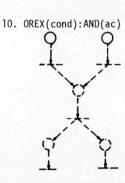

11. OREX(cond):OR(ac)

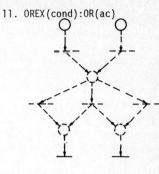

12. OREX(cond):OREX(ac)

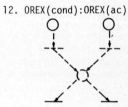

13. OR(cond):EL(ac)

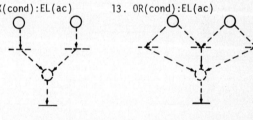

14. OR(cond):AND(ac)

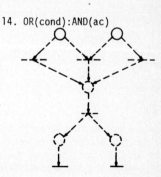

Fig. 2 - Association grammar

As regards the consistency,
an event is consistent with a conceptual schema: S=<D,T,E> if:

1) no other event in E has the same name
2) there are no actions with the same name in other events
3) if a condition is classified as TRANS, it refers to a transaction defined in T.

We are now able to give the definition of *consistent conceptual schema*. A schema S=<D,T,E> is consistent if:

1) D is consistent
2) Every transaction in T is consistent.
3) Every event in E is consistent.

Consistency is an essential condition for a conceptual schema to represent adequately the reality of interest: we show in the following section the way in which INCOD-DTE supports the design in achieving such goal.

3. DESCRIPTION OF SYSTEM'S ARCHITECTURE AND MODULES.

Figure 3 shows the architecture of INCOD-DTE. Each block represents a part of the system responsible of a given function (*module*).

Continuous lines represent logical connections between modules, dashed lines represent interactions between the designer and the system. For each module a special purpose language is defined that allows such interaction. The functions of the modules are the following:

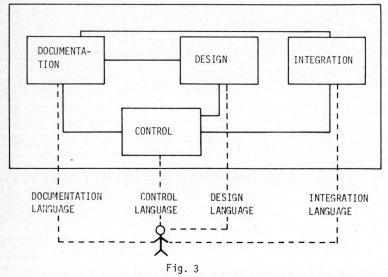

Fig. 3

1. The *control module* supports the designer during initialization of each user schema design, access and release of other modules.
2. The *design module* is used during the design of a user schema, with regard to both the static and the dynamic aspects.
3. The *integration module* is used during user schemata integration.
4. The *documentation module* supports the designer in organizing documentation.

In this section we give more details about the design and integration module; in [2] a detailed description of the system appears.

3.1. The design module

The purpose of the design module is to help the designer to build a user schema by successive enrichments. Such enrichments can be seen as new knowledge obtained by the designer about the application with regard to data, transactions or events.

The allowed enrichments are disciplined in a set of primitives, the commands of the *design language*.

Suppose that a given set of commands has been used to create a partial schema S^+. When a new command (concerning either data or transactions or events) is applied to S^+, the consistency of the resulting conceptual schema is checked. If the schema is inconsistent the command is rejected.

The above concepts will be further explained and detailed in the following three sections, in which we describe respectively data, transactions and events specification commands.

3.1.1 Data specification commands

The operands of the data specification commands are the objects of a given schema; such commands allow:

1. creating and deleting objects (entities, relationships, subsets and generalizations);
2. expanding objects, i.e. refining them into sets of objects that inherit their logical links;
3. giving a structure to entities and relationships by defining their attributes (and identifiers).

As we said, when a command is applied, inconsistencies can occur.

INCOD-DTE aids the designer to solve inconsistencies, providing several scenarios for each type of them. Such scenarios suggest *possible interpretations of the inconsistency*. To each interpretation a consequent consistent schema corresponds. The designer can accept one of the scenarios or reject all of them. In the first case the corresponding solution is automatically performed; in the second case the command that generated the inconsistency is cancelled.

Example 9

Suppose a schema has been obtained in which two entities E_1 and E_2 occur such that the key attribute of E_1 appears in the set of synonyms of E_2. There are at least four interpretations of this naming inconsistency:

a. the key-attributes are homonymous;
b. the entities E_1, E_2 are synonymous;
c. an entity is a subset of the other one;
d. a third entity E_3, generalization of E_1, E_2, must be included in the schema.

Besides *explicit inconsistencies*, INCOD-DTE is able to detect *potential inadequacies*, i.e. situations in which *indications* exist that the data schema may be *incomplete* or *redundant* in representing the reality of interest.

An exaustive analysis of the potential inadequacies that a schema may reveal and the way in which an automatic tool can detect them is beyond the scope of this paper. At present, the following inadequacies are taken into account in INCOD-DTE:

1. homonymies \

2. synonymies
3. hidden hierarchies
4. redundant relationships.

Example 10
Suppose that a schema exists in which a subset relationship is defined between two
entities E_1, E_2 (fig. 4a). Assume a new entity E_3 is created and defined as subset
of E_1 (fig. 4b). Three possible semantic enrichments of the schema in fig. 4b are

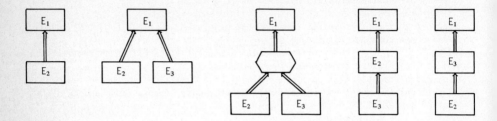

shown in fig. 4c, 4d, 4e:
1. E_1 is the generalization of E_2 and E_3
2. E_3 is subset of E_2
3. E_2 is subset of E_3.
    The system shows to the designer one or more of such enrichments, as a result
of an analysis of the properties (synonyms, keywords, related entities) of the obj
ects.
    A *side effect* of the application of a command concerns the update of the tran-
saction already defined during the design and referring objects involved in the
transaction. The designer can update such transactions with a suitable transaction
specification command (see later). By default, the system "suspends" the transactions, and the designer can defer their update.

3.1.2 Transaction specification commands
    INCOD-DTE allows the definition of transactions at three different levels of re
finement, called *conceptual, navigational and executable,* respectively. The motiva
tion for this choice is twofold:
1. In this way the design of transactions may be carried out by means of successive entichments, in a top-down fashion, similarly to what happens in program design (see fig. 5).

Natural language transaction
↓
Conceptual transaction
↓
Navigational transaction
↓
Executable transaction

Fig. 5

2. In order to check the adequacy of a data schema with respect to a transaction,
   some of the operational details of the transaction are not needed. Moreover, the
   comparison may be performed in two steps:

checking a)that all the objects referred to in the transaction are in the data schema; b)that the corresponding transaction view is consistent with the data schema.
As a consequence, the languages used for the definition of transactions at the first two levels have the following features:
- The Conceptual (Transaction) Language allows a specification of the transactions in which only the names and the types of the involved objects are declared.
- The Navigational (Transaction) Language allows a specification of transactions whose structure is analogous to the executable one but in which only the involved objects and the access path ("navigation") are specified.

The following example shows Conceptual and Navigational specifications of the transaction expressed in the Executable Language in Example 1.

Example 11
```
CONCEPTUAL TRANSACTION bad-students
year: ATT OF attended: REL BETWEEN student: ENT, course: ENT;
passed: REL BETWEEN student, course.

NAVIGATIONAL TRANSACTION bad-students
FIND student
BEGIN THROUGH attended INVOLVING (year)
      HAVING  course   INVOLVING (course-code)
AND   THROUGH passed
      HAVING  course   INVOLVING (course-code)
END.
```

In this framework, the transaction specification commands allow:
1. *creating new transactions* at any level of specification (conceptual,navigational,executable) *and matching them with the current data schema,* i.e. checking their consistency with respect to the schema. If inconsistencies arise, then scenarios are shown suggesting possible solutions: the designer can choose either to suspend the transaction (similarly to what happens when a data specification command is applied, see sec. 3.1.1) or to emend the schema (the data schema or the transaction itself). If the data schema is modified, then other transactions referring to objects involved in the modification must be either updated or suspended.

Example 12
Assume the schema in fig. 6. The following transaction:

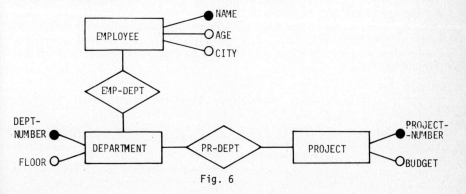

Fig. 6

"Find all the Names of Employees involved in a Project with a given Project-number",
expressed in the language described in section 2.2:

    FIND Employee DISPLAY (Name)
    THROUGH Emp-proj
    HAVING FOUND Project WITH (Project-number = INPUT)

is now matched with the schema. An inconsistency arises because the transaction
refers to a relationship that doesn't exist in the schema.
The possible interpretations of the inconsistency are the following:
a. the logical link represented by the relationship Emp-Proj is missing in the sche‐
   ma: the solution is to create it.
b. the logical link referred to in the transaction is represented in the schema by
   the relationships Pr-Dept and Emp-Dept; the corresponding solution is to emend
   the transaction as follows:

    FIND Employee DISPLAY (Name)
    THROUGH Emp-Dept
    HAVING FOUND Department
            THROUGH Pr-Dept
            HAVING FOUND Project WITH (Project-number = INPUT)

2. *Matching suspended transactions* with the current data schema. The effect of this
   command is analogous to that of the creation command, with the only difference
   that, in case of inconsistencies, the suggestion of suspending the transaction
   is not shown among the scenarios.

3. *Refining* previously defined transactions, in order to obtain versions of them
   expressed at a lower level in the hierarchy of fig. 5. The refinement may be car‐
   ried out just defining the new version of the transaction or asking for a dialo‐
   gue with the system. For example, while passing from a navigational to an execu‐
   table transaction, the system asks the refinement of the clauses "INVOLVING(..)"
   into "WITH(..)" and/or "DISPLAY(..)" clauses.

3.1.3 Event specification commands
    The event specification commands are used by the designer to produce a formal re‐
presentation of the dependency relationships between the events (events graphs).
    Such commands allow:
1. *creating and deleting* events;
2. *composing* events into an events graph;
3. *expanding* events; i.e. refining them into sets of events that inherit the origi‐
   nal logical links. Such an expansion allows the top-down specification of the
   knowledge about an activity of the application in terms a coordinated actions. The
   expansion ends when every specified action corresponds to a defined transaction.
   The handling of inconsistencies is analogous to that described for data specifi‐
cation commands.

Example 13
    We show an example of naming inconsistency. Given the event graph of fig. 7,

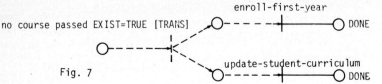

enroll-first-year

no course passed EXIST=TRUE [TRANS]   DONE

update-student-curriculum

Fig. 7   DONE

suppose the following event is declared:

```
EVENT degraded-student
CONDITIONS : (IF accept-course-passed.COUNT< 3 [TRANS] OR IF no-accept-course
              -passed-fundamental.EXIST = TRUE [TRANS])
ACTIONS : (enroll-first-year [MOD] AND update-student-curriculum [MOD])
ACTIVITY : student-statistics
```

An inconsistency is now detected by the system. The designer is asked for renaming the actions of the new event or redefining the previous event.

3.1.4 *The design language*

In table 2 the set of commands of the design language is described.

SYNTAX	SEMANTICS
DATA SPECIFICATION COMMANDS	
D-CREATE <type>:<object> where <type> can be: ENT , REL , ATT	An object (whose name is) <object> is created
D-EXPAND : <obj> INTO <list of obj>	The object <obj> is expanded into the objects in <list of obj>
D-STRUCT : <obj> INTO <list of att>	The attributes of object (entity or relationship) <obj> are specified
D-DELETE : <obj>	The object <obj> and its logical links are deleted
TRANSACTION SPECIFICATION COMMANDS	
T-MATCH <type of trans> TRANSACTION :<trans name> [<transaction declaration>] where <type of trans> can be: CONCEPTUAL,NAVIGATIO-NAL or EXECUTABLE	When <transaction declaration> is present, a new transaction is created and matched with the current data schema; when it is missing, a suspended transaction is matched
T-REFINE <trans name>	A new version of the transaction is built
T-DELETE <trans name>	The transaction is deleted
EVENT SPECIFICATION COMMANDS	
E-CREATE<event declaration>	An elementary graph is created according to the event declaration. An output place with label DONE is created for each action

(continued)

E-DELETE <event name>	The event is deleted
E-COMPOSE <activity name>	The current graphs of the activity are shown to the designer who is now authorized to compose events using special commands (see Appendix)
E-END-COMPOSE	The session opened with the E-COMPOSE command, is closed
E-EXPAND <event name> INTO <event block>	The event is expanded into the events declared in <event block>, structured by sequence, conflict or concurrency, after having verified that all the preconditions of the original event are contained in <event block>. The new structure inherits the logical links of the original event.

TABLE 2

3.2 The integration module

The integration process, in INCOD-DTE, is guided by the system. It takes as input two schemata and builds the integrated schema by incremental aggregation of their objects; three or more schemata may be integrated two at a time by successive integration steps.

The integration process may be logically divided into six steps (see fig. 8)

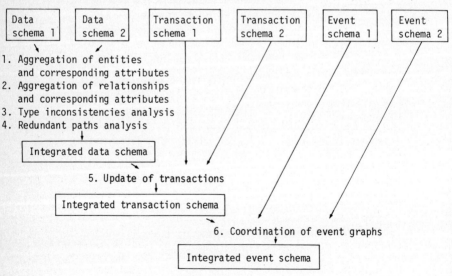

Fig. 8

During the first step, homonymies, synonymies and hidden hierarchies between enti
ties are analyzed: suggestions based on analysis of entity properties (names, synonyms, keywords, attributes, relationships) are shown to the designer.
Similar checks are performed in the second step with regard to relationships. In
the third step type inconsistencies are analyzed and solved. Notice that entity
analysis is anticipated with respect to relationship and type inconsistencies ana
lysis in order to perform as soon as possible the most critical choices, achieve
a first convergence of design and avoid an explosion of decisions. The first three
steps may be iterated in order to achieve a more reliable design.
In the fourth step redundant paths are analyzed. An integrated data schema is obtained at this point.
In the fifth step, all the transactions defined in the schemata are emended accor
ding to the transformations performed in steps 1-4. As a result, the integrated
transaction schema is obtained.

In the sixth step, in order to represent communication between the application activities, the events graphs are coordinated in the integrated event schema.

During integration, all the commands of the design language can be used: fur
ther commands of the integration language are shown in Table 3.

SYNTAX	SEMANTICS
MERGE <obj1>, <obj2>: <obj3>	<obj1>and<obj2>are merged into a unique object, <obj3>
SPLIT <obj> : <obj1>, <obj2>	<obj> is split into the objects <obj1> and <obj2>
COORDINATE <EXT-cond> <action>	An arc is traced from the transition of which the DONE (correspon-ding to the specified action) is an output to the EXT condition factually equivalent. For example: EVENTS-GRAPH A EVENTS-GRAPH B

Table 3: The integration language

4. CONCLUSION AND FURTHER RESEARCH

INCOD-DTE has been developed as a part of a national project sponsored by the
Italian National Research Council, called DATAID. In this framework it is being
implemented and it will be experimented for the design of data bases for the local
administrations. Pratical experiencies and comparisons with other existing tools
and methodologies [21,22], are expected to give us suggestions for improvement of

the system.

   Future research work will be devoted to the following directions:
- the extension of the data model to domain declarations and to a meaningful class
  of integrity constraints to be described by means of a specific language;
- the individuation of tools to be used in the Requirement Analysis phase [16], in
  an integrated environment in which INCOD-DTE be used for the Conceptual Design
  phase.

REFERENCES

[1]   P. ATZENI, C. BATINI, M. LENZERINI, F. VILLANELLI. INCOD-DT: A System for Con
      ceptual Design of Data and Transactions in the Entity-Relationship Model.
      Proc. of the Second International Conference on the Entity Relationship Ap-
      proach. Washington, D.C. 1981.

[2]   P. ATZENI, C. BATINI, V. DE ANTONELLIS, M. LENZERINI, F. VILLANELLI, B. ZONTA.
      A Computer Aided Tool for Conceptual Data Base Design. Extended Description.
      Technical Report. Istituto di Automatica. Roma, Italy. In print.

[3]   P. ATZENI, P.P. CHEN. A Preliminary Definition of the Completeness of Query
      Languages for the Entity Relationship Model. Proc. of the Second International
      Conference on the Entity Relationship Approach. Washington, D.C. 1981.

[4]   P. ATZENI, F. VILLANELLI. A Query and Manipulation Language for the Entity-Re
      lationship Model. Proc. of AICA Congress, Pavia, Italy, 1981.

[5]   J.L. BARRON. Dialogue Organization and Structure for Interactive Information
      Systems. TR.CSRG.108. University of Toronto 1980.

[6]   C. BATINI, M. LENZERINI. INCOD: A System for Interactive Conceptual Data Base
      Design. Proc. of IEEE 18th Conf. on Design Automation. Nashville, Te, June
      1981.

[7]   C. BATINI, G. SANTUCCI. Top-down Design in the Entity-Relationship Model. In
      [9].

[8]   P.P. CHEN. The Entity Relationship Model: Toward a Unified View of Data. ACM
      Trans. on Database Systems, Vol. 1.1. 1976.

[9]   P.P. CHEN (ed.). Entity-Relationship Approach to Systems Analysis and Design.
      North-Holland 1980.

[10] V. DE ANTONELLIS, G. DEGLI ANTONI, G. MAURI, B. ZONTA. Extending the Entity-
      Relationship Approach to Take into Account Historical Aspects of Systems. In
      [9].

[11] V. DE ANTONELLIS, B. ZONTA. Modelling Events in Data Base Application Design.
      Proc. Int. Conf. on Very Large Data Bases, Cannes, 1981.

[12] R. ELMASRI. GORDAS: A Data Definition, Query and Update Language for the Enti
      ty Category Relationship Model of Data Honeywell CCSC Technical Report HR-81-
      -250. Bloomington, Minnesota, Jannary 1981.

[13] A.L. FURTADO, E.J. NEUHOLD, C. DOS SANTOS. A Data Type Approach to Entity Re-
      lationship Model. in [9].

[14] J. HSU, N. ROUSSOPOULOS. Database Conceptual Modelling. In [9].

[15] V.Y. LUM et al. 1978 New Orleans Data Base Design Workshop Report - IBM Report RJ2554 (33154).

[16] S. NAVATIIE et al. Information Modelling Tools for Data Base Design - Data Base Directions. Fort Lauderdale, Florida, 1980.

[17] C.A. PETRI. Introduction to general net theory - in Lecture Notes in Computer Sciences, n. 84, Springer Verlag, 1980.

[18] G. POONEN. CLEAR: A Conceptual Language for Entities and Relationships - ICMOD, Milano, 1978.

[19] A. SHOSHANI. CABLE: A Language Based on the Entity-Relationship Model - Rep. UCID-8005, Univ. of California, Berkeley, 1978.

[20] P. SCHEUERMANN, G. SHIFFNER, H. WEBER. Abstraction Capabilities and Invariant Properties Modelling within the Entity-Relationship Approach. In [9].

[21] H. TARDIEU, D. NANCI, D. PASCOT. "Conception d'un système d'information - construction de la base de données". Edition d'organisation Paris 1979/Gaetan Morin, Quebec 1979.

[22] D. TEICHROEW, E.A. HERSHEY III, M.J. EASTARACHE. An Introduction to PSL/PSA. ISDOS Workshop Paper 86, University Michigan, Ann Arbor, March 1974.

[23] M.D. ZISMAN. Use of Production Systems for Modelling Asyncronous Concurrent Processes - In Pattern Directed Inference Systems, Accademic Press, 1978.

APPENDIX

The commands of event composition

SYNTAX	SEMANTICS
SUPERQUAL <TRANS/EXT/CAL-cond> COMP-TYPE : <type>	Conditions which have the same label are superposed giving rise to a conflict or concurrency structure accor ding to the specified type of composition. For example: CONFLICT CONCURRENCY
SUPEREQUIVAL <list of action>	DONE conditions, corresponding to the actions specified, which are factually equivalent are superposed. For example:

(continued)

TRANSDONE <action>; <list of TRANS-cond> COMP-TYPE : <type>	One or more TRANS conditions are connected to a DONE condition giving rise or to a simple sequence or to a conflict or concurrency structure according to the specified type of composition. For example:
EXT/CAL-DONE <action> <EXT/CAL-cond> COMP-TYPE : <type>	The DONE condition, corresponding to the specified action, is connected to the transition of which the EXT/CAL condition is an input by means of the creation of a new arc or of a concurrency structure, according to the specified type of composition. For example:

Automated Tools for Information Systems Design
H.-J. Schneider and A.I. Wasserman (eds.)
North-Holland Publishing Company
© IFIP, 1982

A Software/Documentation Development Environment
Built From The UNIX Toolkit

M. H. Bianchi

R. J. Glushko

J. R. Mashey

Bell Laboratories
Whippany, New Jersey 07981

ABSTRACT

The popular UNIX* System[1] contains a large kit of tools useful in
software development. Toolkits are easy to learn, use, maintain,
and adapt to different needs and organizations. A good set of tools
works well together, but is not an integrated environment, on
purpose[2]. An integrated environment is often optimal for a
specific situation, and often difficult to move or adapt to new
situations.

We have seen UNIX users develop their own integrated environments.
Most customize the default environment by adding commands of their
own. The early additions simply capture sequences of commands that
they find themselves repeating. Later, they simplify their work
environment by structuring it with directories that contain similar
objects, such as subroutines, main routines, documents, control
files, commands, etc. and then writing commands work within that
structure. Because each organization views its world differently,
customizations differ widely according to local needs. However,
basic concepts keep appearing, even though the environments are
quite different. We've watched the evolution of environments,
observed the concepts they implemented, and generalized those
concepts into a portable environment that overtly supports
customization.

SOLID, a System for On-Line Information Development, is a more
"integrated" programming and documentation environment built from
the UNIX system's tools[3]. It implements the concepts of Source,
where all the source for programs and documents is kept, Product,
where all the executable programs and formatted documents reside,
and Generation Procedures, which translate all types of Source into
all forms of Product. These concepts are implemented as UNIX
command language procedures that combine existing tools. SOLID also
provides Skeletons, the most common outline form of each type of
Source. The developer writing a new module of code or documentation
does not start with an empty file. Instead, they are given an
outline which reduces drudgery and painlessly enforces some
standards of style and content.

SOLID is notable for what it does and what it doesn't do. On the
"does" side, it provides a single environment that is being used to
develop all documentation for computer systems, all programs, and
mixtures of both. It comes with a default environment that is

---

* UNIX is a trademark of Bell Telephone Laboratories.

occasionally used unmodified.

On the other side, it is not a monolith that restricts the user to those options that are built in. Since all SOLID source is under SOLID control, the user can change or extend any of SOLID's capabilities. Some portions, in particular Generation Procedures, are intended to be extended to support new Source and Product types. It provides no editor; people use any that they like. It doesn't enforce any particular programming or documentation methodology, although Skeletons have proved useful in encouraging the methodologies and styles a group prefers.

Although released only recently for internal use, SOLID is now used by a dozen organizations at Bell Laboratories. Some use it for their documentation only, others for their entire product. Because it is based on observing the ways people have customized UNIX to suit their needs, it seems to match the way many groups do business. Because it is designed to be modifiable and is supported by its own mechanisms, people easily extend and customize it to suit their own needs. Because it stands firmly on standard UNIX, as UNIX becomes available on new or different hardware, SOLID is also. Finally, it preserves the tool orientation of UNIX. New capabilities added to UNIX are immediately available to SOLID users.

[1] Ritchie, D. M. and Thompson, K., "The UNIX Time-Sharing System", The Bell System Technical Journal 57, No. 6, Part 2 (July-August 1978) 1905-1929.

[2] Kernighan, B. W., and Mashey, J. R., "The UNIX Programming Environment", Computer 14, 4 (April 1981) 12-24.

[3] Glushko, R. J., and Bianchi, M. H., "On-Line Documentation: Integrated Development, Distribution, and Use", 10th Mid-year Meeting of ASIS, Durango, Colorado, May 14-16, 1981.

Automated Tools for Information Systems Design
H.-J. Schneider and A.I. Wasserman (eds.)
North-Holland Publishing Company
© IFIP, 1982

METHODOLOGICAL AND COMPUTER AIDS
FOR
INTERACTIVE INFORMATION SYSTEM DEVELOPMENT

Alexander T. Borgida[1]
John Mylopoulos
Harry K.T. Wong[2]

Department of Computer Science
University of Toronto
Toronto, Ontario
Canada M5S 1A7

We present an overview of the Taxis project, whose aim is to assist the designer of Interactive Information Systems (abbreviated as IIS) by offering a design methodology, a programming language associated with it, as well as computer aids specifically designed to support them.

The methodology involves *concept specialization* and is particularly well suited for IISs, which generally involve large amounts of unstructured detail that must somehow be integrated into a coherent system. The Taxis programming language offers constructs which enable the designer to define taxonomies of classes representing data structures, transactions, exceptions and their handlers, as well as scripts that specify the patterns of user—system dialogues. The design environment provides facilities for displaying parts of the conceptual structure of systems, class oriented editors and verifiers of semantic consistency; an interpreter used for prototyping and a compiler from Taxis to a conventional programming language and database management system are also included.

The problem domain

The experience of the past two decades in software development indicates that in addition to the task of designing correct and efficient algorithms, the most significant problem is the management of the complexity of descriptions. Traditional efforts in the area have been aimed mostly at the development of universally applicable aids, both in terms of methodologies (e.g., stepwise refinement) and in terms of tools (e.g., editors, general—purpose languages). The survey in [Deutsch and Taft 80] provides a wide ranging view of the types of tools potentially useful in a general experimental programming environment.

Our aim is to provide more powerful aids by restricting attention to a narrower, yet important, problem domain. In particular, we are interested in the design and development of large—scale interactive information systems (IIS). Examples of such systems include (i) administrative record systems for large institutions such as governments, corporations,

---

[1] Current address: Dept. of Computer Science, Rutgers University, NJ08903.

[2] Current address: Lawrence Berkeley Labs, Berkeley, CA.

universities, (ii) materials/product records for manufacturing and warehousing enterprises, (iii) many forms of rental and registration businesses, and in general, most office information systems. The importance of IIS lies in their widespread presence in commercial applications, which will be further accentuated by the increasing acceptance of office automation. The development of such systems by application programmers is in general considered to be a mundane, boring yet error prone process; the algorithms involved tend to be quite simple[3], yet there is a multitude of simple details which have to be captured, with consistency and completeness being at a premium. For these reasons we believe that the domain of IIS a highly useful, yet restricted, subset of general software systems, for which we aim to obtain specific aids.

Finally, we contend that tools for supporting the development of IIS, and in general all programs, should be designed within the framework of a *methodology* of their use. This is not a novel concept (think of the "structured programming" methodology and the Pascal family of languages supporting it) but we feel that it provides useful guidance for research directions.

In the remainder of the paper we will present a methodology for information system design, and then discuss a number of tools which are especially designed to support it.

The methodology of taxonomic design

Foundations

Expanding on [Wasserman 80], we see an IIS as containing at least (a) a large, persistent data base of facts, (b) a collection of transactions for modifying the database, (c) a sizeable collection of semantic constraints on the allowable data base states and the changes which can affect it, (d) query and report generation facilities, and (e) user interfaces. It has been repeatedly observed that a data base, and even the transactions defined over it, constitute in some important and real sense a *model* of some slice of reality, or at least the users' view of it (e.g., [Abrial 74], [Tsichritzis and Lochovsky 81]). In addition, an IIS also contains a model of the interactions of the user with the computer system. We therefore consider the problem of IIS development to be in large part the problem of model description. Furthermore, we are interested in describing models which are closer to the human conceptual view, rather than the machine level, i.e., so-called *conceptual models*. Among the reasons for this is the fact that description at this level is more natural and helpful for the system designer in his effort to organize and integrate details into a coherent whole; the description can also serve as a communication means with prospective users, and can be mapped to the machine level by the use of the computer itself.

At the heart of most software development methodologies lie one or more *abstraction principles*, which allow us to ignore details at some level, plus a *refinement principle* which provides for the guided and gradual reintroduction of details along the abstraction dimension.

---

[3]The detailed storage/retrieval algorithms may be very sophisticated but they are usually hidden inside the database system, not designed by the IIS developers

Using the terminology of [Smith and Smith 80], **aggregation** as an abstraction forms the core of software design methodologies such as "stepwise refinement" (e.g., [Wirth 71], [Dijkstra 72]), and languages such as Pascal which support it. Similarly, the **representation** abstraction is the basis of the abstract machine and abstract data type-related methodologies (e.g., [Parnas 72]) and the languages supporting it (e.g., Alphard [Wulf et al., 77]).

We are interested in formulating a methodology for building conceptual models based on the **generalization** abstraction, which, for example, allows one to suppress the detailed differences of a number of related classes (e.g., ADMINISTRATORS, INSTRUCTORS, STUDENTS) and consider a larger, more general class which contains all their instances and which factors out only the commonalities of the subclasses (e.g., PERSON).

The seminal idea of such a methodology is that a model can be constructed by modelling first, in terms of classes, the most general concepts and tasks in the application area, and then proceeding to deal with special cases through more specialized subclasses. For example, in building a student enrollment system for a university, one might consider first the concepts of student and course, and the task of enrolling a student for a course. Later, the designer can differentiate between graduate and undergraduate students and courses, day and evening classes, full-time and part-time students, etc. and the regulations concerning them. Indeed we believe that most IISs involve *large* amounts of *simple* detail and that taxonomies offer a fundamental tool for coping with such situations.

Design of data and transaction classes

We will expand and illustrate the methodology described above by considering some details of the student enrollment portion of a student record system. In Figure 1, we present a list of semantic conditions on the enrollment of students in Computer Science courses at our university, which would have to be incorporated into the final system. For ease of reference, we have labelled each with a mnemonic name followed by a question mark indicating that each of these will be a constraint predicate. We start, as suggested, by describing the most central and general classes of objects in the domain, which in our case would be COURSES and STUDENTs. Each instance of an object class is characterized by its *properties*, which represent relationships to other objects in the world; in addition, there are a number of constraints which the properties must satisfy, as functions. For example, STUDENT has properties *name, age, student#, address, faculty* and *status*; included among the constraints would be the condition that *age* be a positive integer between 12 and 90, and that *faculty* must be one of "Meds", "GradSchool", etc. The instances of COURSE class would have properties *title, department, limit, size* and *year*, and one of the constraints would specify that *size* can be no larger than *limit*. An important relationship between STUDENTs and COURSEs will be captured by the relation ENROLLMENT, each instance of which will have properties *student, course* and *grade*.[4]

The only event we are considering right now is enrolling a student in a course. Events will also be described using properties; some properties represent participants (parameters) of the

---

[4] The conditions in Figure 1 can be considered as quantified constraints on the ENROLLMENT relationship.

Not-taken-before?	a student cannot take the same course more than once;
Permission?	an undergraduate student requires the permission of the instructor before taking a graduate course;
Part-time-min.?	part time students need not take any courses in any particular year;
At-least-4th-year?	graduate students cannot take first, second or third year courses;
Not-full?	a student cannot enrol in a course whose enrollment limit has been reached;
Undergrad-min.?	a full-time undergraduate must take at least 5 courses each year;
Undergrad-max.?	a full time undergraduate may not take more than 6 courses in one year;
Not-excluded?	there exist groups of mutually exclusive undergraduate courses and an undergraduate may take at most one course from such a group;
Before-deadline?	undergraduates must register in courses by October 13th;
Offered?	a student cannot take a course which is not offered at the time requested;
Has-preparation?	an undergraduate course may have prerequisite courses which an undergraduate student must have taken in previous terms;
Part-time-max.?	part-time students may not take more than 3 courses a year;
Areas-OK?	a graduate Computer Science student must have taken courses in each of three major areas;
Another-1st-year?	at most 6 First Year courses may be counted towards the 22 required for a B.Sc. degree;
Specialist?	Arts & Science students desiring a specialist's degree must have taken the appropriate selection of courses;
Has-coreqs?	certain undergraduate courses may require undergraduates to take at the same time other courses (e.g., in mathematics);
Probation-max.?	an undergraduate student on probation may take no more than 5 courses a year;
Grad-max?	graduate students should not take more than 6 half-courses a year.

Figure 1: Restrictions on enroling in Computer Science courses

activity, while others describe component activities. For the ENROL transaction, we propose two participants s and c, and conditions on them would include the invariance statements that s belong to STUDENT, c to COURSE, and the prerequisite conditions that *Offered?*, *Not-full?* and *Not-taken-before?* be true before the transaction body is executed. The "body" of the ENROL transaction class would involve actions for asserting that s and c are related by ENROLLMENT and incrementing by one the *size* of c. Observe that these properties and constraints apply to all

ENROL events.

In order to introduce further details about ENROL, we can first describe two subclasses of STUDENT, namely GRAD__STUDENT and UNDERGRAD__STUDENT. Since all instances of a subclass are instances of the parent class, it is not necessary to restate all the properties and constraints which have been previously given for the super-class and which are assumed to hold for the subclass as well. This observation, called **inheritance**, can be used as a memory aid in describing models and as an abbreviatory device for reducing the size of a class description. In specializing a class we can (i) 'strengthen' any of the constraints stated for the parent class (i.e. replace a constraint of the parent class, say A, with a stronger one B such that B implies A), (ii) provide additional constraints, and/or (iii) introduce new properties and related constraints. Thus, in defining the subclass of GRAD__STUDENTs we may restrict the *faculty* property to have as value "Grad School", and add new properties *advisor* and *level*, where for example *level* is either "MSc" or "PhD", and we have the additional constraint that all instances of STUDENT with *faculty* value "Grad School" are instances of GRAD__STUDENT. Note that all properties of STUDENT naturally apply to all GRAD__STUDENT instances. UNDERGRAD__STUDENT would be similarly defined.

In the case of transactions we can specialize in a likewise manner the participants and the component events. Thus, we can describe the subclass of ENROL for which its *s* property is restricted to be an instance of GRAD__STUDENT.[5] In this case we also specify that additional prerequisites *Grad-Max?* and *Areas-OK?* should be checked. Along the same lines, the subclass ENROL(*s*:UNDERGRAD__STUDENT, *c*:COURSE) could have additional prerequisites *Before-deadline?* and *Undergrad-Max?*. Continuing, we can distinguish subclasses GRADUATE__COURSE and UNDERGRAD__COURSE of COURSE, and in the case of students enrolling in graduate courses we have a number of additional actions to be done in ENROL, such as printing a computer account number which the student can use in the course.

Assuming joe is an instance of UNDERGRAD__STUDENT and cs2100 is an instance of GRADUATE__COURSE, there are two important points to note here about the interpretation of ENROL(joe,cs2100), which is an instance of ENROL(*s*:UNDERGRAD__STUDENT, *c*:GRAD__COURSE) : by inheritance, this activity will have all the properties of ENROL(*s*:STUDENT, *c*:COURSE), ENROL(*s*:UNDERGRAD__STUDENT, *c*:COURSE), and ENROL(*s*:STUDENT, *c*:GRADUATE__COURSE), and by an obviously useful convention, all inherited prerequisites will be checked before any of the inherited actions will be executed. In this example multiple inheritance is obviously a useful tool for the designer of a system.

Resuming the task of introducing the constraints in Figure 1, we can now consider specializations of ENROL where more that one parameter is specialized. As a result, we add prerequisites *Has-preparation?*, *Not-excluded?* and *Another-first-year?* on ENROL(*s*:UNDERGRAD__STUDENT, *c*:UNDERGRAD__COURSE), as well as *Permission?* on ENROL(*s*:UNDERGRAD__STUDENT, *c*:GRADUATE__COURSE), and *At-least-4th-year?* on

---

[5] Denote this class by ENROL(s:GRAD__STUDENT, c:COURSE).

ENROL(*s*:GRAD__STUDENT, *c*:UNDERGRAD__COURSE).

Finally, by creating additional subclasses PART_TIME_STUDENT and STUDENT_ON_PROBATION of UNDERGRAD__STUDENT, we specialize the *Undergrad-Max?* prerequisite to *Part-time-max?* and *Probation-max?* respectively.

Scripts

The astute reader may have noticed that not all conditions in Figure 1 can be accounted for as prerequisites of the ENROL transaction; examples are checking for co-requisites or conditions involving minimum number of courses, where one needs to know what other courses the student is or will be enrolling in this year. Furthermore, a central attribute of an IIS is the ability to communicate interactively with its users in order to provide the data which "drives" the transactions. We must therefore be able to specify the communication protocols making up the user interfaces.

For the above purposes, we propose to offer *scripts*: processes which have significant duration and which have elaborate communication and synchronization mechanisms. The script formalism used is an adaptation of Zisman's Augmented Petri Nets [Zisman 77] used in office automation systems, and is described in more detail in [Barron 80]. Each script is essentially a Petri net with parameters, local variables, states and state transitions. In turn, each transition consists of conditions, which must be true for the transition to fire, and actions, which are to be carried out if the transition fires. In order to enable communication, scripts can employ operators for *message passing* between a script and a terminal, or more generally between any two scripts. These operators are based on Hoare's primitives **give** and **take** and thus provide further ability for synchronization, especially when the system clock is allowed to send "wake up" messages at desired times. Although much more elaborate communication mechanisms are being currently developed, we will consider here a message to be simply a **form** with possibly some text and slots which can be filled by the user (or some other script) and then sent off.[6]

To illustrate the use of scripts, let us place enrolling in courses into a wider context. At our university, students register first with the university; this includes paying fees, selecting a program of studies which is "correct", etc. However, students take courses directly from the departments offering them, thus allowing the departments to have direct contact with students, in order for example to sell them required lecture notes, lab materials, etc. Consider therefore the TAKE-COURSE script which describes the protocol for taking a course. The script is parameterized by the department *d* which is offering the course, and includes five states, represented by circles. On the transitions, indicated by vertical bars, the conditions have been separated from the actions by ==> . An instance of the TAKE-COURSE script is created by the secretary of the appropriate department whenever a student shows up to enrol in a course. With the initial state on, the script requests a description of the student *s* and the course *c*,

---

[6]See [Tsichritzis 81] for a detailed discussion of the utility of forms as communication means in an office environment.

parameters
    d : DEPARTMENT;
locals
    s . 3TUDENT;
    c : COURSE;

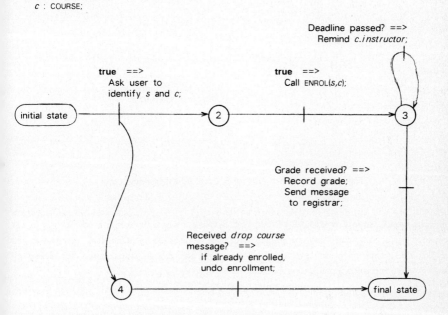

Figure 2: Outline of TAKE-COURSE script

which are properties of the script. Once the student and the course are identified, the script invokes the ENROL transaction, and then awaits the message indicating the grade the student has received in the course. If a deadline is passed, the instructor is sent a reminder that he is late. In parallel with this the script has been waiting, in state 4, for a possible message indicating that the student wants to drop the course, in which case the script is "killed". This is one example of the utility of the underlying Petri-net formalism. We remark that this script "lives" until the final state is reached, which may be several months later, and that every student would have several such scripts, thus requiring sophisticated use of the database for maintaining scripts.

Scripts, like all other constructs, are treated as classes in our methodology. Thus their bodies, i.e. their states and transitions, and also all other information associated with their definition is specified through properties that link a script to other classes. Therefore transitions can be specialized in a manner similar to transactions, and more generally, one can add new states and transitions in order to create a script which applies in more restricted circumstances. For example, the Engineering departments may require a mid-term mark to be recorded and mailed to each student; this could be accomplished by specializing TAKE-COURSE(*d*:DEPARTMENT) to TAKE-COURSE(*d*:ENGINEERING_DEPT) by replacing state 3 by the following script:

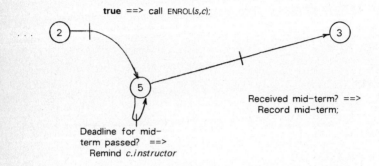

Figure 3:   Additions for TAKE__COURSE(d:ENGINEERING__DEPT)

To summarize, scripts are useful in enforcing dynamic integrity constraints on transaction call sequences (e.g., one can't receive grades until one is enrolled in a course), in defining the format and the protocol of interactions with users, and are a natural place for exception handling, including exceptions arising because of time delays.

Exception Specification

Abstraction is not the only technique useful for dealing with complexity; the ability to *manage exceptions* (i.e., deal with over-abstraction) is characteristic of human behaviour and until recently has been noticeably absent from computer application software.   The traditional view that "abnormal" occurrences be dealt with "in-line" appears to run counter to the "natural" flow of description: one has to constantly take detours from describing how students usually enrol in courses in order to say what is to be done in rare special cases.   A better alternative appears to be to adopt the convention that whenever a constraint (such as a prerequisite) evaluates to false, an *exception object* is raised, i.e., is inserted as an instance of a special class. One can then describe in a separate pass the ways in which exceptions are to be handled. Furthermore, exceptions and exception handlers can be described using the same methodology of concept specialization.

Following [Wasserman 77], each condition (e.g, prerequisite) must specify (or inherit) an exception to be raised when it fails, and we will charge the caller of transaction with handling the exception.   In order to simplify the description, we assume in our example that the exception associated with each prerequisite is labelled by the negation of the condition that raised it (e.g., if *Not-full?* is false then an instance of the exception class FULL is raised).   We chose here to organize the exceptions in a specialization hierarchy of their own, illustrated in Figure 4. This was constructed by answering the question "What can go wrong with enrolling in a course?" at various levels of generality.   Let HANDLE(x:C) be the procedure which is to

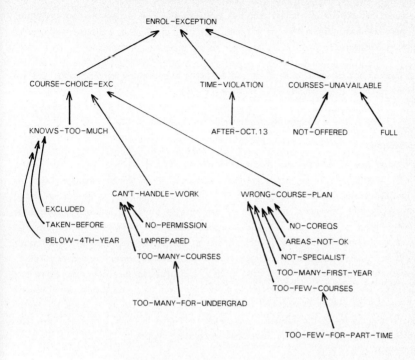

Figure 4: Specialization hierarchy for exceptions

handle instances *x* of some exception class C; in our case this transaction would be attached to the call to ENROL from the TAKE-COURSE script. Then we can start by specifying that HANDLE(*x*:ENROL__EXCEPTION) is to print a message indicating the specific exception raised. By inheritance, this action will then be carried out whenever an instance of any of the exception classes in figure 4 is raised. Turning to the immediate subclasses of ENROL__EXCEPTION, for TIMING__VIOLATIONS students may petition a committee in order to be allowed to register late. The handler in this case could be a script which completes the petition form and then awaits the decision. As far as COURSE__CHOICE__EXCEPTION is concerned, there is nothing we can say that is applicable in all cases; one of the advantages of our methodology over more traditional approaches such as decision tables is that we do not have to say anything if we have no new information to add. However, considering subclasses of COURSE__CHOICE__EXCEPTION, we note that instances of KNOWS__TOO__MUCH should always be handled issuing a "drop course" message to the TAKE-COURSE script since students should not be allowed to pick up credits gratis. On the other hand, HANDLE(*x*:CAN'T__HANDLE__WORK) requires petitioning again. In neither case need we say anything more about the subclasses of these two types of exceptions. Handlers for the other exceptions can be provided in a similar fashion.

We conclude this section by noting that the ability to describe exceptions and exception handlers within the same framework as provided for the normal data, transaction and script classes gives a pleasing uniformity and sparseness to the proposed methodology.

Having presented the principal aspects of our modelling methodology for IIS design, we are now ready to consider tools which would facilitate its use.

Tools supporting taxonomic development of IIS

Linguistic support

In order to be able to express our models in a convenient and precise fashion, we need a language with well defined syntax and semantics. Currently, we offer the language Taxis and its extension ([Mylopoulos et al., 78], [Barron 80]); Taxis integrates within the framework of classes, properties and inheritance, the notion of data classes similar to relations ([Codd 70]), standard Algol/Pascal control structures, and procedural exception handling as in [Wasserman 77]. Taxis is intermediate between a nonprocedural, conceptual requirements specification language and an ordinary application language plus DBMS as used today.[7] It can be used to specify what are known as semantic data models and provides a syntax for expressing commonly used constraints on properties (e.g. domain and key constraints for relational databases), as well as general expressions based on looping and conditional constructs. Rather than dwell on the details of the language, we present in Figure 5 Taxis versions of the class definitions for some of the objects in the student enrollment system.

We feel that the full benefits of a formal language cannot be reached until it is given rigorous semantics, and for this reason we have spent considerable effort in specifying the semantics of Taxis, both denotationally and axiomatically (see [Mylopoulos and Wong 80], [Borgida and Wong 81]). In addition, the Hoare-axioms for the language enable us to prove theorems about the systems developed. For example, we can consider an integrity constraint J ([Hammer and McLeod 75]) as an assertion of invariance. Traditionally, the DBMS would have to check that this constraint holds after every update operation; however if we can prove that every transaction T maintains J, i.e., $J\{T\}J$, then there is no need for runtime validity checks for constraint J.

Development aids

Traditionally, development aids have included, among others, editors, syntax and other static checkers for Programming Languages, version control mechanisms, all these integrated to various degrees. Our proposed development environment is interactive, with a full-screen editor from which one can invoke one of a spectrum of predefined functions; in addition, we feel the need for an interpreter which can simulate the execution of transactions, scripts, etc., however slowly, in order to provide a good *prototyping* facility. In many ways, we embrace the same ideals as the USE system ([Wasserman 80]), and in the remainder of this section we

---

[7]We are currently developing a requirements specification language for conceptual designs, applicable to general software systems, not just IIS ([Borgida and Greenspan 81], [Greenspan 81]).

```
data class STUDENT with
  keys  (name)
  attributes
    name: PERSON_NAME;
    age: 12..80;
    home-address: ADDRESS;
    faculty: {Arts&Science,
            GradSchool, Meds};
    status: {Full-time, Part-time}
end STUDENT;
```

```
data class GRAD_STUDENT is-a STUDENT with
  attributes
    faculty: {GradSchool};
    advisor:PROFESSOR;
    level: {MSc, PhD};
end GRAD_STUDENT;
```

```
transaction ENROL with
params (s,c)
locals
  s: STUDENT;
  c: COURSE;
prerequisites
  Not-full?:  (c.size<c.limit) exception FULL(stud:s,course:c);
actions
  add:  insert object in ENROLLMENT with student:s, course:c ;
  increase:  c.size := c.size + 1;
end ENROL;
```

```
prerequisite At-least-4th-year on (GRAD_STUDENT, UNDERGRAD_COURSE)..enrol
  is   (c.year > 3) exception BELOW-4TH-YR(stud:s, course:c);
```

Figure 5: Examples of Taxis class definitions

will consider only those tools which are specifically designed to support the novel aspects of our methodology, mostly related to taxonomic development.

To begin with, let us consider aids for the *completeness* of descriptions. Foremost among these is a command which expands at a desired moment the abbreviation introduced by inheritance. Thus, when defining a new class (whether data, transaction or script), one can ask for all its inherited properties to be displayed on the screen, once its super-classes are specified. Furthermore, this image can be edited in order to specialize previously defined properties or to add new properties and constraints. This tool removes from the designer the error-prone task of copying identical parts of descriptions, without imposing the burden of remembering what properties would be inherited.

Another problem where memory aids would be useful is in dealing with forward references. For example, following our methodology, the designer would specify first the most central and general classes in the application world; but this description would almost certainly involve references to yet undefined classes (e.g., ADDRESS, AGE, SALARY, etc.) The system could quite easily maintain lists of "stubs" -- classes or properties mentioned but not yet defined. Similarly, in order to ensure completeness, the system could maintain a list of exceptions for which handlers had not yet been specified.

The development environment can also be quite useful in checking the *correctness* of our descriptions. In particular, it can help maintain the consistency of the taxonomies being built whenever properties are being specialized. Thus, in specializing data class A with property *p* whose range is class B, to a class C where *p* has range D, it is necessary that D be a specialization of B; this may be checked by looking at the IS-A hierarchy built until now, or by considering the limits of ranges (e.g., the range 14 to 80 is a subclass of the range 1 to 120). More difficult, but as important, is the ability to verify that specialized assertions, such as transaction prerequisites, imply their more general forms e.g., *Too-many-courses?: (s.#taking <* 5) is a proper specialization of *Too-many-courses?: (s.#taking < 7)* . Related to this is the problem of detecting that one assertion contradicts another, which would result in the class having no instances. These problems are in general undecidable so we must resign ourselves to heuristics which try to detect syntactically when such contradictions arise.

As mentioned before, the ability to prove in advance that an integrity constraint about some class is maintained invariant by all transactions leads to significant run-time savings. In [Wong 81] we illustrate how once we have proven that some transaction T maintains invariant *J*, we can in some cases "inherit" the proof in order to demonstrate that each specialization T" of T also maintains this invariant. The reason for this is that by inheritance T" is in some sense the "sum" of T and some new additional part N; if by some syntactic heuristic we can easily determine that *J{N}J*, then we have that T" also maintains *J* invariant; [Borgida 81] gives a number of such heuristics which can be easily implemented on a computer. Of course, one could couple this to a full program verifying aid (e.g., [Gerhart 80]) in order to achieve a more powerful tool.

Implementation aids

Given a description in a language like Taxis, which is in fact a high-level language with a very elaborate type facility, we could consider developing compilers which would map Taxis programs into efficient, optimized machine code. However this seems to require an enormous amount of work since it includes a traditional compiler and full database management system; furthermore, at best, we will duplicate the work of the most advanced current language and DBMS systems. We have therefore opted, at least for now, for the translation of Taxis descriptions into currently existing DBMS and programming languages.

As an example, given a data class definition, the translator would produce the appropriate DDL schema for the records, etc. needed in the DBMS, and a number of procedures in some DML for manipulating the objects in that class. Following [Abrial 74], these would include procedures for creating, destroying, testing, generating, retrieving, and modifying the property values of instances of the class. Since access to the class instances would be restricted to these procedures, we could maintain the integrity of the database even using a DBMS, like System R [Astrahan, et al., 76], which is "untyped". Based on this, Taxis transactions would be mapped into a control structure skeleton in the application language (e.g., PL/I) on which calls to the procedures defining the data classes are hung. Clearly such transactions could be passed through an optimizer which, for example, eliminated redundant type checking.

We mention here a few words about our experimental system based on these ideas which is currently under development ([Nixon 81], [Nixon and Leung 81], [Hogg and Nierstrasz 81]). In general, starting with various types of Taxis class definitons, we incrementally parse them in an interactive environment, using augmented phrase structure grammars, and generate internal data structures which represent them; these structures are then validated in order to check, for example, that specialization has been correctly carried out. From these structures code is generated in the form of type declarations and procedures in one of a number of languages by invoking the appropriate translator routine. The resulting programs are then compiled or interpreted in order to produce the final or prototype IIS. Until the present, we have carried out modest experiments in a number of environments and configurations, including: (i) Unix on a PDP-11/45 with Yacc and Lex as parsers ([Johnson and Lesk 78]) and C as the target language; (ii) DEC-10 with parser/translator/editor written in Lisp, and Pascal/R ([Schmidt and Mall 80]) or Lisp as the target language. A more complete system, written entirely in Pascla/R and generating Pascal/R code is currently under development. Cobol or PL/I code manipulating any commercially available database management system could, of course, also be generated by different translators.

Summary and conclusions

We have outlined and illustrated the principal elements of a software development project. These include firstly, and most importantly, a design methodology which combines stepwise refinement by decomposition with concept specialization and is intended to help an IIS designer cope with the mass of details that needs to be integrated into his system.

The Taxis methodology suggests that the designer should start by defining the most general naturally occurring classes of objects and events in the domain; this is to be accomplished by the use of named properties which connect related concepts and through the use of assertions which restrict the potential relationships. Further details of the proposed system are then introduced in successive iterations by describing subclasses of already presented classes and specializing transactions and scripts in order to deal with the objects in these classes.[8]

The result is a hierarchy (taxonomy) of object, transaction and script classes on which inheritance operates to abbreviate natural redundancy without losing the benefit of being able to check consistency. Once the usual/normal aspects of the system are described to some level of detail, the designer can describe, using the same methodology, the exceptions raised by the failure of assertions and the exception handling mechanisms for them.

We feel that the above methodology is conducive to a natural style of description because it is oriented toward the *conceptual objects* and *activities* occurring in the user's world. The virtual specialization hierarchy which results when considering the possible specializations of

---

[8]Of course, this does not prevent one from introducing at any stage new classes and transactions, as they are needed.

each parameter for a transaction or script is a convenient conceptual coat rack on which to hang the details of the problem domain, thus providing much needed guidance for the designer. In addition to its role of abridging descriptions, multiple inheritance, as illustrated in our example, allows one to think separately about independent aspects of the world (e.g., undergraduate students and graduate courses) with inheritance taking care of their interaction. We also feel that the systematic treatment of exceptions and exception handlers within the same framework of object and transaction classes supports another important abstraction principle: the ability to disregard the exceptional or unusual situations during the first pass.

The above methodology is supported by a programming language, Taxis, and by an interactive system, currently under development, which provides the designer with a flexible environment for developing and testing prototypes as well as the final application programs. We remark that these tools are useful not only in the development but also the maintenance of IIS, which is considered to be one of the major areas of resource expenditure in software engineering. For example, software structured in inheritance hierarchies, as presented here, is naturally and conveniently extended to deal with special cases, which often come to light later, by introducing even more specialized subclasses at the "bottom" of the hierarchy. Also, if changes occur in a more general class, these filter down to all of its subclasses by inheritance, thus contributing in part to the resolution of the perennial problem of propagating modifications so that the final system is consistent.

In addition to the implementation of the tools mentioned above, our long-term goals include the development of a high-level requirements specification language, methods of specifying user communication media which have some of the attributes of human communication (e.g., a natural syntax, anaphoric references, ellipsis, etc.), and experimental evaluation of the resulting system on actual practical problems, which of course is the ultimate test of the significance of our work.

REFERENCES

[Abrial 74]   J.Abrial, "Data Semantics", in *Data Management Systems*, (Klimbie and Koffeman eds.), North Holland, 1974.

[Astrahan, et al., 76]   M.M.Astrahan, et al., "System R: relational approach to database management" *ACM Transactions on Database Systems 1*, June 1976.

[Barron 80]   J.L.Barron, "Dialogue organization and structure for Interactive Information Systems", MSc Thesis, TR CSRG-108, Department of Computer Science, University of Toronto, 1980.

[Borgida 81]   A.Borgida, "On the definition of specialization hierarchies for procedures and their use for verification", *Proc. Int.Joint Conf. on Artif. Intelligence*, Vancouver, BC., August 1981.

[Borgida and Greenspan 80]   A.Borgida and S.Greenspan, "Data and activities: exploiting hierarchies of classes", *Proc. Workshop on Data Abstraction*, Pingree Park, Colorado, June 1980. (Special issue of SIGART/SIGMOD/SIGPLAN Notices Jan./Feb. 1981).

[Codd 70]   E.F.Codd, "A relational model of data for large shared databases", *Communications of the ACM 13*, June 1970.

[Deutsch and Taft 80]   L.P.Deutsch and E.A.Taft (eds.), "Requirements for an experimental programming environment", Xerox Technical Report CSL-80-10, Xerox PARC, June 1980.

[Dijkstra 72]   E.W.Dijkstra, "Notes on Structured Programming", in *Structured Programming*, O.J.Dahl, E.W.Dijkstra and C.A.R.Hoare, Academic Press, 1972.

[Gerhart 80]   S.Gerhart, et al., "An overview of Affirm: a specification and verification system", Proc. IFIP 80, Australia, October 1980.

[Greenspan 81]   S.Greenspan, "Research on Requirements Modeling", Ph.D. Thesis proposal, Dept. of Compute Science, University of Toronto, March 1981.

[Hammer and McLeod 75]   M.Hammer and D.McLeod, "Semantic integrity in a relational database system", *Proc. 1st VLDB Conference*, Boston, Mass., 1975.

[Hogg and Nierstrasz 81]   J.Hogg and O.Nierstrasz, "An implementation of Taxis scripts", course project, Dept. of Compute Science, University of Toronto, May 1981.

[Johnson and Lesk 78]   S.C.Johnson and M.E.Lesk, "Language Development Tools", *Bell System Technical Journal 57*, #6, July-August 1978.

[Levin 77]   R.Levin, "Program structures for exceptional condition handling", Ph.D. Thesis, Dept.of Computer Science, Carnegie-Mellon University, 1977.

[Mylopoulos, et al., 80]   J.Mylopoulos, P.Bernstein and H.K.T.Wong, "A language facility for designing interactive database-intensive applications", *ACM Transactions on Database Systems 5*, June 1980.

[Mylopoulos and Wong 80]   J.Mylopoulos and H.K.T.Wong, "Some features of the Taxis data model", *Proc. 6th VLDB Conference*, October 1980.   [Nixon 81]   B.Nixon, "The compilation of Taxis programs", M.Sc. Thesis, Dept. of Computer Science, University of Toronto, forthcoming.

[Nixon and Leung 81]   B.Nixon and T.Leung, "Implementing Taxis classes in Pascal/R" course project, Dept. of Computer Science, University of Toronto, May 1981.

[Parnas 72]   D.L.Parnas, "On the criteria to be used in decomposing systems into modules", *Communications of the ACM 12*, December 1972.

[Schmidt and Mall 80]   J.Schmidt and M.Mall, "Pascal/R Report", Berricht Nr.66, Fachbereich Informatik, Hamburg University.

[Smith and Smith 79]   J.M.Smith and D.C.P.Smith, "A database approach to software specification", TR CCA-79-17, Computer Corp. of America, Cambridge MA., April 1979.

[Tsichritzis 81]   D.Tsichritzis, "Form Management", CSRG, University of Toronto, submitted for publication.

[Tsichritzis and Lochovsky 81]   D.Tsichritzis and F.Lochovsky, *Data Models*, Prentice Hall, 1981.

[Wasserman 77]   A.Wasserman, "Procedure-oriented exception handling", TR-27, Faculty of Medicine, University of California, San Francisco, 1977.

[Wasserman 80]   A.Wasserman, "Software tools and the User Software Engineering project", TR 46, Laboratory for Medical Information Science, UC San Francisco, February 1980.

[Wirth 71]   N.Wirth, "Program development by stepwise refinement", *Communications of the ACM 14*, April 1971.

[Wong 81]   H.K.T.Wong, "Design and verification of Interactive Information Systems", Ph.D. Thesis, Dept. of Computer Science, University of Toronto, forthcoming; also, TR-CSRG-129, April 1981.

[Wulf, et al., 76]   W.A.Wulf, R.London, and M.Shaw, "An introduction to the construction and verification of Alphard programs", *IEEE Trans. on Software Engineering SE-2*, 4, December 1976.

[Zisman 77]   M.D.Zisman, "Use of production systems for modelling asynchronous parallel processes", in *Pattern-directed Inference Systems*, (Waterman and Hayes-Roth eds.), Academic Press, 1978.

Automated Tools for Information Systems Design
H.-J. Schneider and A.I. Wasserman (eds.)
North-Holland Publishing Company
© IFIP, 1982

An Automatic/Interactive Software Development System:
Formal Basis and Design

P.A.Subrahmanyam
Department of Computer Science
University of Utah
Salt Lake City, Utah 84112

Abstract

- The conceptual basis and design of an experimental interactive software development system are discussed. The design of the system is based upon a formal theory of program synthesis that views the problem of program synthesis as that of synthesizing implementations of abstract, representation independent problem specifications. The syntax and semantics of the problem, as well as the performance requirements and environment dependent constraints (in particular, frequencies of function invocations), are used to actively guide the overall synthesis strategy. A machine readable history of the development of the implementation is maintained to aid the maintenance phase of software systems.

1. Introduction

This paper discusses the conceptual basis and design of an experimental interactive software development system. The design of this system is based upon a formal theory of program synthesis that views the problem of (automatic/interactive) program synthesis as that of (automatically/interactively) synthesizing implementations of abstract, representation independent problem specifications [30, 34]. The syntax and semantics of the problem, as well as the performance requirements and 'environment dependent' constraints (in particular, patterns of function invocations), are used to actively guide the overall synthesis strategy. The implementations produced are provably correct in a formal sense; in fact, correctness proofs are obtained as a natural by-product of the synthesis. The development history of the synthesis is also recorded in a 're-usable' fashion, so as to facilitate the maintenance phase of software systems.

1.1. Outline of the Paper

We summarize the essential concepts underlying the proposed theory of program synthesis in section 2 and delineate the synthesis paradigm in section 3. The design of an experimental automatic programming system based upon the theory is discussed in section 4; parts of the design have been implemented and some implementation details are mentioned in section 5. In section 6, we illustrate some of the salient features of the system by discussing an extended example -- the automated synthesis of a text editor. Section 7 contains a brief comparison with existing approaches to automatic program synthesis and also outlines avenues for further empirical exploration.

2. Conceptual Basis[1]

Intuitively, the abstraction of several problems can be viewed as consisting of an appropriate set of functions to be performed on an associated set of objects. Such a collection of objects and functions is an "abstract data type" and has the important advantage of providing a representation-independent

125

characterization of problems [11, 14, 21].[2] We stress here the difference between the *use* of data types *in* the specification of (a solution to) a problem, and the specification of (a solution to) a problem *as* an abstract data type.   While it is commonplace to use data types in most forms of programming and/or specification, specifying the *entire* problem as a data type might sometimes require a different perspective on a problem. As an example, [16] illustrates how a symbol table can be viewed *as* a data type; this should be contrasted with the plethora of implementations of symbol tables that might *use* data types (not to be confused with data structures) such as doubly linked lists, circular lists, etc.

We view the process of program synthesis as one of obtaining an implementation for the data type corresponding to the problem of interest (the "type of interest") in terms of another data type (the "representation type" or "target type").   That is, programming is viewed as representing the abstractions of objects and operations relevant to a given problem domain using primitives that are presumed to be already available; ultimately, such primitives are those that are provided by the available hardware.   The rationale underlying this perspective includes the following:

- Program synthesis should proceed from a problem specification that is **representation independent**. This serves to guarantee complete freedom in the program synthesis process, in that no particular program is excluded *a priori* due to an overspecification of the problem caused by representation dependencies.

- Synthesizing correct programs is easier, in general, than verifying *a posteriori* that a given program is consistent with its specification. This is because the parts of a program that are the most difficult to verify are usually those that require the greatest insight into *why* the program was developed a particular way: synthesizing programs provides this "insight" as a natural by-product.

- The synthesis should be guided primarily by the semantics of the problem specification (i.e. the desired functional behavior).   The desired performance requirements and the function application patterns influence the selection of satisfactory implementations.

- The level of reasoning used by a synthesis paradigm should be appropriate to "human reasoning," rather than being machine oriented.   The importance of data abstractions in achieving elegant program organizations was cogently argued by Hoare [18] and their use has, by now, been amply demonstrated.   In addition to making the paradigm computationally more feasible, the perspective we have adopted offers two major advantages:

  - existing paradigms of programming such as "stepwise refinement" can be viewed in a mathematical framework

  - user interaction is facilitated, since the level of reasoning is now "visible" to the user.

An algebraic formulation for program synthesis based on the above principles is detailed in [34, 30]. An important consequence of this decision was that the synthesis paradigm is *independent* of any assumptions relating to the nature of the underlying hardware. In fact, it has since led naturally to target types tailored to specific problems of interest, i.e.   target machine architectures which aid efficient implementations [32].

3. A Paradigm for Program Synthesis

We adopt the view that an instance of a type is completely characterized by its "externally observable behavior".   This is made precise in the notion of extraction (or observable) equivalence of

---

[2]Although the illustrations that most readily come to mind are commonly employed data structures such as stacks, files, queues, symbol tables, etc., any partial recursive function can be presented as an abstract data type [14].

instances of the type [34]. Informally, two terms t1 and t2 are said to be *extraction equivalent* if every sequence of function applications terminating with the application of a function that returns an instance of a "known" type[3] yields the same (or "equivalent") results on the two terms.

The notion of an *implementation* of one data type (the type of interest) in terms of another (the target type) is defined as a map between the functions and objects of the two types which preserves the observable behavior of the type of interest. The objective, then, is to develop methods to automate the synthesis of such implementations based on the specifications of the type of interest and the target type [34, 35, 36].

The synthesis is achieved by analyzing, in a manner which we shall delineate below, both the syntactic and semantic structure inherent in the specified problem and the (abstract) target machine. By the syntactic structure of a problem, we mean the information contained in the syntactic specifications of the functions and objects of the type that specifies the problem. By its semantic structure, we mean the structure of the "smallest" algebra[4] defining the type, where two objects are viewed as being distinct if and only if they exhibit differing observable behavior.

3.1. Synthesis Strategy

The synthesis proceeds by first syntactically categorizing the functions defined on a type into **base constructors** (that serve to spawn new instances of a type), **constructors** (that generate new instances from old), and **extractors** (that return instances of types other than the one being defined). A subset of the base constructors and constructors, called the kernel set, is then identified, serving to generate all representative instances of the type. The semantic characteristics of each function are then examined, as also are the application patterns and performance requirements of the functions defined on the type of interest. In addition, an analysis of the semantics of the functions defined on the target type and their cost specifications is made. Using the results of the preceding analyses, the kernel functions are implemented first, and then the remaining functions. In order to meet the performance requirements of non-kernel function implementations, it may occasionally be necessary to modify the initially synthesized implementations for some of the kernel functions and (or) to augment the target type.

3.1.1. Implementing Kernel Functions.

In order for any target type (henceforth denoted TT) to be able to implement a specified type of interest (henceforth denoted TOI), each distinct object (synonymously, extraction equivalence class) in the type of interest must be represented by a distinct object in the target type. For otherwise, the representations of the two distinct objects will exhibit similar behavior, and as a consequence, the externally observable behavior of the type of interest will no longer be preserved by the implementation.

It follows that if the application of a function (on TOI) produces a distinct instance of TOI, then the implementation of this function must yield a distinct instance of TT. When the goal is one of synthesis, therefore, it is necessary to have a function that acts as a "building block" and enabling construction of distinct instances of TT. Further, when implementing parameterized data types, it is often very desirable to have the ability to encode instances of the parameter types (or "data", if you will) into instances of the target type created by the building block, and to retrieve it if and when needed. A pair of functions ‹f,e› defined on a type, such that f facilitates the generation of distinct instances of a type and the encoding of

---

[3]i.e., a type other than the one being defined, or a "defining type"

[4]Specifically, we mean the algebra under observable (or "extraction") equivalence [34]. All that we require of the input specifications is that they be *sufficiently complete* in the sense of [14].

data, while e enables retrieval of the encoded (or "stored") data is called a *retrievable insertion function pair*.

- **Definition:** A pair of functions f:T,X -› X and e:T -› Set-of-X is said to be a *(weak) retrievable insertion function pair* with respect to X if (i) e(t0)={}, for all base constructors (constants) t0 of type T, and (ii) e(f(t,x)) = e(t) **U** {x} otherwise (for all instances t of type T and all instances x of type X).

- If X is a generic type, then ‹f,e› is an (unrestricted) retrievable insertion function pair.

Intuitively, f provides the ability to encode instances of type X into instances of type T, whereas e provides the ability to retrieve all values encoded by f. A "strong" retrievable insertion function pair allows *identification* of specific instances of X encoded.[5]. The importance of this notion lies in the fact that:

- **Theorem:** A retrievable insertion function pair on TT is sufficient to guarantee the existence of an implementation of TOI in terms of TT.

The proof of the above theorem yields an algorithm to construct an implementation of the kernel functions of TOI in terms of TT. This proof also yields a correctness argument for the implementation synthsized. Intuitively specaking, the kernel functions may be implemented using the insertion function to encode the needed data. The global strategy adopted determines which specific data values are encoded (i.e., what data is "needed") -- the example detailed in section 6 illustrates several instances of this. In essence therefore, an insertion function on the target type serves to generate the needed representative instances (in TT) of all the equivalence classes in TOI, and is therefore sufficient to initially implement the kernel functions.

Given an arbitrary type definition, the identification of a retrievable insertion function pair may be shown to be an undecidable problem in general. We have identified specific classes of type definitions for which it is possible to algorithmically identify retrievable insertion function pairs. The finiteness of real types, as well as complexity considerations are accounted for by introducing the notion of the "capacity" of a type, and a vector of measure functions (one for each performance measure of interest) on the terms of the type. The global strategy is then based on these measures. We postpone a detailed discussion of these issues to a future paper.

3.1.2. Implementing Non-Kernel Functions.

The synthesis of the remaining functions defined on a type is now performed incrementally. In the process, the initial implementation of the kernel functions may be modified for the purposes of meeting the performance requirements of non-kernel function implementations. The overall synthesis strategy is guided by the semantics of the function, and the performance requirements. In particular, the non-kernel functions are synthesized in order of decreasing stringency of their performance requirements.

If the performance of a direct implementation of the function is predicted or computed to be unacceptable then modifications to the existing implementations of kernel functions, and to the target type itself, are made to achieve the desired performance.

If the actual performance of the implementation of some function is better than that required, then an attempt is made to "shift" some of the complexity of (the implementation of) the more inefficient function into the overly efficient one. Alternatively, an additonal component of the target type is introduced, and used to directly encode the needed result, so as to improve its efficiency. All such augmentations need to preserve overall consistency in order to be acceptable to the system.

---

[5]Details of the formalism are outside the scope of this paper. See, for example, [37]

Further optimizations may be achieved by performing "type transformations" by merging common operations between different type components (cf. [39]). Many of the above aspects are illustrated by the example discussed in section 6.

3.2. Some Examples of Applications of the Synthesis Paradigm.

Several programs have been synthesized by applications of the synthesis algorithms developed so far. These include implementations for a Stack, a Queue, a Deque, a Block Structured SymbolTable, an interactive line-oriented Text-Editor and a text formatter. Further, the paradigm has aided in the discovery of some algorithms: these include a tree pattern matching algorithm, and a hidden surface elimination algorithm for graphical displays [33]. Machine architectures appropriate for VLSI have also been obtained by applying the paradigm [32] -- this is achieved by not specifying *a priori* any target type for the implementation.

4. The Design of an Automatic Program Synthesis System

This section outlines the design of an interactive automatic programming system whose conceptual and formal basis we have summarized in section 2. The input specification of the problem consists of

1. *functional specifications* that are assumed to be abstract algebraic data type specifications detailing the syntax and semantics of the functions characterizing the problem;
2. (optional) *requirements specifications* that detail the mandated (or desired) space, time, architectural topology, blockage propagation, paging, ..., costs;
3. (optional) *functional application patterns* that detail the frequency distributions of various function applications (and associated distributions of their parameter values). An ordering on the relative frequencies of applications is also accepted as input, and is in fact easier to provide initially.

The objective of the system design is to facilitate a synthesis of the implementation of the specifications. The development structure of the synthesis is also generated, as also a correctness proof.

4.1. Acquisition of Formal Specifications

In order for any software development system to be a widely used tool, it is important that a friendly environment be provided to its users. Such an environment would, at the very least, include a "front end interface" which helps the user develop a set of formal specifications without his having to know much of the mechanics underlying this process.[6] (We have not implemented such a front-end at the time of this writing, but have a structured editor to facilitate incrementally building up formal specifications.)

Appropriate helpful prompts will be provided by the system to remind the user of the underlying philosophy and methodology involved in specifying a problem as an abstract data type. The specifications generated will be deemed satisfactory if whatever queries the user wants to pose of the specification can be "answered" in a satisfactory manner [15]. This phase benefits from the use of algebraic deduction and simplification systems; currently, our system uses a combination of the Stanford Simplifier [27], and REDUCE [17]. (We are experimenting with a combination of AFFIRM and the Stanford Simplifier as a replacement.)

---

[6]Nevertheless, we have primarily been concentrating on the technical issues relevant to program synthesis, rather than attempting to create a very flexible interface. This is in keeping with the philosophy expressed by McCarthy in [25].

At a later stage, we expect a more sophisticated friendly interface for such a question-answering phase. In the interim, the system may provide a mechanism for keeping track of the queries in both their formal and informal versions, where the translation from an informal query to its formal form would have to be done by the user himself.

4.2. The Synthesis Phase

In what follows, we will assume that the synthesis proceeds in terms of some initially specified target type. There is no loss of generality incurred by this assumption since the system design in fact allows for a library of "candidate" target types, from which a suitable target type is chosen based on some appropriate measure of its "compatibility" with the type being implemented. We now list the functions of some of the major modules that form part of the overall system:

- Analysis of Function Syntax: Base Constructors, Constructors, and Extractors defined on the type of interest are identified.

- Semantic Analysis: A set of kernel functions of the type of interest is deduced. Each of the semantic equations is examined and the semantic descriptions of the refinement sequences for the identification of the extraction equivalence classes are characterized. Inductive reasoning is employed here on the form of the recursion equations.

- An incremental, interactive development of the function implementation is then commenced using the semantics of the target type and the inferences made above. The major modules used during this phase are the complexity computation module for performance analysis, and the semantic analysis module: these are invoked whenever needed (i.e. their invocation is "demand driven"). The primary interactions are maintained as part of a "development tree": this serves to record the actions taken at these steps in machine executable form, along with the rationale for this decision. This allows the possibility for a user later "querying" the system about the development sequence, and allowing an automated execution of a similar development sequence for somewhat differing functionalrequirements specifications.

- In course of the synthesis process, some "auxiliary data types" may be defined by the system in order to aid in the implementation of the initially specified type of interest. A recursive invocation of the synthesis procedure is now performed to implement these types in terms of the originally specified target type.

- Modules to define auxiliary types, and to provide correctness arguments during the incremental synthesis.

At various points during the synthesis process, the system provides for interaction with the user (see section 6). One central theme that we attempt to maintain in all such interactions is that the nature of the interaction is conducted in a tone that is comprehensible to the user.

5. Implementation Details

The basic environment in which the present system resides is that of INTERLISP [19]. Integrated into this environment is a set of tools (c.f. POPART [40]) a structured editor (cognizant of data type definitions), a pattern matcher, and a program development system. In addition, there is an interface to REDUCE [17] (a computer algebra system) that is primarily used for doing most of the symbolic complexity computations required by the synthesizer. We are contemplating incorporating some of the decision procedures in the Stanford Simplifier [22] and AFFIRM [26] into this configuration, but have not yet done so because of address space restrictions in TOPS-20.

5.1. Maintaining the Software Development History

In order to alleviate the problem of software maintenance and modification, it is important to record the history of decisions (and their rationale) leading to the development of a specific implementation [1]. This is motivated by our hope that such automatic documentation that is created by, and hence "readable" by, the automatic programming system itself, will facilitate future modifications to the program. This is implemented by building on the "history list" mechanism provided by INTERLISP, and makes use of some of the features available in POPART [40].

6. Implementation of an Interactive Line-oriented Text-Editor

To illustrate some aspects of the paradigm for program synthesis outlined in section 3, we discuss the synthesis of an interactive line-oriented text editor. We do this by elaborating on an edited version of a transcript illustrating the synthesis. The definition of a Text Editor as an abstract type appears near the beginning of the interaction with the system. (As mentioned in section 4, this definition was obtained using a syntax directed editor that is cognizant of data types. We will not, however, elaborate any more on this facet of the system interaction here.)

If we are given a library of target types, it is possible, if desired, to select a target type that is 'closely matched' to the specified type of interest (here, the TextEditor). We will, however, for the sake of simplicity, assume here that the target type is initially specified to be a CircularList; the definition of a CircularList is included in the transcript. This definition is a slightly modified version of that defined in [16] in that it includes some additional functions e.g. LEFT, RIGHT*, and LEFT*.

The discussion of this example reviews some of the rationale for the various steps taken in obtaining the synthesis, and points out the places where alternative decisions are possible. This serves to illustrate some of the variations that are possible within the scope of the basic synthesis paradigm.

It is important to note that whenever alternative decisions are available to the synthesis algorithms, a correct implementation is guaranteed no matter what decision is made -- the difference lies in the efficiency of the resulting implementation, and therefore its appropriateness in differing environments of use. (It is here that the performance requirements and application patterns play a critical role in guiding the overall synthesis strategy.) More importantly, it should be noted that almost all of the steps here are completely automatable; there is, however, great leeway for interaction, as will be pointed out below. Due to lack of space, we do not detail the algorithms that exist for the various steps (see however, [34, 37]). Instead, we merely sketch the result of applying the algorithms and attempt to provide some of the underlying intuition.

6.1. An Edited transcript

We continue this discussion using an edited transcript of the synthesis of a TextEditor in terms of a target type that is initially specified to be a CircularList. (The current implementation does not support target type libraries.) It will turn out that this target type needs to be augmented in order to meet the desired performance requirements.

Remarks within braces have been inserted for added explanation and are not meant to be part of the program output.

```
------------------------->-------------------------------------------------------
....
```

{This is an edited transcript of the synthesis of a text editor in terms
of a circular list.}

> Please Input the Name of the Type of Interest (TOI): TextEditor
> Please Input the Name of the Target Type (TT): CircularList

> AcquireSpecifications TextEditor

Specification acquisition phase beginning...

{We omit all of the interactions involved in acquiring the specifications
of the TextEditor. We remark that it is possible to read in specifications
from an existing file; in fact, when dealing with large type specifications,
this is often a more convenient mode of operation, as it permits a natural
temporal partitioning of the specification acquisition and synthesis phase.
The final definition of Type TextEditor acquired via the Specification
Acquisition phase is summarized below using the 'PrettyPrint' command of the
syntax directed editor.}

> PrettyPrint

Type TextEditor

Syntax

```
NEWTEXT :  -> Text;
        -- spawn a new instance of a TextEditor i.e. start
        -- edits for a new file;
INPUT : Text, Line -> Text ;
        -- insert a new line at the current position into the
        -- existing text;
SCROLLUP : Text, Integer -> Text ;
        -- scrollup the text by a specified number of lines;
PEEKUP : Text, Integer -> Text ;
        -- Create a temporary "window" of 1 line at an
        -- intermediate point in the text to facilitate
        -- deletion/insertion at that point. The window
        -- 'vanishes' after insertion/deletion, unless it is
        -- desired to further SCROLLUP or SCROLLDOWN,  in
        -- which case, the temporary move is maintained.
DELETELINE : Text -> Text ;
        -- delete the line at the current position;
SCROLLDOWN : Text, Integer -> Text;
        -- scroll down the text by a specified number of lines;
TOP : Text -> Text;
        -- move to the top of the text;
BOTTOM : Text -> Text;

        -- move to the bottom of the text;
CURRENTLINE : Text -> Line;
        -- return ('display') the line of text at the current position;
LINENUMBER : Text -> Integer;
        -- return the line-number of the current line of text;
```

```
NUMBER_OF_LINES: Text -> Integer;
        -- return the number of lines in the text;
```

{Remark: The following are examples of derived functions that are defined on the TextEditor. In the interest of brevity, however, we will not discuss the implementations of these functions here.}

Derived Functions

```
LOCATESTRING : Text,string -> Text;
        -- locate the occurrence of a specified string in the text;
REPLACE : Text,string,string -> Text;
        -- replace the occurrences of the first string by the second;
TEXT_UPTO_CURSOR : Text -> Text;
        -- retrieve the portion of text that extends from the top
           of the text upto (and including) the current position;
TEXT_FROM_CURSOR : Text -> Text;
        -- retrieve the portion of text that extends after the
           current cursor position;
APPENDTEXT : Text,Text -> Text;
        -- append two pieces of text;
```

Semantics

```
Variables t:TextEditor,l:Line,l1:Line,n:Integer,n1:Integer;

INPUT(PEEKUP(INPUT(t,l),n),l1) = if n = 0
                                 then INPUT(INPUT(t,l),l1)
                                 else INPUT(INPUT(PEEKUP(t,n-1),l1),l);
        -- The window created by PEEKUP is "temporary"
INPUT(SCROLLUP(t,n),l) = SCROLLUP(INPUT(PEEKUP(t,n),l),n);
        -- The window created by SCROLLUP is persistent.

PEEKUP(NEWTEXT,n) = NEWTEXT;
PEEKUP(PEEKUP(t,n),n1) = PEEKUP(t,n+n1) ;
PEEKUP(t,0) = t;
        -- PEEKUP(SCROLLUP(t,n),n1) is an unreduced term.

SCROLLUP(NEWTEXT,n) = NEWTEXT;
SCROLLUP(SCROLLUP(t,n),n1) = SCROLLUP(t,n+n1) ;
SCROLLUP(PEEKUP(t,n),n1) = SCROLLUP(t,n+n1) ;
        -- this makes TOP, BOTTOM, etc. work naturally;
SCROLLUP(t,0) = t;

DELETELINE(NEWTEXT) = NEWTEXT;
DELETELINE(INPUT(t,l)) = t;
DELETELINE(PEEKUP(INPUT(t,l),n)) =
                if n = 0
                then t
                else INPUT(DELETELINE(PEEKUP(t,n-1)),l);
DELETELINE(SCROLLUP(t,n)) = SCROLLUP(DELETELINE(PEEKUP(t,n)),n);

SCROLLDOWN(NEWTEXT,n) = NEWTEXT;
SCROLLDOWN(INPUT(t,l),n) = INPUT(t,l);
SCROLLDOWN(PEEKUP(t,n),n1) = if n1=0 then SCROLLUP(t,n)
                            else SCROLLDOWN(SCROLLUP(t,n-1),n1-1);
```

```
SCROLLDOWN(SCROLLUP(INPUT(t,l),n),n1) =
                              if n1=0
                              then SCROLLUP(INPUT(t,l),n)
                              else SCROLLDOWN(SCROLLUP(INPUT(t,l),n-1),n1-1)

CURRENTLINE(NEWTEXT) = UNDEFINED;
CURRENTLINE(INPUT(t,l)) = 1;
CURRENTLINE(PEEKUP(INPUT(t,l),n)) = if n = 0
                                    then 1
                                    else CURRENTLINE(PEEKUP(t,n-1));
CURRENTLINE(SCROLLUP(INPUT(t,l),n)) = if n = 0
                                      then 1
                                      else CURRENTLINE(SCROLLUP(t,n-1));


LINENUMBER(NEWTEXT) = ZERO;
LINENUMBER(INPUT(t,l)) = LINENUMBER(t) + 1;
LINENUMBER(SCROLLUP(INPUT(t,l),n)) = if n = 0
                                     then LINENUMBER(t) + 1
                                     else LINENUMBER(SCROLLUP(t,n-1));
LINENUMBER(PEEKUP(INPUT(t,l),n)) = if n = 0
                                   then LINENUMBER(t) + 1
                                   else LINENUMBER(PEEKUP(t,n-1));

NUMBER_OF_LINES(NEWTEXT) = 0;
NUMBER_OF_LINES(INPUT(t,l)) = NUMBER_OF_LINES(t) + 1;
NUMBER_OF_LINES(SCROLLUP(t,n)) = NUMBER_OF_LINES(t);
NUMBER_OF_LINES(PEEKUP(t,n)) = NUMBER_OF_LINES(t);

TOP(t) = SCROLLUP(t,LINENUMBER(t));
```

{Remark: We omit the semantics of the other derived functions here.}

Function Application Patterns:

   {Remark: The function application patterns can either be probabilities of
(the frequency of) function applications, or a partial ordering indicating
function application frequencies.}

```
NEWTEXT = 1;
INPUT ~ CURRENTLINE > Most Others;
SCROLLUP ~ SCROLLDOWN;
```

Performance Requirements:

Complexity Vector = <TIME, SPACE>;

   {Remark: The Complexity vector is arbitrary in that other performance
criteria may be stated. "Constant" in the complexity field implies
independence of the complexity from the actual value of the parameters.
"Arbitrary" implies that the actual complexity value can be arbitrarily large
and still meet the performance requirements. "O(n)" implies the complexity
function can at most be a linear polynomial in n.}

```
TIME(NEWTEXT) = Constant;
SPACE(NEWTEXT) = Constant;

TIME(INPUT(t,l)) = Constant;
SPACE(INPUT(t,l)) =   SPACE(t) + SPACE(l);
```

```
TIME(SCROLLUP(t,n)) = O(n);
SPACE(SCROLLUP(t,n)) = SPACE(t);

TIME(SCROLLDOWN(t,n)) = O(n);
SPACE(SCROLLDOWN(t,n)) = Arbitrary;

TIME(CURRENTLINE(t)) = Constant;
SPACE(CURRENTLINE(t)) = Arbitrary;

TIME(LINENUMBER(t)) = Constant;
SPACE(LINENUMBER(t)) = Constant;

TIME(NUMBER_OF_LINES(t)) = Arbitrary;
SPACE(NUMBER_OF_LINES(t)) = Arbitrary;
```

{Remark: It is possible to have a library of types and select a potential target type from this library dependent on a compatibility measure. This feature is not implemented as yet; we do not elaborate on it here, and presume a CircularList has been specified as the initial Target Type.}

{The specifications of a CircularList are summarized below.}

> PrettyPrint CircularList

Type CircularList

Syntax

```
NEWCL: -> CircularList;
        -- spawns a new instance of a CircularList;
INSERTCL : CircularList, item -> CircularList;
        -- inserts a new element into the current position
        -- of the CircularList;
LEFT : CircularList, Integer -> CircularList;
        -- "rotate" the CircularList Left;
DELETECL : CircularList -> CircularList;
        -- Delete the element at the current position;
VALUECL : CircularList -> Item;
        -- display the value at the current position in
        -- the CircularList;
ISEMPTYCL : CircularList -> Boolean;
RIGHT : CircularList -> CircularList;
        -- "rotate the CircularList right;
```

Derived functions:

```
LEFT* : CircularList, Integer -> CircularList;
        -- rotates the CircularList left a specified number of times;
RIGHT* : CircularList, Integer -> CircularList;
        -- rotates the CircularList right a specified number of times;
```

Semantics

Variables c:CircularList; c1:CircularList; i:Integer; x:Item;

```
VALUECL(NEWCL) = UNDEFINED;
VALUECL(INSERTCL(c,x)) = x;
VALUECL(LEFT(INSERTCL(c,x))) = if c = NEWCL then x
                                  else VALUECL(LEFT(c));
```

```
ISEMPTYCL(NEWCL) = TRUE;
ISEMPTYCL(INSERTCL(c,x)) = FALSE;
ISEMPTYCL(LEFT(c)) = ISEMPTYCL(c);

LEFT(NEWCL) = NEWCL;
LEFT(INSERTCL(c,x)) = INSERTCL(DELETECL(LEFT(INSERTCL(c,x))),
                               VALUECL(LEFT(INSERTCL(c,x))));

RIGHT(NEWCL) = NEWCL;
RIGHT(INSERTCL(NEWCL,x)) = INSERTCL(NEWCL,x);
RIGHT(INSERTCL(INSERTCL(c,x),x1)) = INSERTCL(RIGHT(INSERTCL(c,x1)),x);
RIGHT(LEFT(c)) = c;

DELETECL(NEWCL) = NEWCL;
DELETECL(INSERTCL(c,x)) = c;
DELETECL(LEFT(INSERTCL(c,x)) = if c = NEWCL then NEWCL
                               else INSERTCL(DELETECL(LEFT(c)),x);

LEFT*(c,i) = if i = 0 then c else LEFT*(LEFT(c),i-1);

RIGHT*(c,i) = if i = 0 then c else RIGHT*(RIGHT(c),i-1);
```

{We omit the details of the performance specifications (assumed costs) for the CircularList.}

Synthesis proceeding...

> CategorizeFunctions TextEditor

Analyzing the function syntax of TextEditor Specifications...

Base Constructors: NEWTEXT

Constructors: INPUT, PEEKUP, SCROLLUP, SCROLLDOWN, TOP

Extractors: CURRENTLINE, LINENUMBER, NUMBER_OF_LINES

Kernel Functions: NEWTEXT, INPUT, PEEKUP, SCROLLUP

> AnalyzeSemantics TextEditor

Commencing Semantic Analysis of TextEditor...

> PossibleRecursions TextEditor

Recursion occurs in...

SCROLLUP(INPUT(t,l),n)

PEEKUP(INPUT(t,l),n)

> ComputeEllipticForms TextEditor

Computing elliptic representations of TextEditor...

NEWTEXT

```
INPUT(NEWTEXT,<11,...,ln>)

SCROLLUP(INPUT(NEWTEXT,<11,...,ln>),n1)

PEEKUP(INPUT(NEWTEXT,<11,...,ln>),n1)
```

{Remark: The internal form for representing elliptic forms used by the program is slightly different from the printed expressions above, although isomorphic.}

{Remark: We omit the details of most of the semantic analysis that is done at this stage.}

> CategorizeFunctions CircularList

Analyzing the function syntax of CircularList Specifications...

Base Constructors: NEWCL

Constructors: INSERTCL, RIGHT, LEFT

Extractors: VALUECL

Kernel Functions: NEWCL, INSERTCL

> AnalyzeSemantics CircularList
... {Remark: we omit details}...

> ComputeRetrievableInsertionFunctions CircularList

Synthesizing a Retrievable Insertion function pair defined on a CircularList...

Retrievable Insertion Function Pair defined on a CircularList:
        < INSERTCL(c,x), VALUECL(INSERTCL(c,x)))>
where c:CircularList; x:Item;

{Remark: These are computed by a definition driven pattern match routine.}

> Do you wish to suggest an alternative Retrievable
Insertion Function Pair? (Please answer Y/N)...No

> ImplementKernelFunctions TextEditor CircularList

Synthesizing Implementations of Kernel Functions defined on a TextEditor...

Synthesized Implementation of Kernel functions:

THETA(NEWTEXT) = NEWCL

THETA(INPUT(t,l)) = INSERTCL(THETA(t),<1,l>)

THETA(PEEKUP(t,n)) = INSERTCL(THETA(t),<2,n>)

THETA(SCROLLUP(t,n)) = INSERTCL(THETA(t),<3,n>)

> CorrectnessArguments TextEditor

The inverse Homomorphism (Representation Function) that
guarantees correctness is given by:

TextEditor_Represented_By(NEWCL) = NEWTEXT;
TextEditor_Represented_By(INSERTCL(c,<n,x>)) =
            case
              n=1 : INPUT(TextEditor_Represented_by(c),x)
              n=2 : PEEKUP(TextEditor_Represented_by(c),x)
              n=3 : SCROLLUP(TextEditor_Represented_by(c),x)
            end;

    {Remark: This follows directly from the algorithm guiding the
implementation generated above.}

> *** There is potential for alternative implementations at this stage.
Do you wish to specify an alternative Implementation here?

(Please answer Y or N) ...No

> AnalyzeImplementationComplexity TextEditor
Complexity analysis commencing...

> ComputeComplexities TextEditor

Computing Complexity of Implemented Functions...

    {Remark: Complexities of NEWTEXT, INPUT, PEEKUP, and SCROLLUP will be
computed and displayed here. The complexity computation package is being
implemented at this time; the results here are interactively supplied.}

> PredictDirectImplementationComplexities TextEditor

Attempting to predict direct implementation complexities
for Non-kernel functions defined on type TextEditor...

Non-kernel functions: CURRENTLINE, LINENUMBER, TOP,
NUMBER_OF_LINES.

Direct Implementation Complexities:

TIME(CURRENTLINE(t)) = Constant when the normal form is NEWTEXT;
                       Constant when the normal form is INPUT(t,l);
                       $O(n)$ when the normal form is PEEKUP(t,n);
                       $O(n)$ when the normal form is SCROLLUP(t,n);

    {Remark: The "predictions" are approximate, and are based upon the
syntactic form of the defining equations. In contrast, "actual" complexities
are computed from synthesized implementations. A package for asymptotic
complexity computations [28] is also being implemented. Other details
complexity computation are omitted here.}

> ******* The predicted complexities suggest that a direct
implementation of CURRENTLINE will not meet the desired
performance criteria.

{Remark: This is done by comparing predicted complexity O(n) with the
desired complexity which is Constant.}

> ******* The predicted complexities suggest that a direct
implementation of LINENUMBER will not meet the desired
performance criteria.

> Do you want detailed complexities to be computed? (Y/N)...No

{Remark: The performance of all other functions is satisfactory in this
implementation.}

From the assumed costs, the retrieval function on the type
CircularList has constant performance

Analysis for CURRENTLINE...

Performance degradation suspected when the normal form(s) is(are)

SCROLLUP(INPUT(t,l),n)
PEEKUP(INPUT(t,l),n)

{Remark: This is obtained from the complexity computations above.}

> Do you wish to suggest any implementation at this point?
(Please answer Yes/No)...No

> Are there any additional constraints on function applications
you want to add? (Yes/No/?)...Yes

Adding Constraints...

> Please input type of constraint:
(Type D for Done, or ? for options)...HiddenFunction PEEKUP.

> Please input type of constraint:
(Type D for Done, or ? for options)...Done

> AnalyzeConstraintRamifications TextEditor

{Remark: The fact that PEEKUP is a "hidden function" [23, 29, 38] implies
that PEEKUP will never be explicitly applied by a user.   This has two
important ramifications for synthesis:

- This fact may be used to optimize the resulting implementation.
  More important, what would have otherwise been an incorrect (and
  therefore unacceptable) implementation, now becomes acceptable.

- This form of exploiting the constraints imposed by hidden functions is feasible only in the synthesis process, and not in a pure a posteriori correctness proof. This is yet another reason why synthesizing correct implementations is easier than proving correctness a posteriori.}

> AnalyzeImplementationPossibilities CURRENTLINE

Analyzing Implementation Possibilities for CURRENTLINE...
    {Remark: This is inferred from the fact that CURRENTLINE(SCROLLUP(t,1),n) has O(n) complexity.}

Potential sources(s) of inadequate performance for CURRENTLINE:
Normal form SCROLLUP(INPUT(t,1),n).

* The performance criteria state that SCROLLUP is allowed more complexity than CURRENTLINE.

To satisfy the constant performance requirement, it is possible to

                - Transfer complexity of CURRENTLINE implementation to SCROLLUP
                - Encode the required results in an auxiliary type

> Attempting to transfer complexity into SCROLLUP

> Do you wish to suggest an alternate implementation at this stage?
(Please answer Yes/No)...No

    {Remark: Again, the performance criteria dictate the path to be pursued: SCROLLUP is allowed more time complexity than CURRENTLINE -- therefore SCROLLUP may be made "slower", within bounds. This illustrates how the performance specifications guide the search for a suitable synthesis; in this case, the application pattern is merely a partial order. NEWTEXT, INPUT, and SCROLLUP are the only remaining kernel functions that need be implemented. The preceding inference implies that the integer argument "n" of SCROLLUP must be separated from any of the other encodings. An auxiliary target type component Integer is therefore introduced for this purpose: the augmented target type now becomes <CircularList, Integer>. Further, an added optimization is now possible since there now exists only one kernel constructor viz., INPUT, that must be encoded as a CircularList. Thus, the tupling with the Integer component can be eliminated.

    We now summarize the remainder of the synthesis. It is necessary to

- deduce a normal form configuration required of the representation of SCROLLUP(INPUT(t,1),n)   such   that VALUECL(THETA(SCROLLUP(INPUT(t,1),n)))   yields   the   result CURRENTLINE(SCROLLUP(INPUT(t,1),n));

- confirm that the implementation generated satisfies the desired performance criteria.

In general, to maintain correctness while synthesizing implementations incrementally, it is necessary to ascertain that

- all extractors function correctly on the existing state (i.e., that observable behavior is preserved);
- the application of all constructors yield "correct" resulting configurations.

Let $THETA(t) = <c,i1>$. The modified implementations for NEWTEXT and INPUT are

```
THETA(NEWTEXT) = <NEWCL, ZERO>
THETA(INPUT(t,l)) = <INSERTCL(c,l), i1>
```

The implementation for SCROLLUP is now synthesized to be:

```
THETA(SCROLLUP(t,n)) = SCROLLUPTT(<c,n>)
        -- the second component of the representation is the
        -- argument of SCROLLUP.
SCROLLUPTT(<c,n>) = if n=0 then <c,ZERO>
                    else SCROLLUPTT(<RIGHT(c),PRED(n)>)
```

The inverse Homomorphism induced is:

```
TextEditor_Represented_By(<NEWCL,0>) = NEWTEXT;
TextEditor_Represented_By(<INSERTCL(c,l),n>) =
        if n=0 then INPUT(TextEditor_Represented_By(<c,0>),l)
        else SCROLLUP(INPUT(TextEditor_Represented_By(<c,ZERO>),l),n);
```

If $THETA(t) = <c,i1>$, then the conditions that are asserted are:

```
i1 = ZERO.
if t = NEWTEXT then c=NEWCL.
```

The second component is actually redundant since i1 is always ZERO except during immediate reduction of $SCROLLUPTT(<c,i1>)$; it may therefore be eliminated.}

> Implementation for CURRENTLINE

```
THETA(CURRENTLINE(t)) = VALUECL(c)
```

Performance Requirements for SCROLLUP, and CURRENTLINE are now satisfied, but not for LINENUMBER.

> *** For constant performance of LINENUMBER, it is advisable to record the needed result dynamically.

{Remark: The alternative chosen is to introduce an auxiliary data type which encodes the desired result. Intuitively, the result of LINENUMBER is "carried along" as dictated by the semantics of LINENUMBER.

{Remark: This illustrates the effect of performance requirement on synthesis route. Also, the order in which non-kernel functions are synthesized

is on a "maximum performance first" basis; among functions that have
comparable performance requirements, an arbitrary choice is made.}

Thus, the TT is extended to <CircularList, Integer, Integer> where the
first Integer represents the argument to SCROLLUP, and the second represents
the value of LINENUMBER. the implementation is extended to:

```
THETA(NEWTEXT) = <NEWCL,ZERO,ZERO>;
THETA(INPUT(t,l)) = <INSERTCL(c,l),i,SUCC(i)>;
       -- because LINENUMBER(INPUT(t,l)) = LINENUMBER(t)+1;
THETA(SCROLLUP(t,n)) =
<already defined tuple for SCROLLUP,LINENUMBER(SCROLLUP(t,n)>
       -- because LINENUMBER(SCROLLUP(INPUT(t,l),n)) =
               if n=0 then LINENUMBER(t)
               else LINENUMBER(SCROLLUP(t,n-1))
```

It is possible to combine the processing of LINENUMBER(SCROLLUP(t,n))
with the processing of the first tuple.

The final implementation generated is given below. An extra component is
introduced in the target type for recording the number of lines, while the
integer component introduced for SCROLLUP can be eliminated as mentioned
above. TRIPLE is a 3-tuple, with projection functions TPROJ(t,i) yielding the
components of the 3-tuple for i=1,2,3 respectively.

Intuitively, the first component of the representation is the
CircularList (used to encode the Line parameter), the second component is an
Integer (used to encode the value of LINENUMBER), the third component is an
Integer (used to encode the value of NUMBER_OF_LINES). For ease in reading, we
write THETA(t) = <c,i1,i2>.

Implementation of Type TextEditor
Using RepresentationType CircularList X Integer X Integer;

```
 THETA(NEWTEXT) =  TRIPLE(NEWCL,ZERO,ZERO);

 THETA(INPUT(t,l)) =
           TRIPLE(INSERTCL(c,l),
                  SUCC(i1),
                  SUCC(i2));

 THETA(SCROLLUP(t,n)) = SCROLLUPTT(THETA(t),n);

 SCROLLUPTT(TRIPLE(c,i1,i2),n) =
        CASES   (n=0) -> TRIPLE(c,i1,i2);
                (n <> 0) & (i1=0) -> TRIPLE(c,i1,i2);
                (n <> 0) & (i1 <> 0) -> SCROLLUPTT(TRIPLE(RIGHT(c),
                                                   PRED(i1),
                                                   i2), PRED(n))
        END;

THETA(DELETELINE(t)) = TRIPLE(DELETECL(c),PRED(i1),PRED(i2));

THETA(SCROLLDOWN(t,n)) = SCROLLDOWNTT(THETA(t),n);
```

```
SCROLLDOWNTT(TRIPLE(c,i1,i2),n) =
            CASES
                (n = 0) -> TRIPLE(c,i1,i2);
                (n <> 0) & (i1 = i2) -> TRIPLE(c,i1,i2);
                (n <> 0) & (i1 <> i2) ->
                        SCROLLDOWNTT(TRIPLE(LEFT(c),
                                            SUCC(i1),
                                            i2), PRED(n))


            END;

THETA(TOP(t)) = THETA(SCROLLUP(t,LINENUMBER(t)));

THETA(CURRENTLINE(t)) = VALUECL(c);

THETA(LINENUMBER(t)) = i1;

THETA(NUMBER_OF_LINES(t)) = i2;
```

{The types Integer and Boolean are "known types", and therefore the implementation map acts as the identity on these.}

```
THETA(ZERO) = ZERO;

THETA(UNDEFINED) = UNDEFINED;
THETA(TRUE) = TRUE;
THETA(FALSE) = FALSE;

PRED(ZERO) = ZERO;
PRED(SUCC(I)) = I;
ISZERO(ZERO) = TRUE;
ISZERO(SUCC(I)) = FALSE;

THETA(SUCC(X)) = SUCC(THETA(X));
THETA(PRED(X)) = PRED(THETA(X));

End Implementation;
```

A "summary" of the history of development of the implementation is also produced, but is omitted here. The level of detail contained in this summary may be controlled by the user.

7. A Brief Comparison

The current research is related to former work in automatic programming, program transformation systems, software engineering and programming methodology (e.g. [1, 2, 5, 6, 7, 9, 12, 10, 13, 20, 24] etc.); it also is relevant to recent advances in design methodologies for VLSI systems [32, 31]. The underlying concepts are also applicable in the design of data base information systems (cf. discussions in [4]).

Although there have been several attempts at program synthesis under the general umbra of "automatic programming," (see [3], [8] for reviews) only a few of these are general in their scope. In summary, most earlier approaches to program synthesis were either based on a general theorem prover, or on a principle of gradual refinement of the initial specifications based on some knowledge base of programming rules. Thus, it was the case that either a theorem prover was burdened with the brunt of this problem, or *ad hoc* heuristics were used to fill this lacuna.

Unfortunately however, at the current stage of development, approaches relying primarily on theorem proving are not of great pragmatic relevance (and the prognosis is not very optimistic.) Further, the kind of "reasoning" that was largely involved in theorem proving systems was more at the level of the machine, rather than at the level of the human; thus it was difficult to incorporate interaction into a system based on theorem proving strategies. On the other hand, the "level of reasoning" portended by the current paradigm is more akin to human reasoning, and therefore makes interaction with the system more viable.

It must be noted that the approach adopted differs from the common "generate and test" paradigm in a very crucial sense. Heuristics are not used to prune the search space to be 'tested'; rather, the algorithms yield ways to "expand" the synthesis tree with all leaves leading to acceptable results. An important distinction from most transformation based systems is that the refinement is guided by the semantics of the functions defined on the type of interest, rather than by a fixed set of rules e.g. as in [2]. An analogy may be drawn to the difference between the computation of an integral using a table of integrals and the computation of the same integral using the basic principles of integration. While both methods are of value in practice, what we are seeking here is best viewed as the basic "principles of program synthesis" which may in turn be *used* to build "tables of transformations" applicable in different contexts. We believe that providing a theoretical framework for program synthesis, which directly incorporates principles that characterize "good" program development, will help provide a formal characterization of some of the pivotal steps in the synthesis process. In turn, this will help pin-point those stages of the synthesis process where there is leeway for making alternative choices based upon the functional and/or performance requirements of the specification, as well as the dependence of these choices on (i) the patterns of function invocation on the type of interest, and (ii) the semantics and cost measures on the target type (/architecture/abstract machine).

Further, a clear separation of the constraints imposed by

- the structure inherent in the problem specification (i.e. the syntax and semantics of the functions);
- the performance requirements;
- the constraints imposed by the context of use (i.e. the function application patterns);
- the semantics of the target type; and
- the cost measures on the target type;

serves to naturally partition the synthesis task. It becomes possible now to build relatively independent modules which attempt to aid in each of these tasks. This is particularly important, since the components of the cost measures that may be relevant vary widely depending upon the level of granularity of functions (e.g. Is the exact number of bits used critical?), the architecture and the underlying technology (for instance, time and space are important metrics in von Neumann architectures; interprocessor communication traffic in distributed systems, chip area and interconnection topologies in VLSI systems, ...), etc.

8. Conclusions

In order to obtain a significant improvement in the quality and reliability of software, it is imperative to have a sophisticated program development tool that is based on a coherent theory of program synthesis. In this paper, we have discussed the design of an experimental software development system that goes some way towards meeting this goal. The formal mathematical framework underlying our theory is algebraic. Most of the deduction performed by the system can be done by using *fast* decision procedures for restricted theories (see [27]). The programs synthesized are primarily applicative in nature; they are provably correct. The underlying synthesis strategy directly allows for the incorporation of different "environment dependent" criteria relating to the "efficiency" of implementations. Our initial empirical evidence has been encouraging but has also served to point to some of the areas that need further attention: these include non-deterministic specifications and the synthesis of concurrent programs.

References

1. Robert M. Balzer. Transformational Implementation: An Example. Tech. Rept. TR 78, USC/ISI, 1979.. To appear in IEEE Transactions on Software Engineering

2. D.R.Barstow. *Knowledge-based Program Construction.* Elsevier North-Holland, New York, 1979.

3. A.W.Biermann. Approaches to Automatic Programming. In M.Rubinoff, M.Yovits, Ed., *Advances in Computers, Vol. 16*, Academic Press, N.Y., 1976, pp. 1-64.

4. Ed. M.Brodie and S.Zilles. Proceedings of the Workshop on Data Abstraction, DataBases and Conceptual Modelling. SIGPLAN Notices, Vol 16, Number 1. ,January 1981.

5. R. Burstall and J. Darlington. "A Transformation System for Developing Recursive Programs." *JACM 24*, 1 (January 1977), 44-67.

6. Burstall, R.M. and Goguen, J.A. Putting Theories Together to Make Specifications. IJCAI5, IJCAI, August, 1977, pp. 1045-1058.

7. Thomas E. Cheatham,Glenn H. Holloway, and Judy A. Townley. Symbolic Evaluation and Analysis of Programs. Tech. Rept. TR-19-78, Harvard, NOV, 1978.

8. R.Elsclager and J.Phillips. Automatic Programming. Tech. Rept. Report Number STAN-CS-79-758, Stanford Artificial Intelligence Laboratory, August, 1979.

9. Gerhart, Susan L. Knowledge about programs: a model and a case study. Proceedings of an International Conference on Reliable Software, IEEE, June, 1975, pp. 88-95.

10. J.A.Goguen and J.J.Tardo. An Introduction to OBJ: A Language for Writing and Testing Formal Algebraic Program Specifications. Proceedings Of A Conference On Specifications Of Reliable Software, IEEE, April, 1979, pp. 170-189.

11. J.Goguen, J.Thatcher,E.Wagner. An Initial Algebra Approach to the Specification, Correctness, and Implementation of Abstract Data Types. In R.Yeh, Ed., *Current Trends in Programming Methodology, Vol IV*, Prentice-Hall, N.J, 1979, pp. 80-149.

12. Goldman, Neil and Wile, Dave. GIST(Internal Report). Unpublished, USC/ISI, September 1980

13. Cordell Green, Richard Gabriel, Elaine Kant, Beverly Kedziersk, Brian McCune, Jorge Phillips, Steve Tappel, Stephen Westfold . Results in Knowledge Based Program Synthesis. Proc. 6th Int. Joint Conf. on Artificial Intelligence, Vol. 1, IJCAI, August, 1979, pp. 342-344.

14. J.V.Guttag. *The Specification and Application to Programming of Abstract Data Types.* Ph.D. Th., Computational Sciences Group, University of Toronto, 1975.

15. J.V.Guttag and J.J.Horning. Formal Specifications as a Design Tool. Proceedings of the Seventh ACM Symp. on the Principles of Programming Languages, ACM SIGPLAN, Jan, 1980.

16. J.Guttag, E.Horowitz, D.Musser. "Abstract Data Types and Software Validation." *CACM 21* (1978), 1048-64.

17. A.C.Hearn. REDUCE Users Manual. University of Utah, 1973.

18. C.A.R.Hoare. "Proof of Correctness of Data Representations." *Acta Informatica 1* (1972), 271-281.

19. Warren Teitelman. *Interlisp Reference Manual.* Xerox-PARC, 3333 Coyote Hill Road,Palo Alto,Calif. 94304, 1975.

20. Kant, E. *Efficiency Considerations in Program Synthesis: A Knowledge-Based Approach.* Ph.D. Th., Stanford University, Palo Alto, California, September 1979.

21. B.Liskov, S.Zilles. "Specification Techniques for Data Abstractions." *IEEE Trans. on Soft. Engg. SE-1* (1975), 7-19.

22. D.C.Luckham et al. Stanford Pascal Verifier User Manual, Edition 1. Stanford University, April, 1979.

23. Majster, M. "Limits of the Algebraic Specification of Abstract Data Types." *SIGPLAN Notices 12*, 10 (October 1977), 37-42.

24. Manna, Z. and R. Waldinger. "A Deductive Approach to Program Synthesis." *ACM Transactions on Programming Languages and Systems 2*, 1 (January 1980), 90-121.

25. J.McCarthy. Comments on 'The State of Technology in Artifical Intelligence'. In P.Wegner, Ed., *Research Directions in Software Technology*, M.I.T.Press, Cambridge, Mass., 1979, pp. 814-815.

26. David R. Musser. A Data Type Verification System Based on Rewrite Rules. USC/Information Sciences Institute, October, 1977.

27. G.Nelson and D.C.Oppen. "Simplification by Cooperating Decision Procedures." *ACM Trans. on Programming Lang. and Systems 1*, 2 (Nov. 1979), 245-257.

28. Stoutemyer, David R. "Automatic Asymptotic and Big-O Calculations via Computer Algebra." *SIAM Journal of Computing 8*, 3 (August 1979), 287-299.

29. Subrahmanyam, P.A. "On a Finite Axiomatization of the Data Type L." *SIGPLAN Notices 13*, 4 (April 1978), 80-84.

30. Subrahmanyam, P.A. A Basis for a Theory of Program Synthesis. Proceedings of the First Annual National Conference On Artificial Intelligence, AAAI, August, 1980, pp. 74-76.

31. Subrahmanyam, P. A. and Organick, E. I. Perspectives on Transforming Ada Programs into Silicon. Unpublished

32. Subrahmanyam, P.A. Abstractions to Silicon: A New Design Paradiogm for Special Purpose VLSI Systems. Internal Memo, February 1981.

33. Putnam, K. and Subrahmanyam, P.A. Computation of the Union, Intersection, and Difference of n-dimensional Objects. Submitted for publication, November 1980.

34. P.A.Subrahmanyam. *Towards a Theory of Program Synthesis: Automating Implementations of Abstract Data Types.* Ph.D. Th., Department of Computer Science, State University of New York at Stony Brook, Aug. 1979.

35. P.A.Subrahmanyam. On Proving the Correctness of Data Type Implementations. Dept. of Computer Science, University of Utah, September, 1979.

36. P.A.Subrahmanyam. Nondeterminism in Abstract Data Types. Dept. of Computer Science, University of Utah, December, 1979. Also in, Proceedings, International Colloquium on Automata, Languages and Programming, 1981, Haifa, Israel

37. P.A.Subrahmanyam. A Formal Basis for Program Synthesis. Dept. of Computer Science, University of Utah, February, 1980.

38. J.Thatcher,E.Wagner,J.Wright. Data Type Specifications: Parameterization and the Power of Specification Techniques. Proceedings, Tenth SIGACT Symp. , ACM,SIGACT, April 1978, 1978, pp. 119-132.

39. Wile, D. Type Transformations. Submitted for Publication

40. Wile, Dave. POPART: A Producer of Parsers and Related Tools, System Builder's Manual. Unpublished, USC/ISI, June 1980.

Automated Tools for Information Systems Design
H.-J. Schneider and A.I. Wasserman (eds.)
North-Holland Publishing Company
© IFIP, 1982

CEMS - A CONTINUOUS USER FEEDBACK MONITORING SYSTEM FOR INTERACTIVE APPLICATIONS SOFTWARE DESIGN AND DEVELOPMENT

Lloyd R.E. Loisel   Robert L. Probert

Computation Centre   Software Reliability Research Group
National Research Council   Department of Computer Science
of Canada   University of Ottawa
Ottawa, Canada   Ottawa, Canada

CEMS is a continuous evaluation and monitoring system
which supports the responsible evolution of highly
interactive applications software.   CEMS provides
effective data collection, display, and communication
services among end-user, system, and system
designer/maintainer.   In particular, CEMS can gather
and report both voluntary and involuntary user
feedback about the suitability of a prototype.   This
feedback is used to facilitate both user acceptance
and designer responsiveness.   Experiences using CEMS
are reported.

INTRODUCTION

A common paradigm for software development is given in Figure 1.
Although oversimplified, this sequence of life cycle phases contains
the major components of an idealized software development process
(Myers (1979)).   However, such a decomposition of all development
processes can often be inappropriate.   An alternate representation
of the software development process which we shall denote
evolutionary software development (Gilb (1981))   is shown in Figure
2.

Figure 2 depicts a realistic development process in which user
requirements evolve based on feedback obtained from "trying out" the
system (actually a prototype of the system).   After a number of
repetitions of a system modification cycle consisting of user-
evaluation, requirements modification, and design modification, the
detailed design or prototype of the system can be frozen, and a
production (release) version of the system can be developed.   We
propose that this model of the software process is more realistic
because it more accurately reflects the high proportion of
maintenance or re-design activities in the software life-cycle.   In
fact, maintenance as depicted in Figure 1 can often involve system
re-design as user requirements evolve or misunderstandings about
user requirements are recognized and corrected.   This corresponds in
Figure 2 to a potentially unbounded number of repetitions of the
system modification cycle, i.e., the detailed design is never
frozen.

It is widely accepted that maintenance activities comprise
approximately fifty percent of the typical software development
process.   In addition it is well known that the earlier in the life
cycle errors are diagnosed and corrected, the lower the cost of
correction (Boehm (1975)).   Thus, life-cycle validation is vital to

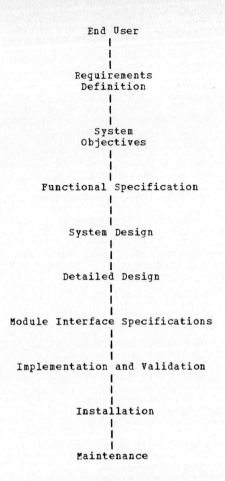

Figure 1 : The Software Life Cycle
(Traditional Model)

the cost-effective production of high quality software (Osterweil
(1981)). However, the ultimate authority on an error in
specifications is the user, and that person often cannot precisely
define system requirements without some experience on a prototype or
subsystem. Moreover, over the life of the applications system, user
requirements are likely to change, and system functions must be
modified to incorporate such changes. This is particularly true in
highly interactive systems, where some modules become a working set
or basis for constructing interactive applications programs (Hunt
and Prentice (1981), Wasserman (1981), Osterweil (1981)). Thus, the
user should participate fully in the production process especially
to require and evaluate design modifications. Rapid prototyping

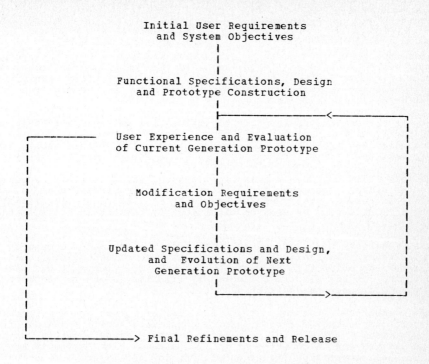

Figure 2 : Evolutionary Software Development Model

encourages this user participation; however some effective support mechanisms must be provided to collect and communicate user feedback. This is a main objective of CEMS.

The first part of the paper will present an overview of CEMS capabilities, a brief description of the major interfaces, and a summary of related work in the area. In the remainder of the paper, we give functional specifications, design considerations and a sketch of CESMS design. Then we illustrate the use of CEMS in developing and maintaining GRAFIX, a graphics application package. Finally, experiences using CEMS (to evolve GRAFIX) are summarized, and conclusions regarding the usefulness of CEMS-like systems are given.

Note that the term "user" will be used henceforth to represent a wide class of individuals or organizations. Thus, "user", may represent an applications programmer, or a user's representative rather than an individual end-user. Similarly, the term "designer" may refer to support and maintenance personnel as well as system designer.

OVERVIEW OF CEMS CAPABILITIES

CEMS is a continuous software evaluation and user monitoring system. Both evaluation and monitoring capabilities are provided through the use of communication mechanisms. These mechanisms support a user/designer interface by providing both a user/system and system/designer interface.

First, the mechanisms supports the collection of "feedback" that may be analysed to provide patterns of user actions and reactions. Secondly, the mechanisms provide for the display of this analysis to the designer.

As well CEMS provides a means for communicating designer responses to the users. Moreover the history of user requirements and of the dialogue between the user and designer is recorded automatically. These records can be used to significantly assist in configuration control.

The feedback to produce an improved requirements document is collected in two fashions. The data may be collected involuntarily through the collection of errors committed or by examing the user's profile. It may also be collected by voluntary means in the form of requests or comments submitted at will by the user.

The feedback session reports assist the user learning process.depending on Errors of low complexity merit a "likely fix" suggestion, while high complexity errors demand both directing information and a committment to response. High severity errors must be accompanied by reassurances to the user and priority requests to the designer/maintainer.

Finally user feedback and responsiveness of maintenance personnel can be critical to the success of software developed strictly according to the paradigm of Figure 1. Thus, CEMS can also be used effectively as a maintenance support tool after system installation.

USER/SYSTEM/DESIGNER INTERFACE

CEMS may be viewed as providing support for the critical user/designer interface activities during both the design and maintenance phases. The table in Figure 3 lists some of these activities. Note that several kinds of user/system interaction can occur. CEMS is designed to document and respond to such interactions. These interactions are brought about by

• Inappropriate User Action - The user is still learning how to use the system.

• Careless User Errors - The entering of simple, typographical errors.

• Serious User or System Errors - This includes users causing physical (usually file) damage and unplanned system software changes.

```
ACTIVITY             MODE          COMMUNICATION MEDIA

Processing User    Automatic       CEMS Error History,
Actions & Major                    Log-on Reports,
or Minor System                    Log-off Reports
   Errors

Gripe Processing   User-Initiated  Message to Designer,
                                   Acknowledgement
                                      to User

    User           Designer-       Log-on Report
 Counselling,      Initiated          to User
   System
 Maintenance


           Figure 3 : User/Designer Interface
              Activities Supported by CEMS
```

- User Requests or Comments (henceforth denoted "gripes").

In many instances of "straightforward" (first and second type) actions, CEMS can respond immediately with useful correction information. In instances of more complex (third or fourth type) actions, CEMS can respond immediately with "directing" prompts, and reassuring responses to the user, then pass error, gripe, and/or enviroment information to the designer for processing. It appears that the timeliness, and focussing capabilities of CEMS will enhance user/designer communication.

Interface considerations play an crucial part in the design of any interactive system. A system may be as internally complex as required be but should always appear simple and logical on the outside. We distinguish 4 basic types of interface.

- Communications Interface - Communication between components of the software development system. Information passed should be precise and brief.
- User Interface - Should be in plain English, or a subset there of. It should only have access to the higher levels (that is, no priviliged commands). Commands should be brief, preferably menu supplied.
- Designer Interface - Should have access to all levels. Should be precise and direct, an English shorthand.
- Management Interface - Like the user interface it should also be outwardly simple. Its vocabulary should be a cross between that of the users and that of the designers. It should be accessible to all but the the lower levels.

To summarize, the user's interface to the system involves the reply report, the session report, automatic error collection, and demand-

initiated comments.   The designer interface to the system before
instrumentation involves the insertion of reply calls,   session
calls,   probes and the design of classification schemes.   Post
instrumentation   services   involve   report generation and reply
procedures.

RELATED WORK

A number of investigators have pointed out difficulties in managing
software development (Mills (1980)),   Hayes et al (1981),Schwartz
(1975)).   Several other investigators have defined requirements or
proposed designs for specific systems for supporting software
development, with particular emphasis on interactive applications
enviroments and life-cycle tools (Negus et al (1981), Wasserman
(1981),   Osterweil (1981),   Gutz et al (1981), Bratman (1975),
Osterweil et al (1979), Schofield et al (1980)).

Effective interaction during the software life cycle is emphasized
in more than one paper.   Mills (1980) redifines software as the
logical doctrine for the harmonious cooperation in a system of
people and machines.   There are few systems produced to date to
monitor data relating to the degree of harmony in order to "fine
tune" the software and improve relations.   A partial reason for
existing   disharmony   arises   from   the   reliance   on   incorrect
information supplied during any life cycle phase, particularly
during requirements definition, to guide the software production
process. Similarly Hayes et al (1981) point out the difficulties of
expecting a system to understand a user's request, and that this
difficulty is compounded by the system's inability to pinpoint the
cause of the lack of understanding.

We take the above issues one step further and consider the problem
of communicating such difficulties to a designer.   A practical
solution to these problems is provided by CEMS messaging and
reporting capabilities.   Several of the above papers are concerned
with deficiencies in existing approaches such as a lack of robust,
meaningful communication among user, system, and designer (Negus et
al (1981)).   This will be seen to be taken into account in the
design of CEMS. Other considerations in the design of CEMS included
widespread use of logs as in Negus et al (1981), personalization
(Negus et al (1981)),   continuity of support (Osterweil (1981)),
improved visibility (Osterweil (1981),   Schwartz (1975),   Bratman
(1975)), cost-effectiveness (Osterweil (1981)), compatability (Gutz
et al (1981)),   the provision of support for configuration control
(Bratman (1975)), and ease of evaluation of system by users (Gutz et
al (1981)).   In fact, CEMS meets many of the interface requirements
of MM/1 (Schofield (1980)).

Finally, Stavely (1978) argues that feedback presented early in the
design process is invaluable to the quality of the resulting
software product.   However, he discusses tools only for aiding the
designer in evaluating his own design. Important as such tools are,
they do not support more important functions associated with user
interfaces,   such as modifications of requirements,   and user
evaluation of the current design.   What is refreshing about CEMS is
that it provides such desirable and useful functions via an
extremely straightforward design.

SUMMARY OF REQUIREMENTS

During either evolutionary system development, or the maintenance phase of software development (in the traditional paradigm), information on system development status may be generated or required by any or all of the project manager, the designer, or the user. CEMS will provide regular access to this information via its mechanisms. One method is through the use of automated functions to reduce the amount of human intervention needed to produce

- Management Reports - Several different forms of reports are produced at various frequencies, depending on individual installation practices. There are many different forms of reports, the most necessary being team reports (software deficiencies), management reports (cost expenditures), and system reports (system status and behaviour).
- Summary Reports - Though perhaps difficult to produce, summaries should include basic software statistics (perhaps gathered through an error frequency or type count), and evaluations (gathered through a user gripe severity count). An important addition to summaries would be the recommendations and conclusions of management and teams for completed stages of project development.
- Analyses - This includes analyses of reports, summaries, and the actual code to see if the specifications have been fulfilled, analyses of user behaviour to check progress rate of both user and software, and cross checks to evaluate rate of improvement. This involves, for example, classification schemes for involuntary feedback data.
- Session Reports - Produced at the end of a run, they aid in the user learning cycle. An important factor in the learning process is re-enforcement, by either repetition or by review. Produced at the beginning of the session, a session dump is useful in passing helpful hints to the user, as well as replies to questions asked at an earlier time.

The fact that these functions are automatically performed ensures information flow between parties such as user and designer, whether or not action is required for a particular stimulus or problem is up to the parties concerned. To request a response, either party can initiate a demand for an appropriate response. These demands are serviced by the CEMS functions described below.

A second mechanism to provide information is through the use of demand-initiated functions. The demand action does not guarantee a reply, but an acknowledgement or request for clarification will be displayed. The following functions should be available to any party on demand.

- Message Passing - This includes the passing of mail (user to user), gripes (user to designer), and replies.
- Configuration Control - This may be accomplished through the use of system logs, and/or production logs.
- Collection of specific data related to a project - Where appropriate, information about any type of a software or user behaviour, should be made available.

- Extended Information Enquiry Capabilities - This provides
  another communication channel from the designer to the user.

Another mechanism is the use of logical aids.   The permanent system
should possess at least some set of logical aids.   This is to
suppliment the previously mentioned interfaces of each of the
concerned parties and to provide more sophisticated services such as
the following.

- Cross Checks - History searching.
- Counselling - This includes assistance in preliminary
  planning, planning, team selection, coding, testing, utility
  selection, debugging, and post-production monitoring.
- Case Behaviour Analysis - To establish equivalence classes
  of errors, user profiles, etc..

An initial assumption was that the only way to judge if users were
having difficulty with the commands was to monitor all the errors
they committed.   In order to do this several objectives were set
forth.

(1) To keep a log of all errors. This includes command errors
    produced by the user and errors produced by improper
    coding.   These errors would include everything from
    improper command sequencing and typing errors to improper
    data and improper arguments for the commands.

(2) Provide precise responses to these errors.   Though this
    may sound necessary, one must remember that a majority of
    the users may not have an error description manual at hand
    and many of the users may be novices (common in turnkey
    systems).   The error reply facilities should also possess
    the capability of elaborating the error messages.

(3) Produce session reports for re-inforcing the user's
    learning process.   A person will learn more if he sees a
    review of the mistakes that he has made over a period of
    time.   Also it provides the user with a permanent history
    of his errors or misunderstandings should he wish to
    consult personally with a knowledgable authority.

(4) Produce user feedback reports for the designer. The CEMS
    methodology will not function if the designer never
    studies data collected from the monitor devices.   The
    reports should be produced on a regular basis, but could
    also be done if desired on a demand basis.

(5) Allow the designer to respond with corrective suggestions
    through the software itself.   This completes the
    communication chain between user and designer.

Objectives (1),(2) and (3) are to be fully automatic. Objective (4)
should be automatic but production on demand is sufficient if done
responsibly.   Objective (5) relies on designer intervention, thus
making it a manual process though it has the capability of being
conditionally automatic.

In order not to interfere with the host software package, CEMS must
contain the following additional features.

(6) Logging of errors should be invisible to the user.

(7) Any commands must be compatible with the host software commands. In the case of GRAFIX (the example application), the commands should be of the same type and they should be entered in the same fashion as GRAFIX commands. This implies keyboard or screen menu input.

To summarize, the main goal of CEMS is to provide the designer with useful information on the software under development. A side goal was to train the user how to use the graphics package and to monitor his progress.

There were also the usual considerations of keeping the complexity down for both execution, interfaces, insertion and design. CEMS must have the capability of being able to be expanded as well as being included in the expansion of other systems such as a configuration management system. CEMS must also blend with the host system (invisibility) and take advantage of the host systems capabilities and the capabilities of existing tools (like editors).

Above all, people using CEMS should require little knowledge of both CEMS and the host system in order to use it.

OVERVIEW OF DESIGN CONFIGURATION

The CEMS/host configuration can take two forms. In the first, Figure 4, the monitoring system acts as a back end to the

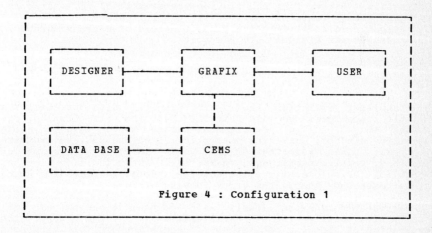

Figure 4 : Configuration 1

applications software package (e.g. GRAFIX). All user requests are transmitted through the host software. This may require modification of the software package but if the monitor is to remain with the package for its entire life cycle then the details of the architectural relationships between CEMS and the applications software may not be a major consideration. GRAFIX and CEMS are presently in this configuration. An alternate form is shown in Figure 5. The monitoring system becomes a front end to the software package. This requires less code modification in the application

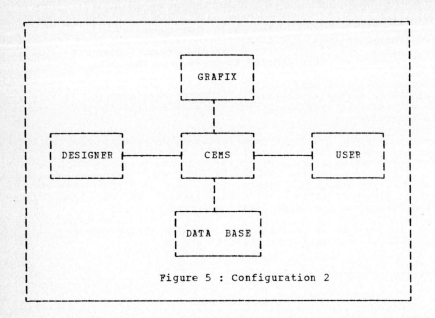

Figure 5 : Configuration 2

software itself. Plans are presently under way to produce a version in this form. Either form can provide the same level of monitoring. But regardless of the configuration the general construction of CEMS is identical. To facilitate the classification of tasks the support system ideally was divided into 3 sections.

- The Counsellor
- The Facilitator
- The Enforcer

The Councillor solicites the use of logical aids or utilizes heuristic techniques to aid primarily in the pre-planning and planning stages. The pre-planning stage would involve doing feasibility studies, gathering statistics, studying surveys and case histories. The planning stage would involve selection of algorithms, testing techniques, teams, etc. The councillor also has the duty of using classification schemes, data searches and doing history researches during the error logging process.

The Facilitator concerns itself with communications between all participating parties via the 4 interfaces. It can support the organization of testing activities, generation of test harnesses etc. by, for example providing standard guidelines and checklists.

The Enforcer would concern itself with cross checks, output reports, and periodic audits. It would provide reports, and any fully automated functions. It would also be in charge of audits and making sure that the data base remains consistent. The Enforcer makes sure that duties get done according to a designer or user standards and on schedule.

Figure 6 : A General Monologging Process

CEMS utilizes data logging as an information gathering tool. Since,
for the automated features, the bulk of the information is passed in
one direction with significantly less data returned, we refer to
this process as "monologging". Figure 6 shows the general structure

of the monologging process used in CEMS. Portions of both the
Councillor and Facilitator can be found in the monologging process.

DETAILED DESIGN CONSIDERATIONS

To achieve the above goals the following design was derived. We
list the design requirements for each of the components below.

(1) An error condition control block will be added to each
    user-defined procedure.   This is the Classifier of Figure
    6.   Errors occuring in a procedure would be detected and
    classified by this block.   It enables errors within each
    procedure to be handled in an individualized manner. An
    error of type A in procedure Z may warrant a different
    handling than an error of type A in procedure Y.

    The error condition block may be quickly inserted into the
    code at code design time, coding time, or during post-
    production maintenance. Since the modules are stored in a
    standardized, pre-coded form they may be manually inserted
    into the code in full form by using a standard text editor
    or by using pre-processor statements (like %INCLUDE).
    Insertion usually occurs after normal procedure
    declarations.   One probe is usually inserted but is is
    possible to insert more.

    Standardized probes may be inserted into the code
    automatically,   customed designed probes will require
    manual insertion.   Also, to perform certain functions,
    such as termination of procedure after error detection,
    the code of the host may have to be modified slightly (for
    example the addition of labels for branching).

(2) A response and decision mechanism will be needed. This is
    the Searcher and Researcher of Figure 6. This will likely
    involve an error display procedure accessible by any
    module in the host system. This is basically for the
    benifit of the user.

    Using this display procedure, system error messages may be
    replaced by messages which are tailored to the user's
    needs.   It may also contain standardized, well-proven
    error messages that are known and understood by the user.
    This type of display procedure may be inserted
    automatically. More complex Searchers and Researchers may
    contain automated councilling capabilities, alternate
    solution reporting mechanisms, history researching aids or
    the ability to converse in meaningful dialogue with the
    user.

Points (3), (4), and (5) pertain to the Recorder in Figure 6.

(3) A cataloging procedure will be needed. This cataloging
    procedure should be versitile enough to be used for
    purposes other than error cataloging (like file
    cataloging). The cataloging procedure will be activated
    either an automatic or a demand-driven basis.

    The procedure can provide printing and update facilities,

as well as insertion and deletion facilities. Being driven automatically means that the procedure may produce different reports at varied frequencies. The cataloging procedure will support both the designer and the search/research procedures.

(4) A data base will be created to store the CEMS-related information. The data base will be on some fast direct access device, because most data base I/O will be accomplished in the background, transparent to the user, with minimal execution time overhead.

The data base holds not only error information but also information on files or data. It is protected from accidental misuse, and is readily accessible by the designer. The CEMS data base resembles the GRAFIX data base in order to save time. The data base of CEMS need not resemble the data base of the host.

(5) The CEMS system will maintain a system log of "unexpected errors", a system log of "expected errors", and a "user gripe" log on a permanent secondary storage device.

In this way CEMS is capable of compiling data on three major classes of errors. These are the class of "expected errors", those that can be forseen because of some incorrect action taken on the part of the user, the class of "unexpected errors", those errors that occur and can not be forseen as been caused by some action taken on the part of the user (both the above are collected automatically), and "gripes", the set of actions taken on the part of the user to express his feelings about a certain circumstance (they may or may not be forseen by the designer).

The reports are duplicated to safeguard against accidental loss of reports. This is accomplished by using the cataloging procedures described above.

(6) A report generator for feedback reports is necessary. It will have the capability of generating reports automatically and semi-automatically. Automatic reports are reports where the data is displayed automatically on a regular basis. Semi-automatic reports are viewed at the discretion of the designer.

The report generator is responsible for producing session diagnostic reports (to the user) at sign-off, in a simplified format. The report generator could be expanded to provide stastical analysis and even conclusions based on the stastical analysis and pre-defined limits. Limited report generation will be allowed at the end of each session for the benifit of the user. The session report generator will be called near the end of the session. It will be inserted in the same fashion as the probe.

(7) A reply mechanism will be made available to the designer. It should take advantage of the facilities provided by the cataloging procedures to produce a gripe reconciliation report (to the user) at sign-on.

Replies are entered manually by the designer. It would be
desirable to have an expert automatic reply system, but
the present semi-automated system appears to work well.
The replies would be viewed at the beginning of a session
so that the user can use the information during that
session. It should be inserted in the same fashion as the
probe.

The Figures in Appendix A illustrate possible implementations of
some of the above specifications. Figure A.1 shows a general
purpose probe. It was designed to pick up four different types of
involuntary errors. These were conversion, record, key, and
undefined-file errors. In this example, messages are printed from
within the probe, and then an additional error display procedure is
called. Normally one would simply call a universal error message
display procedure to print the message.

Figure A.2 shows a typical message display procedure. The one
displayed here serves two purposes. It prints out error messages
and it prints out debugging information. The error cataloguer is
called after the message is printed to register the error.

Figures A.3 and A.4 show simple probes inserted into the code.
Notice that the probes remain separate from the code in general.
This code separation simplifies code analysis.

Appendix B also shows some of the error data collected. Figures
B.1, B.2, and B.3 are all CEMS data.

GENERAL APPLICABILITY OF CEMS

The CEMS concept could be applied to most interactive software
packages, but it is most effective in software that demands
intensive user participation, such as highly interactive software.

Turn-key interactive systems are ideal candidates for a CEMS-like
software monitor. These systems are usually heavily used. The
users of these systems vary from the inexperienced novice, to the
casual user, to the well-seasoned expert. CEMS would have the
capacity to gather feedback from all these users on a continuous
basis allowing changes to be made that would improve software
quality for all users, not just users of one particular level of
expertise.

Remote work stations controlled by a centrally located processor are
also candidates. Here distance is a prime factor in user/designer
communication difficulties. CEMS removes the distance factor by
supplying data to the central processor and hence the designer.

Most interactive graphics systems could make fruitful use of a CEMS-
like system. This includes CAD/CAM systems. These many be turn-key
or evolutionary packages, local or remote. The more advanced
packages are screen-menu driven. CEMS would fit quite nicely into
this enviroment. Computer aided instruction systems could also
benifit from a CEMS-like system. It is ideally suited for the
monitoring of student progress. It could also be used in software
development studies as a tool for studying the effect of programming
techniques in the production of software.

In general, any software package with a large command vocabulary is also a candidate. A CEMS-like system is an extremely appropriate mechanism for gathering user feedback on what commands they want implementod.

CEMS was written in PL/1, so as a result it may be integrated quickly into any host system that is written in PL/1. The initial reason for using PL/1 was two-fold. First, GRAFIX was written in PL/1 so the integration could proceed with minimal difficulty. Secondly the PL/1 language had the necessary tools to provide the error monitoring capability. So CEMS as it stands now may be used in almost any system written in PL/1 or in systems contain some PL/1 code. However the CEMS design is language independent and therefore widely applicable.

In summary, CEMS appears to be ideally suited to the evolutionary paradigm of software development (Gilb (1981)).

AN EXAMPLE APPLICATION OF CEMS TO GRAFIX

CEMS was developed primarily to gather user feedback on a graphics package called GRAFIX. GRAFIX started out as a modest graphics package consisting of only one to two thousand lines of code and being driven by only five to ten simple commands which were all entered from the keyboard (commands, or action requests, were submitted as 2 or 3 letter symbolic codes, like whose of a text editor). But GRAFIX evolved to meet a natural demand to approximately four thousand lines of code with twenty to twenty five driving commands. It became much more interactive, for example, it was adapted to handle menu-based input.

As GRAFIX began to mature it was used by more people. It became obvious that an automated software logging device was needed. Thus CEMS was added to GRAFIX as a back-end. At first, interaction of GRAFIX and CEMS was kept to a minimum. Only automatic logging of involuntary feedback was monitored. This was a logical first step, as the addition of this feature was invisible to the user and resulted in negligible execution time increase. An error recording sequence was as follows:

    user -> error -> logging facility -> error file

The logging facilities were then updated. The sign-on reports were then added. This enabled the following communication sequence:

  designer file -> display procedure -> display -> user

The logging facilities were then updated again. The log off session reports were added, yielding the sequence:

  error file -> display procedure -> display -> user

EXAMPLE SESSION 1

The following is an example of an error producing session. Though the example is a simple one, it is representative of a frequently committed type of error.

GRAFIX

```
>>--------<<
>> GRAFIX << SUN 24 MAY 1981  12:22:36
>>--------<<

RESPONSES REGISTERED (IF ANY) ::
I.D.    TIME      RESPONSE
TAH     4084830   THE HP PLOTTER IS NOW FUNCTIONAL

>> MAXIMUM NUMBER OF LEVELS : 12 <<
OUTPUT(TEK-1,RAST-2,HP-3)/UNIT(NORM-0,FILE>0)/BAUDRATE(DEVICE) ::
:
3 0 1200

>> HP CHOSEN <<
MENU NAME ::
:
TYPE1
```

Here the user (TAH) signs on the system by entering "GRAFIX". The
software responds with a time stamp. Then any outstanding designer
reponses are printed. In this example there is a message to TAH
(printed to TAH only) that the HP plotter has been serviced and
deemed functional. So TAH proceeds, and specifies that he wants the
HP plotter, running normally (no file output), at a speed of 1200
BAUD. GRAFIX then prompts for a menu type (menu "TYPE1" is a
general purpose menu).

```
COMMAND ::
:
AF 1 ; IF ADD FUSELAGE

## COMMAND ERROR ##
--> AF 1 ; IF ADD FUSELAGE
    **

COMMAND ::
:
AC 1
```

TAH enters the commands AF 1 and IF ADD FUSELAGE. But he really
meant to enter AC 1. GRAFIX prints an error message and aborts the
following command. He corrects the mistake by typing in AC 1 (this
"ACtivates" level #1 viewing screen).

```
COMMAND ::
:
IF ADD FUSELAGE

COMMAND ::
:
DR
```

TAH then "ADDs" an "Input File" whose identifier is "FUSELAGE", (on
the next input prompt), and asks for a "DRaw".

```
COMMAND ::
:
Q

  >>--------------<<
  >> DIAGONISTICS <<
  >>--------------<<

  LINE SEGMENTS DRAWN ::      437

  ERRORS REGISTERED (IF ANY) ::
  I.D.    TIME      ERROR#    CONTEXT
  TAH     3072407    32    ->
  TAH     4122739     1    -> AF 1 ; IF ADD FUSELAGE

  >>---------<<
  >> GRAFIX << 12:45:05
  >>---------<<
```

The figure is then drawn on the HP plotter so he quits by typing
"Q". Upon quiting a session report is printed. The first error is
coded "32" which means he submitted a null response. This is an
error committed during a previous session. The second error (the
one just committed) is coded "1" and implies a command error ("AF"
instead of "AC", a typographical error). The context of the error
is also shown. He then sees another time stamp which means he has
left GRAFIX.

To display these errors to the designer is a simple matter. CEMS
has a report generator, which is tied to its data base, called UDACS
(a User Defined Auxiliary Cataloging System). To print the gripes
stored in the file GR.GRIPES.AUTO the following is entered:

```
UDACS
 NOTE : "OUT" AS INPUT GETS OUT
 COMMAND (ADD/UPD/DEL/PRT/OUT) & FILE NAME ?
:
PRT GR.GRIPES.AUTO
NNA     1131145     1    -> WI -10 10 -10 10 10 -1A 20
ABH     1131147     1    -> AF 1
ABH     1133846     1    -> AJ 1
ABH     2133847     1    -> AJ 1
TAH     3072407    32    ->
TAH     4122739     1    -> AF 1 ; IF ADD FUSELAGE
 COMMAND (ADD/UPD/DEL/PRT/OUT) & FILE NAME ?
:
OUT GR.GRIPES.AUTO
```

The following points should be noted from this example:

(1) All feedback data at this stage was accumulated as a result of
    an involuntary error condition being raised.

(2) The user can expect to see
    (i) Nothing during the involuntary feedback collection, except
    for a verification message (error message).
    (ii) A session report at sign-off.
    (iii) Perhaps a sign-on reply from the designer at next sign-on.

(3) The designer can expect to see the user's error on the next
    error report.

EXAMPLE SESSION 2

The following is an example of gripe submission.

```
GRAFIX

  >>--------<<
  >> GRAFIX << WED 19 APRIL 1981  11:03:12
  >>--------<<

  RESPONSES REGISTERED (IF ANY) ::
  I.D.    TIME       RESPONSE
  NNA     3122812    PLEASE CATALOG YOUR FILES BEFORE LOADING

  >> MAXIMUM NUMBER OF LEVELS : 12 <<
  OUTPUT(TEK-1,RAST-2,HP-3)/UNIT(NORM-0,FILE>0)/BAUDRATE(DEVICE) ::
  :
  1 0 1200

  >> TEK CHOSEN <<
  MENU NAME ::
  :
  TYPE1
```

The user (NNA) signs on the system by entering "GRAFIX".   The
software responds with a time stamp.   Then any outstanding designer
reponses are printed.   In this example there is a message to him
(only) that he should catalog all his files before loading them in
GRAFIX.   He has had this problem before, and so the message has been
printed out to remind him to do so.   NNA proceeds, and specifies
that he wants the TEK display screen, running normally (no file
output), at a speed of 1200 BAUD.   GRAFIX then prompts for a menu
type (menu "TYPE1" is a general purpose menu).

```
COMMAND ::
:
GR PLEASE SEND ME A "GRAFIX" MANUAL

> YOUR GRIPE HAS BEEN RECORDED <
FOR URGENT PROBLEMS OR IF YOU DO NOT RECIEVE A
REPLY WITHIN ONE DAY CALL 993-0240 - THANK YOU
```

NNA then enters his Gripe.   In this case, he is in need of a manual.

```
COMMAND ::
:
Q

  >>-------------<<
  >> DIAGONISTICS <<
  >>----7---------<<

  LINE SEGMENTS DRAWN ::        0
```

```
ERRORS REGISTERED (IF ANY) ::
I.D.    TIME      ERROR#    CONTEXT
NAA     4031231    34    -> IF ADD ZAP

  >>--------<<
  >> GRAFIX << 11:10:14
  >>--------<<
```

NNA then signs off ("Q" command). Upon quitting a session report is printed.　It shows that (in the past)　he has made an error.　The error is　coded "34" and　implies a　file command error (file "ZAP" does not exist).　The context of the error is also shown.　He then sees another time stamp which means he has left GRAFIX.

The procedure for　displaying the gripes is the same　as for viewing the errors.


```
UDACS
  NOTE : "OUT" AS INPUT GETS OUT
  COMMAND (ADD/UPD/DEL/PRT/OUT) & FILE NAME ?
  :
PRT GR.GRIPES.USER

  ABH     5131905 GRIPE    ->  PLEASE SEND ME A MANUAL.....
  NNA     9110803 GRIPE    ->  PLEASE SEND ME A "GRAFIX" MANUAL
  JKU     5132437 GRIPE    ->  PLEASE ADD "COPY MIRROR" COMMAND
  TIM     5133832 GRIPE    ->  IS TEK4112 TERMINAL INSTALLED????
  COMMAND (ADD/UPD/DEL/PRT/OUT) & FILE NAME ?
  :
OUT GR.GRIPES.USER
```


There were a few points that should be noted from this example:

(1) All feedback data at this stage was accumulated as a result of a voluntary error condition being raised.

(2) The user can expect to see
(i) Nothing during the voluntary feedback collection, except for an acknowledgement message (error message).
(ii) A sign-on reply at a following session.

(3) The designer　can expect　to see　the user's　gripe on　the next gripe report.

EXPERIENCES

During both a controlled and uncontrolled test of CEMS, results were most　favourable.　Most　of the　undesirable points were not　that serious and could be eliminated by minor modifications.　We present a review　of some favourable　points of　CEMS while in　a controlled enviroment, that is, while being used by knowledgable people.

- The　response　time　increase　for　command　prompt　was negligible.

As a designer, when any problems arose as a result of human or
software error, a time lag or break in servies was expected. The
time increase, though negligible, was welcomed in order to digest
error information.

- The sign-on report was useful as duty reminders for code
  additions, code deletions, and code modifications.

It seems that sometimes the only way to get certain things done is
to constantly remind people (and this includes the designer). The
report provided a useful way to pass design or other information for
next sign-on.

- The sign-off report was useful as session reminders. The
  number of typographical errors committed was remarkable. If
  knowledgable users cannot handle the command language, the
  inexperienced and naive users probably will not be able to.
  It was also surprising to see the number of errors that were
  repeated over and over again. Perhaps this is due to a
  "tourist communication mechanism". A tourist trying to
  speak to someone may think that if he repeats his words and
  speaks slowly, then the listener will understand. But this
  approach will not improve communication with a menu-driven
  system. Happily the number of unknown errors decreased
  rapidly and most errors could be diagnosed quickly.

The only message here is that reinforcement is a powerful tool. It
was relieving to find that many of the errors were caused by the
users lack of typing ability, not in the software design.

Under uncontrolled conditions, use by untrained and naive users, the
results were found to be much the same.

- The response time increase was not noticed by users.

- Most users were surprised to learn that CEMS was implemented
  and functioning as part of GRAFIX.

One can argue, at this point, whether or not the user should be made
aware of the automatic monitoring features of CEMS. It is quite
possible that users may object to the presence of CEMS as an
invasion of privacy. Others may welcome its presence and use it
fully.

- The errors most commonly committed were mispelling of
  commands, improper command arguments, and improper command
  sequencing.

These were indications that the command system of the host needed
minor improvements.

The gripes produced a large quantity of interesting information,
indicating that the users were not afraid of using the gripe system.

- The gripes usually matched the preceeding automatically
  collected errors. After a certain number of attempts and
  errors, the user became frustrated and sent a gripe.

This way the sending of the gripe was a pressure outlet for the
user. The user would leave knowing that the problem was at least

being investigated by a knowledgable party.

- The gripes fell into three classes. The first class was "User Confusion" (represented by repeated gripes), the second was "User Lack of Knowledge" (manifested by ignorance on how to sequence commands or by not knowing command capabilities), and the third was "Requests" (for manuals and other material).

Being able to isolate the classes of gripes helps in analysing the design faults that exist in the software. It also allows the designer to assign a priority scheme to the problems.

There were several undesirable points that arose during the construction and testing of CEMS.

- The error reports often lay neglected for a period of time.

This implies that the report producer process should be automated. This represents a straight-forward enhancement.

- The lack of logical aids hindered in the production of quick and effective replies.

This implies again, that automation would be helpful especially those aids which would allow the designer to avoid mundane data history searches.

- The reply messages were not produced as regularly as they should have been.

As the reply process demands designer intervention, total automation would be difficult. Here, we suggest the inclusion of an automated designer prompter to facilitate prompt replies.

The gripes had some of the same undesireable features that the automated error collection facilities had.

- The gripe reports as viewed by the designer of GRAFIX were not dumped frequently enough and were they were not analysed as thoroughly as they should have been and they were not replied to as quickly as they should have been.

The primary cause for this was outright laziness.

The same problem exists here as with the automatic error collection reports. Response at this point though is even more crucial than the other as the user expects to receive a response within a certain time.

- The gripes were limited to one line of text forcing the user to sometimes use more than one gripe call.

The one line gripe was ment to persuade the user to be more to the point in the explanation of the problem. In many cases the problem can not be described in one line, perhaps not in a paragraph, nor even a novel. For these cases personnal contact with the designer is desired.

The integration of CEMS into GRAFIX was found be be quite trivial. The calls to the reply procedures and to the session report

procedures was simple as both consisted of a single PL/1 call
statement. The insertion of the probes demaned a bit more work, but
it still remainded to be a simple task.   The probes were prestored
in data sets in memory and could be loaded in and inserted using a
standard text editor.   If the blocks were to be customed design (
which may involve the addition of print statements or statistical
calculations) . then the standard probe must be edited.   The custom
designing may also involve the scanning of the host code to
determine what sections of code may need scrutiny (probable areas of
high error).   Also, superfluous tests in the probe may not be
necessary and be removed.

In general, then, experiences have been extremely favorable, with
the possible exception of forcing a designer response to a gripe.
This potential problem has been addressed by a recent modification.
To force the designer to review the reported problems and gripes,
CEMS will not allow the designer to log off until all such mail has
been accessed.   If necessary, a priority scheme could be invoked to
aid the designer in identifying problems perceived as critical.

SUGGESTIONS AND CONCLUSIONS

Many extensions to CEMS are possible.   Though presently under
development, it is suggested that configuration 2 be tested.
Configuration 1 requires more modifications to the host system than
does the other.   Also configuration 1 forces the user (in a mild
sense) to provide data.   Configuration 2 allows the user and
designer to deal directly with CEMS.

It would also be of benifit to add CEMS to a software configuration
management system.   At this point studies could be undertaken to
determine if CEMS could be easily integerated and to see what the
true benifits would be as CEMS contributes to an existing system.

More of CEMS features should be made fully automatic. These include
an automated feature to insert the parameterized probes, the calls
to session report procedures and the reply procedures. The printing
of the reports to the designer should be made fully automatic along
with responses.

Statistical calculation capabilities should also be added and
heuristics should be used.   These features could be utilized to aid
in everything from customized reports for all parties or to
intelligent councilling services for the user (while he is using the
system), for the designer (while he is responding to gripes) or to
management (while they are performing audits or progress reports).

It is clear that CEMS has addressed some of the major points that
were described as being absent from present software development
tools.   CEMS has considerable breadth of scope.   It is reusable,
adapting either to a central data base or the data base of the host
software package. It is designed to be user friendly, and offer him
continuous support.

CEMS also has a wide area of applicability.   It would be
indispensible for the the customizing of off-the-shelf software.
This is evident by its ability to monitor individual user's needs.
Used in rapid prototyping or evolutionary development, it would aid

in customizing software. CEMS can simplify the user interface for software packages, hence ease user acceptance of produced software. In general, CEMS appears to be both a useful design aid and an effective post-delivery software support tool.

REFERENCES:

[1] H.D. Mills, The Management of Software Engineering Part1: Principles of Software Engineering, IBM Systems Journal, Vol. 19, No. 4 (1980) 415-420.

[2] Phil Hayes, Eugene Ball, and Raj Reddy, Breaking the Man-Machine Communication Barrier, Computer, March (1981) 19-30.

[3] B. Negus,M.J. Hunt, and J.A. Prentice, Dialog: A Scheme for the Quick and Effective Production of Interactive Applications Software, Software Practice And Experience, Vol. 11, (1981) 205-244.

[4] Anthony I. Wasserman, Automated Developement Environments, Computer, April (1981) 7-10.

[5] Leon Osterweil, Software Environment Research: Direction for the Next Five Years, Computer, April (1981) 35-43.

[6] Steve Gutz, Anthony I. Wasserman, and Michael J. Spier, Personal Developement Systems for the Professional Programmer, Computer, April (1981) 45-53.

[7] Jules I. Schwartz, Construction of Software: Problems and Practicalities, in: E. Horowitz (ed.), Practical Strategies for Developing Large Software Systems, (1975), 15-53.

[8] Barry W. Boehm, The High Cost of Software, in Practical Strategies for Developing Large Software Systems, Ed. by E. Horowitz, 1975, 3-14.

[9] Harvey Bratman, Automated Techniques for Project Management and Control, in Practical Strategies for Developing Large Software Systems, Ed. by E. Horowitz, 1975, 193-210.

[10] Leon J. Osterweil, John R. Brown, and Leon J. Stucki, ASSET: A Life Cycle Verification and Visibility System, The Journal of Systems and Software, 1, 1979, 77-86.

[11] D. Schofield, A.L. Hillman, and J.L. Rodgers, MM/1, A Man-Machine Interface, Software-Practice and Experience, Vol. 10, 1980, 751-763.

[12] Glenford J. Myers, The Art of Software Testing, Wiley-Interscience, 1979.

[13] Tom Gilb, Evolutionary Developement, Software Engineering Notes, ACM Informal Newsletter of the Special Interest Group on Software Engineering, Vol. 6, No. 2, April (1981) 17.

[14] Allan M. Stavely, Design Feedback and Its Use in Software Design Aid Systems, Software Engineering Notes, ACM Performance Evaluation Review, Vol. 3, No. 5, November 1978, pp.72-78.

APPENDIX A

Each of the following figures contains example applications (GRAFIX)
code which has been modified or inserted to interface with the CEMS
system.

```
/*******************************/
/*                             */
/* ERROR HANDLING BLOCK        */
/*                             */
/*******************************/
ON ERROR
   BEGIN;
   TYPE = 0;
   /*                     */
   /* SIGNALED CONVERSION ERROR */
   /*                     */
   IF ((ONCODE >= 600) & (ONCODE <= 629))
   THEN DO;
       PUT SKIP FILE (SYSPRINT) LIST
           (' >> CONVERSION ERROR :: ',ONCODE,' << ');
       TYPE = 1;
       END;
   /*                 */
   /* SIGNALED RECORD ERROR */
   /*                 */
   IF ((ONCODE >= 20) & (ONCODE <= 24))
   THEN DO;
       PUT SKIP FILE (SYSPRINT) LIST
           (' >> RECORD ERROR :: ',ONCODE,' << ');
       TYPE = 2;
       END;
   /*                     */
   /* SIGNALED UNDEFINEDFILE ERROR */
   /*                     */
   IF ((ONCODE >= 80) & (ONCODE <= 84))
   THEN DO;
       PUT SKIP FILE (SYSPRINT) LIST
           (' >> UNDEFINEDFILE ERROR :: ',ONCODE,' << ');
       TYPE = 3;
       END;
   /*             */
   /* SIGNALED KEY ERROR */
   /*             */
   IF ((ONCODE >= 50) & (ONCODE <= 57))
   THEN DO;
       PUT SKIP FILE (SYSPRINT) LIST
           (' >> KEY ERROR :: ',ONCODE,' << ');
       TYPE = 4;
       END;
   CALL DISPLAY (TYPE);
   END;
```

FIGURE A.1 : An Example Standard Error Block

```
/****************************************************************/
/*                                                            */
/* PROCEDURE DISPLAY                                          */
/* FUNCTION - DISPLAY ERROR MESSAGES AND DUMP MESSAGES        */
/* CALLED FROM - DATAIOT DRIVER FILES  DUMPIT TRNSFRM ADDE ALPHABE */
/*               NUMERIC DEL    POP    BININP ROTATE  PUSH BINOUT */
/*               BUFLUSH DUMPIO SELOUT                        */
/* CALLS PROCEDURE(S) - NONE                                  */
/*                                                            */
/****************************************************************/
DISPLAY:PROCEDURE (NUMBER);
        DECLARE NUMBER FIXED DECIMAL (2),
                EBUFFER CHARACTER (80) EXT,
                ERROPLT (0:32) CHAR (35) VARYING INITIAL
                /* 00 */  ('UNKNOWN ERROR',
                /* 01 */   'COMMAND ERROR',
                           'NO QUERY POSSIBLE',

                                  .
                                  .
                                  .
                                  .
                                  .

                           'ERROR - NO ACTIVE LEVEL',
                /* 30 */   'ERROR - NO INPUT FILE',
                           'REGION LIMIT REACHED',
                           'SUBREGION LIMIT REACHED'),
                DISPLT (16) CHAR (25) VARYING INITIAL
                /* 01 */  ('PRE-CLEAR',
                           'CLEAR SCREEN',

                                  .
                                  .
                                  .
                                  .

                           'CTRL-CHAR-GRAPHICS MODE',
                /* 15 */   'BUFFER DUMP BY BFLUSH',
                           'BUFFER DUMP BY BININP');
        /*                                    */
        /* IF NEGATIVE NUMBER THEN ERROR      */
        /*               ELSE MESSAGE         */
        IF (NUMBER <= 00)
        THEN DO;
            PUT SKIP FILE (SYSPRINT) EDIT
                    (' ## ',ERRORLT(-NUMBER),' ## ') (A);
            CALL CATALOG ('AUTO     ',CHAR(-NUMBER,7),EBUFFER);
            END;
        ELSE PUT SKIP FILE (SYSPRINT) EDIT
                    (' @@ ',DISPLT(NUMBER),' @@ ') (A);
        END DISPLAY;
```

FIGURE A.2 : An Application-Specific
Message Display Procedure

```
/**************************************************/
/*                                                */
/* PROCEDURE TRNSFRM                              */
/* FUNCTION - TO HANDLE TRANSFORMATION COMMANDS   */
/* CALLED FROM - DRIVER                           */
/* CALLS PROCEDURE(S) - DISPLAY SCALE TRANS       */
/*                      ROTATE INITIAL            */
/*                                                */
/**************************************************/
TRNSFRM: PROCEDURE (COMMAND) ;
        DECLARE (SCFACTORS(3) ,TRFACTORS(3)) FLOAT BINARY (10),
                                  .
                                  .
                                  .
                COMMAND CHAR (2) ;
         /*                            */
         /* ERROR - HANDLING BLOCK     */
         /* ARITHMETICS VALUES NOT VALID */
         /*                            */
         ON ERROR
           BEGIN;
           TYPE = 0;
           IF (ONCODE = 612)
           THEN DO;
              PUT SKIP FILE (SYSPRINT) EDIT
                (' ## THE DATA ASSOCIATED WITH COMMAND  "',COMMAND,
                '" IS IN ERROR ## ') (A);
              TYPE = -31;
              IBUFFER = ' ';
              END;
           CALL DISPLAY (TYPE);
           GO TO ERROR;
           END;
         /*-------------------------------*/
         /* COMMAND = 'SC'                */
         /* FUNCTION - SCALE OBJECT       */
         /*-------------------------------*/
         IF (COMMAND = 'SC')
         THEN DO;
              SCFACTORS(1) = GET_STR (IBUFFER);
              SCFACTORS(2) = GET_STR (IBUFFER);
              SCFACTORS(3) = GET_STR (IBUFFER);
              CALL SCALE (SCFACTORS);
              END;
                          .
                          .
                          .
                          .
                          .

         ERROR:  /* ABORT COMMAND */
         END TRNSFRM;
```

FIGURE A.3 : Probe Inserted Into Code

```
/**********************************************************************/
/*                                                                  */
/* PROCEDURE ENVRMNT                                                */
/* FUNCTION - HANDLES ENVIROMENT FOR WINDOWING, VIEWPORT,EYE-VIEW   */
/*            AND ACTIVATION OF LEVELS                              */
/* CALLED FROM - DRIVER                                             */
/* CALLS PROCEDURE(S) - ACTIVE WNDW VWPRT                           */
/*                                                                  */
/**********************************************************************/
ENVRMNT:PROCEDURE (COMMAND);
        DECLARE NLEVEL FIXED BINARY (5) EXT,

                          .
                          .
                          .

              CHANGE BIT (8) EXT;
        /*                          */
        /* ERROR - HANDLING BLOCK   */
        /* REVISED FOR CONVERSION ERROR */
        /*                          */
        ON CONVERSION
          BEGIN;
          TYPE = -31;
          PUT SKIP FILE (SYSPRINT) EDIT
            (' ## THE DATA ASSOCIATED WITH COMMAND  "',COMMAND,
             '" IS IN ERROR ## ') (A);
          CALL DISPLAY (TYPE);
          IBUFFER = ' ';
          GO TO ERROR;
          END;
        /*----------------------------------------------------------*/
        /* COMMAND = 'AC'                                           */
        /* FUNCTION - LOAD NEW INSTANCE TO ACTIVE INSTANCE          */
        /* ARGUMENTS - INSTANCE NUMBER -> NUMBER 1 -12              */
        /*----------------------------------------------------------*/
        IF (COMMAND = 'AC')
        THEN IF (QUERY)
            THEN PUT SKIP FILE (SYSPRINT) LIST (NLEVEL);
            ELSE DO;
                /*                          */
                /* GET NEW INSTANCE NUMBER AND ACTIVATE */
                /*                          */
                NLEVEL = GET_STR (IBUFFER);
                CALL ACTIVE;
                END;

                          .
                          .
                          .
                          .
                          .

        ERROR:/* COMMAND ABORTED */
        END ENVRMNT;
```

FIGURE A.4 : Probe Inserted Into Code

APPENDIX B

The following figures show some simple data formats utilized
by both CEMS and GRAFIX.

User I.D.	Time Stamp	Error I.D.	Error Context
GRL	1084940	31	-> TR 5 5
GRL	1085617	31	-> TR 5 5
GRL	1094805	31	-> TR 4 4
NNA	2111249	31	-> SC 3
NNA	2112348	31	-> RO 3
TIM	4132937	1	-> DF
LRL	4132958	29	-> DR
ZNA	4133033	31	-> TP 5 6

FIGURE B.1 : COLLECTED INVOLUNTARY ERRORS

User I.D.	Time Stamp	Error I.D.	Error Context
GRT	6093004	GRIPE	-> DATA FILE "WING" WILL NOT LOAD - WHY?
LRL	6120111	GRIPE	-> REMEBER TO ADD MIRROR COMMAND

FIGURE B.2 : COLLECTED VOLUNTARY ERRORS

User I.D.	Time Stamp	Error I.D.	Error Context
ALL	0115630	MESSAGE	-> PLEASE SEND A "GRIPE" IF IN TROUBLE
LRL	4125821	MESSAGE	-> SEE TGJ AS SOON AS POSSIBLE

FIGURE B.3 : RECORDED REPLY MESSAGES

Automated Tools for Information Systems Design
H.-J. Schneider and A.I. Wasserman (eds.)
North-Holland Publishing Company
© IFIP, 1982

An Interactive Applications Development System
and
Support Environment

N. Adam Rin

Applied Data Research, Inc.
Orchard Road and Route 206, CN-8
Princeton, New Jersey 08540
U.S.A.

An interactive applications development system
called IDEAL and its related automated
development support environment is presented.
This paper describes a set of integrated video
terminal based facilities and a language for
interactive development of online and database
applications. It also summarizes the features of
an integrated online support environment
specifically oriented towards development
activities of this facility and language.

1. Introduction

This paper describes an interactive application development
system called IDEAL* and its related automated development
support environment. The system has two objectives. One, is to
provide an online application design and development facility,
especially for database and online commercial business
applications. The second, is to provide an associated automated
support environment for the design, development, maintenance, and
execution activities. Both objectives strive to improve
productivity and reduce the amount of expertise required to
develop complex applications. Furthermore, the aim is to provide
this in an environment that is highly interactive, user-friendly,
self-teaching, "intelligent" and sensitive to the development
facilities and language, and oriented to the widely used video
display terminals (e.g., IBM 3270 and compatible display
terminals).

----

*IDEAL (which is an acronym for Interactive Development
Environment for an Application's Life-Cycle) is designed and
partially implemented at Applied Data Research, Inc. (ADR),
Princeton, N.J. It will be available in 1982.

The system and this paper consist of two major parts:

(A) the application design and development facility; and (B) the automated interactive support environment. The major features of these two aspects are summarized briefly here and are discussed in length in Sections 2 and 3, respectively.

A.   The application design and development facility

   This is a facility consisting of a set of inter-related video terminal based tools and a language. Unlike traditional programming textual languages, the approach in IDEAL has been to use

      (1) special-purpose fill-in-the-blank screen formats that are displayed on a video terminal and are processed interactively for the declarative or descriptive portions of applications design and development (e.g., for data definition, report specification, screen format specification, etc.); and

      (2) a unified, structured, and very high level language for design and development of application logic, computations, and non-procedural database reference and maintenance.

   The facilities are oriented towards the development of database and online commercial business data processing applications. The language and other facilities are designed to lessen the amount of expertise needed to develop database applications by providing a structured language that interfaces to a relational view database. Beyond the simplicity of database usage, emphasis was placed on seeing that the language was comprehensive enough for even complex applications -- complete with arithmetic, logical, reporting, and interactive capabilities.

   The facilities and language are compatible with and designed to support modern structured design and development methodologies, resulting in applications that are more readable, maintainable, and reliable.

   The facilities are highly interactive making heavy use of the visual effects of using a video display terminal.

   These facilities will be described in Section 2 by way of example, followed by a more detailed feature description and comparison to other languages and facilties.

B. <u>The automated development support environment</u>

An integral part of the philosophy of this system is an automated online support environment specifically oriented towards this facility and language. This includes the following:

* a powerful command language for the experienced user to request services;

* a set of menus for the inexperienced user to request services;

* a set of online "help" facilities that decrease the need for using manuals;

* split screen capability for performing two or more related activities on one video display terminal;

* a host of supporting services for displaying, browsing, printing, copying, deleting, renaming, inquiring, and otherwise managing the various components of an application such as data definitions, report specifications, procedures, etc.;

* specialized "intelligent" editors that have knowledge of the facilities and language and are sensitive to syntax, format, and structure during the editing process;

* online validation, compilation, debugging, and a run-time system for execution;

* a centrally-maintained data dictionary, application directory, and library available online to application developers;

* authorization and security mechanisms that are oriented towards the facilities of the system;

* complete interactive control from design through development and production.

2.   Interactive Applications Development Facility & Language

2.1   General Comments

This section starts with some general comments regarding IDEAL's
approach and development facilities.   Then, following a brief
explanation on how the user perceives the logical data
organization (Section 2.2), the application development
facilities are presented via two sample applications.   The first
(Section 2.3) is a simple retrieval and reporting problem, while
the second (Section 2.4) is a more complex online screen-oriented
transaction processing and database update problem.   Section 2.5
summarizes the main features of the language and provides a
comparison to other languages and facilities.

In IDEAL's framework, a commercial application is divided into
the following components:

   (1) General declarative information.   This includes the
   following:

      (a) a declaration of the external inputs and outputs;

      (b) the logical database definition (or traditional file
      record layout for applications that use conventional file
      access methods);

      (c) possible report definitions;

      (d) screen layouts and definitions for online
      screen-oriented applications;

      (e) input and output parameters.

   (2) The application program itself, which consists of:

      (a) the definition of working data (data local to the
      program) and;

      (b) the logic, computations, terminal interaction and
      database maintenance rules, procedures, and actions.

Since all but the last component (2b) are highly declarative or
descriptive in nature, the approach in IDEAL has been to use
special-purpose screen formats.   These screens are for all the
components of the application definition, are processed
interactively, and replace a textual language.   All logic,
computations and database maintenance are expressed in a
language, and in a way that solves some traditional problems by

offering a comprehensive, yet simple, unified, structured, and very high level language.

2.2 The Data-View Concept

A "data-view" is a logical view of data shared across many applications. The user perceives the data as a set of "flat" tables or relations, such as the example in Figure 1. The underlying database management system is ADR's DATACOM/DB, an inverted file system used by IDEAL to effectively simulate a relational database. A subset of the system can also be used effectively to process data on traditional files using file access methods.

From the application developer's point of view, a "data-view" is a named collection of fields (or data elements) with a related common purpose. These fields could, in a simple case, comprise a record of a physical file or, at the opposite end of the spectrum, could be a set of non-contiguous fields from an underlying physical structure. A developer can display a data-view definition via a simple command at the terminal as shown in Figure 2, with a resulting display as shown in that figure.

Data-view definitions are stored in a central online data dictionary, which plays an integral role throughout IDEAL. It is intended that the data-view definitions be established and maintained by the enterprise's "data administrator," using screen formats similar to that in Figure 2 that are processed interactively. Those forms are somewhat more involved than most other IDEAL screen formats in that not only are the logical data-views defined but the underlying physical file definitions and structure are defined as well.

In addition to using the central data dictionary for displaying data definitions to the application developers, the system also uses the dictionary to process the application itself, both during compilation and during execution. The result is a high degree of data independence.

INVENTORY-ITEM					
ITEM-NO*	ITEM-DESC	UNIT-PRICE	QTY-ON-HAND	QTY-ON-ORDER	REORDER-POINT
10100	WIDGET	5.00	95	0	80
10200	WHATSIT	15.95	150	90	170
...	...	...	...	...	...

Figure 1: "DATA-VIEW" from Application Developer's Viewpoint

```
DISPLAY DATA-VIEW INVENTORY-ITEM

IDEAL   DATA-VIEW INVENTORY-ITEM              DISPLAY

LEVEL  FIELD-NAME        TYPE LENGTH DP OCCUR KEY

       ITEM-NO           X      5                *
       ITEM-DESC         X     20
       UNIT-PRICE        N      5    2
       QTY-ON-HAND       N      5
       QTY-ON-ORDER      N      5
       REORDER-POINT     N      5
```

Figure 2: Sample Data-view Definition Display

2.3 A Simple Retrieval and Reporting Example

To illustrate the basic application development facilities of this system, consider the following problem. Given the inventory item data-view described in Figure 2, for each inventory item whose price is less than five dollars, produce a report like that shown in Figure 3, showing its item number, description, price, quantity on hand, and value on hand (price times the quantity on hand). Also show the average price and value.

In IDEAL's framework, this simple application consists of two parts: a definition of the desired report, and the request for the selected items. Defining a report is accomplished by asking the system to display a set of forms for report definition. A request to display the main report definition form and its result is illustrated in Figure 4, where each line of the form is used to describe an item across the report. This formatted screen-based form, like all the other screens in the system, allows the user to tabulate or move the cursor to the portions of the form that need to be filled. The concept of "filling-in-the-blanks" is not new and goes back to commercial systems such as MARK IV or RPG. The difference here is that these forms are displayed on a video terminal in an interactive user-friendly environment and more importantly, this is not a standalone report generator package, but part of an integrated and complete system for application development.

Often a user needs to display or edit two or more aspects of an application on the same screen simultaneously. For example, before proceeding to fill in the form with the desired items, the user may wish to see the data-view definition again and simultaneously work on the report definition form. This is an example of the usefulness of a dual screen or "split screen" mode. After splitting the screen with a command (or a program function key), the user can display the inventory data-view definition in one half and the report definition detail form in the other half of the screen. The commands and the resulting screen are illustrated in Figure 5a. The user would now proceed to fill in the report detail definition form as illustrated in Figure 5b. Each line of the form consists of a description of an item across the report. The entry consists of the source of the data item desired and the user in this case also checks off the desired summary functions. In a more complex application, there are facilities in the forms to describe control breaks, sorting, headings, footings, etc.

FOR EACH INVENTORY ITEM WHOSE PRICE IS UNDER $5,
PRODUCE A REPORT SHOWING ITS ITEM NUMBER,
DESCRIPTION, PRICE, QUANTITY ON HAND, AND THE
VALUE ON HAND (QUANTITY ON HAND TIMES PRICE).
SHOW AVERAGE PRICE AND AVERAGE VALUE.

```
                                          PAGE __

           INVENTORY LIST OF SELECTED ITEMS

  ITEM NO    ITEM DESC        PRICE      ON HAND VALUE
  _____    _____       _____    _____ _____
  _____    _____       _____    _____ _____
  _____    _____       _____    _____ _____
  _____    _____       _____    _____ _____
  _____    _____       _____    _____ _____
  _____    _____       _____    _____ _____
  _____    _____       _____    _____ _____

  AVERAGE                     _____            _____
```

Figure 3: Example 1: Simple Retrieval and Reporting

```
  EDIT   REPORT INVENTORY-REPORT DETAIL

  IDEAL        REPORT DETAIL DEFINITION      FILL-IN

  FIELD NAME   SORT   BREAK   FUNCTION   COLUMN   EDIT
               L A    L H S   T M M A    H W  T
               V /    V D K   O A I V    D ID A
               L D    L G P   T X N G    G TH B
  _____   _ _    _ _ _   _ _ _ _    _ _ _   _____
  _____   _ _    _ _ _   _ _ _ _    _ _ _   _____
  _____   _ _    _ _ _   _ _ _ _    _ _ _   _____
  _____   _ _    _ _ _   _ _ _ _    _ _ _   _____
  _____   _ _    _ _ _   _ _ _ _    _ _ _   _____
  _____   _ _    _ _ _   _ _ _ _    _ _ _   _____
```

Figure 4: Sample Report Definition Form

```
1 DISPLAY DATA-VIEW INVENTORY-ITEM
2 EDIT REPORT INVENTORY-REPORT DETAIL

IDEAL    DATA-VIEW INVENTORY-ITEM              DISPLAY

LEVEL  FIELD-NAME        TYPE LENGTH DP OCCUR KEY

       ITEM-NO           X      5              *
       ITEM-DESC         X     20
       UNIT-PRICE        N      5    2
       QTY-ON-HAND       N      5
       QTY-ON-ORDER      N      5
       REORDER-POINT     N      5
```
```
IDEAL       REPORT DETAIL DEFINITION         FILL-IN

FIELD NAME      SORT   BREAK   FUNCTION   COLUMN    EDIT
                L A    L H S   T M M A    H W  T
                V /    V D K   O A I V    D ID A
                L D    L G P   T X N G    G TH B
_____   _ _    _ _ _   _ _ _ _    _ _ _ ____
_____   _ _    _ _ _   _ _ _ _    _ _ _ ____
_____   _ _    _ _ _   _ _ _ _    _ _ _ ____
_____   _ _    _ _ _   _ _ _ _    _ _ _ ____
_____   _ _    _ _ _   _ _ _ _    _ _ _ ____
_____   _ _    _ _ _   _ _ _ _    _ _ _ ____
```

**Figure 5a: Simultaneous Data Definition Display
        and Report Definition Form Display**

```
1 DISPLAY DATA-VIEW INVENTORY-ITEM
2 EDIT REPORT INVENTORY-REPORT DETAIL

IDEAL     DATA-VIEW INVENTORY-ITEM                DISPLAY

LEVEL  FIELD-NAME          TYPE LENGTH DP OCCUR KEY

       ITEM-NO             X      5                   *
       ITEM-DESC           X     20
       UNIT-PRICE          N      5    2
       QTY-ON-HAND         N      5
       QTY-ON-ORDER        N      5
       REORDER-POINT       N      5

IDEAL       REPORT DETAIL DEFINITION           FILL-IN

FIELD NAME    SORT    BREAK   FUNCTION    COLUMN    EDIT
              L A     L H S   T M M A     H W  T
              V /     V D K   O A I V     D ID A
              L D     L G P   T X N G     G TH B
ITEM-NO       _ _     _ _ _   _ _ _ _     _ __ ___
ITEM-DESC     _ _     _ _ _   _ _ _ _     _ __ ___
UNIT-PRICE    _ _     _ _ _   _ _ _ S     _ __ ___  ____
QTY-ON-HAND   _ _     _ _ _   _ _ _ _     _ __ ___
VALUE-ON-HAND _ _     _ _ _   _ _ _ S     _ __ ___  ____
              _ _     _ _ _   _ _ _ _     _ __ ___  ____
```

**Figure 5b: Report Definition Filled in by User
While Displaying Data-view Definition**

An application request is made via a language we call IDEAL/PDL
(Procedure Definition Language). The language is entered and
edited using a screen-editor that is language-intelligent (see
Section 3.4). Assuming for now that the application has already
been written, it can be displayed via a command as shown in
Figure 6. This simple example illustrates one of the structured
language constructs, the "FOR EACH", which is used to apply a set
of computations, decisions, database actions, or reporting
actions, to a selected set of data-view "rows." In this case,
each item where the price is less than five dollars has one
computation as shown plus the production of a detailed line of
the report that was already defined in the previous report
definition transaction (in Figure 5b).

```
DISPLAY PROGRAM LIST-INVENTORY


FOR EACH INVENTORY-ITEM

    WHERE   UNIT-PRICE < 5

    SET VALUE-ON-HAND = QTY-ON-HAND * UNIT-PRICE

    PRODUCE INVENTORY-REPORT

ENDFOR
```

Figure 6: Application Procedure for Example 1

Although this is a simple example, it illustrates several
objectives and features of IDEAL/PDL:

* It is intended to be both easy to read and easy to learn.

* It allows the user to perceive the data being processed in the
  tabular view presented earlier, and to specify or select the
  desired set of records non-procedurally. Like some query
  languages, this one has a self-contained easy-to-use language
  to access the database without having to learn a complex
  callable interface with complex parameters. However, unlike
  query languages, the database retrieval and update
  capabilities are unified into a comprehensive programming
  language, complete with arithmetic, structured constructs for
  logic, screen-oriented interactive capabilities, and a
  reporting facility (all of which will become more apparent in
  the second example) without using a "host" programming
  language. For example, the FOR EACH construct in this example
  has a scope to the "ENDFOR", meaning that every statement in
  that scope applies to each selected entry in the data-view.
  In a more complex example, the body of that construct could
  have had computations, invocations of lower level processes,
  or nested structured constructs for logic (such as,
  IF...THEN...ELSE...ENDIF or a LOOP...WHILE...ENDLOOP).

- The overall intent is to provide an easy database user
  interface facility within the language. The language style
  and structure is, on the one hand, suited for simple query and
  reporting problems, and on the other hand fits well within a
  uniform style and structure of a comprehensive language for
  complex commercial applications.

2.4 A More Complex On-Line Database Application

To illustrate some other advanced features of IDEAL, the
following order-entry problem will be used. It is a screen-based
online transaction processing and database update problem.
Admittedly, the problem is not as realistic as an actual
order-entry situation nor is the solution complete; however, it
is intended only as a vehicle to present various system features.
The application processes customer orders entered online on an
ORDER-FORM at a video terminal as shown in Figure 7 and produces
an INVOICE for the order like that shown in Figure 8. It updates
the INVENTORY-ITEM data-view that we used in the previous example
(whose description is repeated in Figure 9) reflecting the
reduced quantity on hand due to the order for each item, and it
uses the CUSTOMER master data-view displayed in Figure 10. It
also produces, as another output, an accounts receivable record
(displayed in Figure 11).

The order processing procedure might informally be specified as
follows:

Process each order form when the operator hits "enter" and
continue doing so until the operator hits "program function
key" number 1 (PF1). When the operator hits the "enter" key,
each form is processed as follows:

For each item ordered, check whether there is sufficient
quantity on hand for the order, and if so, update the
inventory item's quantity-on-hand to reflect that order.
Additionally, the line in the invoice is produced.

Also produce an accounts receivable record.

When the operator hits "PF1", the session is over.
When the operator hits "PF2" a fresh form is displayed.

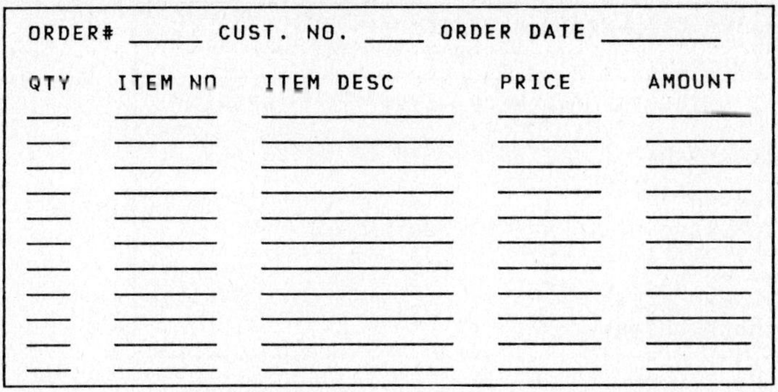

```
ORDER#  _____  CUST. NO. ____  ORDER DATE _____

QTY     ITEM NO   ITEM DESC        PRICE      AMOUNT
___     _____    _____     _____     _____
___     _____    _____     _____     _____
___     _____    _____     _____     _____
___     _____    _____     _____     _____
___     _____    _____     _____     _____
___     _____    _____     _____     _____
___     _____    _____     _____     _____
___     _____    _____     _____     _____
___     _____    _____     _____     _____
```

Figure 7: "ORDER-FORM" Screen Map for Example 2

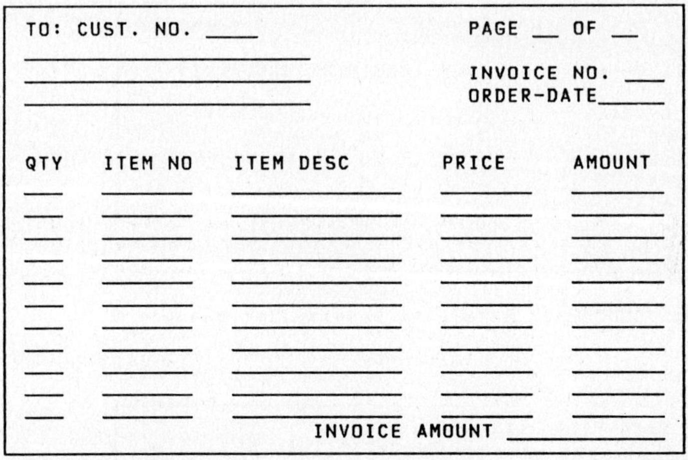

```
TO: CUST. NO. ____                PAGE __ OF __

_____              INVOICE NO. ___
_____              ORDER-DATE_____


QTY     ITEM NO   ITEM DESC        PRICE      AMOUNT
___     _____    _____     _____     _____
___     _____    _____     _____     _____
___     _____    _____     _____     _____
___     _____    _____     _____     _____
___     _____    _____     _____     _____
___     _____    _____     _____     _____
___     _____    _____     _____     _____
___     _____    _____     _____     _____
                   INVOICE AMOUNT  _____
```

Figure 8: "INVOICE" Report for Example 2

```
DISPLAY DATA-VIEW INVENTORY-ITEM

IDEAL        DATA-VIEW INVENTORY-ITEM            DISPLAY

LEVEL FIELD-NAME         TYPE LENGTH DP OCCUR KEY

      ITEM-NO            X      5                  *
      ITEM-DESC          X     20
      UNIT-PRICE         N      5    2
      QTY-ON-HAND        N      5
      QTY-ON-ORDER       N      5
      REORDER-POINT      N      5
```

Figure 9: Inventory-item Data-view Display for Example 2

```
DISPLAY DATA-VIEW CUSTOMER

IDEAL        DATA-VIEW CUSTOMER                   DISPLAY

LEVEL FIELD-NAME         TYPE LENGTH DP OCCUR KEY

      CUST-NO            N      4                  *
      NAME               X     20
      ADDRESS            X     20
      CITY               X     15
      STATE              X      2
      ZIP                N      5
```

Figure 10: "CUSTOMER" Data-view Display for Example 2

```
DISPLAY DATA-VIEW ACCT-RECEIVABLE

IDEAL        DATA-VIEW ACCT-RECEIVABLE            DISPLAY

LEVEL FIELD-NAME         TYPE LENGTH DP OCCUR KEY

      CUST-NO            N      4                  *
      DATE               N      8
      INVOICE-NO         N      5
      AMOUNT             N      7    2
```

Figure 11: "ACCT-RECEIVABLE" Data-view for Example 2

There are several steps in the development of this application, as in other applications:

Database and data-view definition
For brevity, we will assume that this has already been done.

Data-view definition display
The user developing the application can display the data-view definitions or get printouts of them in a form as shown in Figures 9, 10, and 11.

Application Creation
The user needs to identify to the system information about the program and its authorized logical resources (the data-views it uses, the reports it produces, authorized users, etc.).

Screen Definition
The layout of the ORDER-FORM and a definition of its fields needs to be accomplished.

Report Definition
The INVOICE report needs to be defined.

Application Process Definition
The application logic specified above needs to be expressed formally in the IDEAL/PDL language.

After database definition, the first step is the creation or identification of the application to the system. The other steps, screen definition, report definition, procedure definition, can be accomplished in any order convenient to the developer. All of these application development steps are illustrated in this section.

2.4.1 Application Creation

A user begins to create a new application via a command (shown in Figure 12) which results in a form displayed on the video terminal (also shown in Figure 12). In IDEAL's framework, the task of creating an application is a separate authorized activity from the writing of the application. It is intended that in some organizations these two tasks would be accomplished by two different people, although the same person may be authorized to create and write the application. Essentially, this form allows the application creator to establish the program, to establish who is authorized to control, update, and run the application, and to provide some descriptive commentary about the program.

The user is then immediately prompted, via another online form shown in Figure 13a, for the names of the data-views, screen maps, report definitions, and programs that this program uses, transmits, produces, and calls, respectively. In effect, the authorized application creator, intended to be a database administrator, a project manager, or the developer, is establishing which resources this application is authorized to use. Figure 13b shows how the user filled in this form for this problem, indicating the names of the data-views, etc., used by the new program.

```
 _____
|                                                               |
|  CREATE PROGRAM                                               |
|_____|
|                                                               |
|  PROGRAM _____                                            |
|                                                               |
|  CONTROL AUTHORIZATION _____ |
|  UPDATE AUTHORIZATION _____ |
|  RUN AUTHORIZATION _____ |
|  LANGUAGE IDEAL                                              |
|  DESCRIPTION                                                 |
|         _____ |
|         _____ |
|         _____ |
|         _____ |
|         _____ |
|         _____ |
|         _____ |
|_____|
```

Figure 12: Application Creation for Example 2

```
SPECIFY THE DATA-VIEWS, MAPS, REPORTS, PROGRAMS
THAT THIS PROGRAM USES:

DATA-VIEW        MAP NAME    REPORT NAME      PROGRAM NAME
_____      _____    _____      _____
_____      _____    _____      _____
_____      _____    _____      _____
_____      _____    _____      _____
_____      _____    _____      _____
_____      _____    _____      _____
_____      _____    _____      _____
_____      _____    _____      _____
_____      _____    _____      _____
_____      _____    _____      _____
```

Figure 13a: Application Creation for Example 2

```
SPECIFY THE DATA-VIEWS, MAPS, REPORTS, PROGRAMS
THAT THIS PROGRAM USES:

DATA-VIEW        MAP NAME    REPORT NAME      PROGRAM NAME

CUSTOMER         ORDER-FORM  INVOICE          _____
INVENTORY-ITEM   _____    _____      _____
ACCT-RECV        _____    _____      _____
_____      _____    _____      _____
_____      _____    _____      _____
_____      _____    _____      _____
_____      _____    _____      _____
_____      _____    _____      _____
_____      _____    _____      _____
_____      _____    _____      _____
```

Figure 13b: Above Form Filled in by User

2.4.2   Screen Definition

The screen in our example, the ORDER-FORM described in Figure 7,
is laid out directly on a blank screen as shown in Figure 14.
The screen designer is then prompted with a split screen as shown
in Figure 15, with the screen layout in the top half and a
corresponding table in the bottom half. The table is used to
designate names of fields (which the user will reference in the
procedure portion), screen attributes, data type attributes,
decimal places, and occurrences. Although certain entries in the
table are pre-filled with defaults, Figure 15 shows the form as
the user would have filled it out. The user may also specify
built in validation rules, such as specifying that a field is
required, specifying a range check, and other available rules
that are enforced by the run-time system.

Screen definition mode is entered via a simple command or menu
selection.

```
┌────────────────────────────────────────────────────────┐
│ ¬ORDER#¬_____ ¬CUST. NO.¬_____ ¬ORDER DATE¬_____;  │
│                                                        │
│ ¬QTY    ITEM NO    ITEM DESC        PRICE      AMOUNT;  │
│ ¬___; ¬_____; ¬_____; ¬_____; ¬_____; │
│                                                        │
│                                                        │
│                                                        │
│                                                        │
└────────────────────────────────────────────────────────┘
```

Figure 14: "ORDER-FORM" Screen Map Definition

```
¬ORDER#¬_____¬CUST. NO.¬_____¬ORDER DATE¬_____;
1       2       3          4     5              6

¬QTY    ITEM NO    ITEM DESC        PRICE     AMOUNT:
7
¬___; ¬_____; ¬_____; ¬_____; ¬_____;
8     9        10                11        12
```

CMD	NO.	NAME	ATTR	T	LEN	DP	OCC	VALIDATION/EDIT
	1	_____	PS	_	6	__	__	_____
	2	ORDER-NO	U	N	5	__	__	_____
	3	_____	PS	_	9	__	__	_____
	4	CUST-NO	U	N	4	__	__	_____
	5	_____	PS	_	10	__	__	_____
	6	ORDER-DATE	U	X	8	__	__	_____
	7	_____	PS	_	20	__	__	_____
		ORDER-ITEM		_	___	__	10	_____
	8	ORDER-QTY	U	N	3	__	__	_____
	9	ITEM-NO	U	X	7	__	__	_____
	10	ITEM-DESC	PS	X	20	__	__	_____
	11	UNIT-PRICE	PS	E	7	2	__	_____
	12	AMOUNT	PS	E	7	2	__	_____

Figure 15: "ORDER-FORM" Screen Map Definition (cont.)

2.4.3 Procedure Definition Language

Whether we define the procedure next or the details of the
INVOICE report definition next is immaterial, but let us assume
that from the point of view of stepwise refinement, it is more
convenient to define the procedure.

Procedure entry and editing is accomplished by using the editor
via an "EDIT PROGRAM" command or menu selection. The editor is
"language intelligent" in that it is sensitive to the syntax of
the language, helping the user with formatting, structure, syntax
checkout, and shorthand -- allowing the user to enter a program
very conveniently. More will be said of this in Section 3.4.

The specification for the logic of this application was described
earlier in Section 2.4. The overall logic can be restated more
formally as follows:

```
        LOOP

                TRANSMIT ORDER-FORM

        UNTIL    PF1

                Process-the-order-form

        ENDLOOP

        End the session and TRANSMIT final signoff screen
```

The upper case letters are actually part of the IDEAL/PDL
language. The LOOP ... UNTIL ... ENDLOOP is a variant of the
"DO WHILE" or "DO UNTIL" that is found in a number of other
"structured" languages such as PASCAL [1]. Our form, based on
Weinberg et   al. [2], allows the UNTIL or WHILE to appear
anywhere in the scope of the loop thereby permitting
"n-and-a-half" loops. Another convention we followed in our
language design consistently throughout each construct, was to
end each construct with the construct name prefixed by "END".
The TRANSMIT statement is the one that sends the pre-defined
formatted screen "ORDER-FORM" to the user and receives the input.
The language has a number of built-in functions, some of which
deal with the widely used video terminals (IBM 3270 and
compatible terminals). The PF1 function here tests whether
program function key #1 was depressed by the user.

Refining the overall logic slightly, the user may enter the "top level" logic using the system's editor, resulting in the text as shown in Figure 16a. (Actually, skeletons of the various constructs can be inserted by the editor by using a shorthand described in Section 3.)

```
LOOP

   TRANSMIT ORDER-FORM

UNTIL    PF1              :  End of session

   SELECT
   WHEN   ENTER-KEY
      DO    PROCESS-ORDER
   WHEN   PF2
      DO REFRESH-SCREEN
   WHEN   PF3
      ...
   WHEN   OTHER
      DO REPORT-ERROR-KEY
   END-SELECT

ENDLOOP

DO END-SESSION

TRANSMIT SIGNOFF-SCREEN
```

Figure 16a: Application Logic for Example 2 Using IDEAL/PDL

"Process-the-order-form" in the previous frame has been refined into a SELECT construct in Figure 16a, which in its most general format is an extension of the classical CASE construct. The WHEN clauses here are evaluating which key was depressed by the user by using the built-in keyboard oriented functions.

In each case, a lower level process was invoked. IDEAL/PDL recognizes two classes of modularity: (1) a CALL to a separate sub-program with parameters; and (2) another class which is shown here, a "DO" or an invocation of a lower-level "local" process which can share common data. The former is encouraged in keeping

with the methods of structured design; however, we felt that the
latter is quite pragmatic, useful, and efficient for smaller
"chunks" of processing logic for which a formal sub-program
philosophy may be impractical.

Two sample sub-PROCEDUREs are shown in Figure 16b (the remaining
sub-PROCEDUREs have been left out intentionally for the purposes
of this paper). PROCESS-ORDER is invoked once per order form,
whereas PROCESS-ORDER-ITEM is invoked once per line item. All
the names used here are names of fields in the INVENTORY-ITEM and
CUSTOMER data-view or names of fields in the ORDER-FORM screen
map. The "FOR THE CUSTOMER ... " construct in the PROCESS-ORDER
PROCEDURE, establishes or selects a single CUSTOMER entry or row,
which in this case corresponds to the CUST-NO on the ORDER-FORM.
It also establishes a scope that the CUSTOMER is "current,"
meaning it can be referenced or updated (there is also a "FOR
FIRST n" and a "FOR EACH" variant, the latter of which has been
illustrated).

The inner FOR EACH traverses the ORDER-ITEM repeating group in
the ORDER-FORM; i.e., each iteration processes one line item in
the ORDER-FORM, invoking the lower level process,
PROCESS-ORDER-ITEM. Note the interchangeability of memory tables
and data-views of relations in that the same FOR EACH construct
is used here to traverse and reference an in-core table (actually
a repeating group in the ORDER-FORM screen map) as is used to
traverse a set of entries of a data-view (relation). This
interchangeability helps make data-views appear to the user as
tables that can be immediately referenced by using a FOR
construct.

The PROCESS-ORDER-ITEM PROCEDURE invoked here establishes the
INVENTORY-ITEM that corresponds to the current ITEM-NO on the
ORDER-FORM via a FOR construct which again has a scope to the
corresponding ENDFOR. Within that scope, all references to that
entry are valid. A feature of this language is that an entry can
be updated "virtually" simply by moving values into the current
entry. Note, for example, that the ORDER-QTY is SUBTRACTed FROM
the QTY-ON-HAND, which happens to be a field in the
INVENTORY-ITEM data-view. This, in effect, virtually updates the
amount with no need for input/output statements or calls to a
database system. The database, in effect, becomes an extension
to the user's addressable space, using the FOR and other
constructs to "position" to the proper logical "window" in the
database. Also, the system detects, upon compilation of such a
program, that an update is made; so exclusive control over the
record is performed automatically for the scope of the FOR
construct up to the ENDFOR.

The various statements in this example illustrate the "record at
a time" level language interface to a relational view database
that is provided and is unified into the general style of
IDEAL/PDL. This example illustrates selection and updating.
Although not shown in this example, there is a "DELETE data-view"
statement that can appear in the scope of a FOR to delete an
entry; likewise, there is a construct for the insertion of new
entries in a data-view.

The IF...THEN...ELSE...ENDIF construct is also illustrated in
this sub-process and should be self-explanatory.

Finally, the PRODUCE statement is responsible for the production
of one detail line of the named report, in our case the INVOICE.
Each time the PRODUCE is executed, another detail line of the
INVOICE report, which we have yet to define, is generated. The
control breaks, page breaks, summary functions, etc., are
produced by the report writer according to the report
specifications. For example, on each page break, a page heading
could be defined to include the name and address of the customer.

```
PROCEDURE PROCESS-ORDER


FOR THE CUSTOMER
    WHERE CUSTOMER.CUST-NO = ORDER-FORM.CUST-NO

  DO    INIT-INVOICE

  FOR EACH ORDER-ITEM
      DO PROCESS-ORDER-ITEM
  ENDFOR

ENDFOR


PROCEDURE PROCESS-ORDER-ITEM

FOR THE INVENTORY-ITEM
    WHERE INVENTORY-ITEM.ITEM-NO = ORDER-FORM.ITEM-NO

  IF QTY-ON-HAND > ORDER-QTY
    THEN
      SUBTRACT ORDER-QTY FROM QTY-ON-HAND
      PRODUCE INVOICE-ITEM
    ELSE
      DO BACKORDER
  ENDIF

ENDFOR
```

Figure 16b: Application Logic for Example 2 (cont.)

2.4.4 Report Specification

To finish our example, the report is specified by using a set of
online forms that are filled in by the user. There is one form
for definition of general report parameters (such as width,
depth, forms, justification, page numbering, date, etc.), another
form for specifying page headings, and a third form for
specifying a report detail line as shown in the previous example.
Figure 17 illustrates how the user might fill in the report
detail definition form for the INVOICE report. The names entered
here are names of fields in the ORDER-FORM or are calculated
fields. A similar form is used for the page heading, which in
the case of the INVOICE in our problem would be the customer name
and address, etc.

```
┌──────────────────────────────────────────────────────────────┐
│ IDEAL        REPORT DETAIL DEFINITION         FILL-IN          │
│                                                                │
│ FIELD NAME      SORT    BREAK    FUNCTION   COLUMN    EDIT      │
│                 L  A    L  H  S  T  M  M  A  H  W  T            │
│                 V  /    V  D  K  O  A  I  V  D  ID A            │
│                 L  D    L  G  P  T  X  N  G  G  TH B            │
│ ORDER-QTY      __ __   __ __ __  __ __ __ __  __ __ ___  _____  │
│ ITEM-NO        __ __   __ __ __  __ __ __ __  __ __ ___  _____  │
│ ITEM-DESC      __ __   __ __ __  __ __ __ __  __ __ ___  _____  │
│ UNIT-PRICE     __ __   __ __ __  __ __ __ __  __ __ ___  _____  │
│ UNIT-PRICE *   __ __   __ __ __  S  __ __ __  U  __ +10  _____  │
│  ORDER-QTY     __ __   __ __ __  __ __ __ __  __ __ ___  _____  │
│                __ __   __ __ __  __ __ __ __  __ __ ___  _____  │
│                __ __   __ __ __  __ __ __ __  __ __ ___  _____  │
└──────────────────────────────────────────────────────────────┘
```

Figure 17: Report Definition for Invoice Detail Line

2.5 Summary and Comparison of Language Features

IDEAL/PDL is a structured, very high level language with an
integrated database sub-language, facilities for modularization,
structured control constructs, arithmetic, report definition,
screen-oriented interactive capabilities, and error-handling.
Its features were designed to support the following capabilities:

Structured Design and Development

The control structures and modularization aspects of the language
have been motivated by the large amount of literature on
structured design and development techniques, and languages of
the past decade. Conceptually, the control structures are of the
capability of languages such as PASCAL [1] or ADA [3], but our
language syntax choice has been motivated by that found in
Weinberg, et al. [2], which is somewhat more general
(for example, the CASE has been generalized into a more extensive
SELECT, which the reader can find in the cited reference), and
whose human engineering, in our view, is more consistent and
attuned to the background of commercial applications developers.
For example, each construct begins with a keyword and ends with
"END" plus the keyword. Also there is no GO TO in IDEAL/PDL,
which enforces use of the constructs. An additional construct
beyond that in Weinberg et al., is the FOR EACH for iteration
and traversal of a data-view, table, or traditional file.

Two levels of modularity are provided, as explained in our second
example: the formal external CALL with parameters, which is
encouraged for structured design techniques; and invocation of
local procedures via a "DO", for very local abstraction,
division, and other pragmatic uses. The structured control
constructs, the CALL, the creation of sub-programs, and the
declaration of parameters as being either "input only" or
"updatable" in one of the program creation forms for parameter
declaration (illustrated in Figure 18) -- are all compatible with
and can be used to implement a number of the "structured design"
and "top-down" development methodologies in the literature.
These methodologies include Myers' "composite design" [4],
Yourdon and Constantine's "structured design" [5], Warnier [6],
and Orr's [7] methodologies, Wirth's "step-wise refinement" [8],
and others.

It can be argued that one can use IDEAL's language, along with
its other online facilities, as a program design tool. A systems
analyst might use IDEAL, defining the inputs and outputs via the
screen forms, and then proceed to define the high-level portion
of the logic in a formal "pseudocode" using IDEAL/PDL. One can
view IDEAL/PDL as an implementation of a variation of such

structured design language notation as Orr's SDL [7], which we
discovered was similar to our language.

While modern general-purpose structured programming languages
such as PASCAL and ADA certainly support "structured design and
programming" methodologies, we contend that they are not suited
to database and online oriented applications. Access or update
to a particular underlying DBMS or tele-processing monitor, a
CALL must be made to the services of the package. In other
words, those programming languages were not designed to have
knowledge of any particular DBMS, and invoking the services of a
DBMS through a CALL or through a distinct sub-language results in
two incongruous languages within one application. In IDEAL/PDL
an attempt to unify the database sub-language with the structure
and style of one integrated language is discussed below.

```
┌─────────────────────────────────────────────────────────────┐
│ EDIT PROGRAM X PARMS                                         │
│                                                             │
│                                                             │
│   IDEAL     PARAMETER DEFINITION              FILL-IN        │
│                                                             │
│  LEVEL FIELD NAME    T LENGTH   DP OCCUR U K VALUE          │
│  ____ _____ _ ____  __ _____ _ _ _____                │
│  ____ _____ _ ____  __ _____ _ _ _____                │
│  ____ _____ _ ____  __ _____ _ _ _____                │
│  ____ _____ _ ____  __ _____ _ _ _____                │
│  ____ _____ _ ____  __ _____ _ _ _____                │
│  ____ _____ _ ____  __ _____ _ _ _____                │
│  ____ _____ _ ____  __ _____ _ _ _____                │
│  ____ _____ _ ____  __ _____ _ _ _____                │
│  ____ _____ _ ____  __ _____ _ _ _____                │
│                                                             │
│  T=FIELD TYPE: X=ALPHANUMERIC, N=NUMERIC, C=COND.,          │
│               F=FLAG.                                        │
│  DP=DEC.PLACES. U=UPDATABLE PARM. K=KEYWORD PARM.           │
└─────────────────────────────────────────────────────────────┘
```

Figure 18: **Screen Format for Declaring Parameters
            of a Sub-program**

Database Sub-language

The database portion of the language has been inspired by the
database work of Codd [9], a programmer's interface language by
Date [10], informal "pseudocoding language" notations used in the
industry, and our own experience with what we consider to be
appropriate human engineering for commercial application
developers.

The design objective was to provide an easy database user
interface within the language with style and structure that is,
on the one hand, suited for simple query and reporting problems,
and on the other hand, powerful and comprehensive enough for
complex commercial applications. A main human engineering
consideration has been to unify the style of the two parts of the
language in terms with which a commercial programmer could
relate. There really is no "database sub-language" at all, but
rather a naturally integrated language.

The data model allows the user to perceive the data relationally
via "data-view" definitions. The database sub-language provides
the user with referencing and updating capabilities via a
structured language. We feel this gives the user greater
control, flexibility, yet ease for development of complex
commercial applications, than, for example, a relational
algebraic interface would have.

Unlike network DBMSs, navigation through a network structure is
unnecessary. Unlike a hierarchical DBMS such as IMS, the
limitations inherent in a hierarchy plus the more complex,
cumbersome CALL-level interface is replaced by a simple
structured language that is unified into a general purpose
programming language for commercial applications with uniform
style and structure.

Like some query languages, such as SQL [11], this has a
self-contained easy-to-use language to access the database
without having to learn a complex callable interface with formal
parameters. However, unlike most query languages, the database
retrieval and update capabilities are unified into a
comprehensive programming language -- complete with arithmetic,
logical, reporting, and interactive capabilities. It is true
that one can embed CALLs to a query language system such as SQL
in a traditional COBOL or PL/1 program, but again this leaves the
problem that the user is faced with two levels of non-unified
languages: the database sub-language, and a different host
language for computations, logic, reporting, etc.

To summarize IDEAL/PDL's database statements, the "FOR EACH"
construct shown in the examples enables selection by a general
Boolean expression of any fields in the data-view. The "FOR
FIRST" or "FOR THE" construct makes a single entry in a data-view
"current" or available for reference or immediate updating.

Updating and exclusive control over records is automatic in that records are virtually updated by moving values into the data elements of the logical view of data.

A DELETE statement on a current record is available for deletion, and a FOR NEW statement (not shown in the examples) is available for insertion. In addition, a CREATE statement is planned for the dynamic creation of derived relations at an aggregate level -- functionally equivalent to the relational algebra but in an easier set-oriented notation.

Transparent File Support and Table Handling

A subset of the data sub-language can be used to process tables and traditional files. The same FOR statements used to position or select entries of a data-view can also be used to access in-core tables (as was illustrated in the second example). This applies to traditional sequential and indexed sequential files as well. IDEAL knows from its data dictionary whether a reference is to a database file or a traditional file, and the underlying access method is transparent to the user. The language has no READ and WRITE statements for file access; input/output is implicit.

Screen Orientation

Video display terminals are used and supported at two levels. (1) There are specialized statements in the language to support the processing of screens that the user previously defined and formatted for the data entry portion of the application, such as the ORDER-FORM shown in our second example. In the procedure language a designated screen can be sent and received by the TRANSMIT statement that was illustrated in the example, and there are specialized symbolic built-in functions to test the location of the cursor, to test which fields were entered, which program function keys were depressed, and so on. Another form of the TRANSMIT statement allows sending and receiving of unformatted data when there was no pre-formatted screen defined by the user. A statement such as

    TRANSMIT OUTPUT 'PLEASE TYPE YOUR NAME:', INPUT NAME

can be used for conversational programming.

(2) At another level, facilities oriented towards the video terminal are an integral part of the application development "language," replacing the traditional textual language as the medium for data definition, screen formatting, report specification, parameter declaration, etc. These forms, some of which were illustrated in this paper, are easier to use than a textual language due to the tabulation and cursor capabilities and the pre-written prompting of the "keywords" already on the form.

Report Specification

This aspect of IDEAL was illustrated in our examples, with reports defined not via a textual language, but by specifying entries in a form displayed on a screen. The idea for using a form for report specification was motivated by the manual forms used in various commercial packages such as MARK IV or RPG. We submit that IDEAL's human engineering is easier than using a textual language for this purpose, especially when interactive prompts and validating plus on-line help exist, as described in Section 3.

Arithmetic Capability, Built-in Functions, and Other Areas

The arithmetic capability is traditional with computational "assignment statements" and built-in functions. There are also built-in functions and statements for string handling, screen processing, error-handling, and other areas that cannot be covered in the scope of this paper.

Other Comparative Remarks

In the course of the implementation of IDEAL, the description of other languages and systems were examined. One of these is the programming language PLAIN [12], whose goals are somewhat similar in that it complements a PASCAL-like language with database and interactive capabilities. Some of the differences between the two are IDEAL's heavy use of visual effects (using forms dislayed on a video terminal) for the declarative portions of the language, rather than a textual language; IDEAL's use of a central data dictionary, which is intended to be maintained by a "data administrator" and shared by the various application developers in an organization; a syntax and structure with human engineering towards the commercial applications developer; and an alternative to the relational algebraic approach to interfacing with a relational database management system.

A final difference is the assertion that a facility and language such as IDEAL could not really survive the 1980's without a comprehensive companion online development support environment specifically designed to facilitate development of such applications, a topic covered in the next section.

3. Application Development Support Work Station

There are many fine examples of general purpose online systems
for development of applications. For example, the UNIX
programming support environment has received notable attention
[13].

What makes IDEAL's support environment unique is that it is
specifically designed and oriented to support the activities in
developing applications with IDEAL's facilities and language.
These activities include the definition and maintenance of all
the components of an IDEAL application; editing, displaying,
browsing, copying, compiling, debugging, executing, establishing
authorization, inquiring, printing, etc.

The following are some of the facilities of the online
development support environment.

3.1 Commands vs. Menus

A development environment of the 1980's such as that of IDEAL,
which offers a wide range of facilities, must have more than one
approach for addressing its variety of users. IDEAL has a
complete command language oriented towards the user already
experienced and familiar with the system's facilities, as well as
a tutorial set of menus and fill-in forms for the unfamiliar or
infrequent user.

Commands and menus exist for requesting each of the online
services or for entering any of the modes or activities. Both
are specifically designed for the facilities, language, and
activities of the system. First, to illustrate commands, an
example of a system-specific command is

     DISPLAY REPORT INV-REPORT DETAIL

which displays the detail line specification of the designated
report, or

     EDIT PROGRAM INV-UPDATE PROC

which positions the start of the procedure portion of the
INV-UPDATE application to the top of the screen. As the program
is already being edited, a user might enter

     EDIT PARAMETERS

which would position the parameter declaration portion of the application definition (the completed formatted screen of Figure 18) to the top of the display. In other words, the commands are sensitive to the format of the objects on which they operate. There is a comprehensive set of commands for all services such as displaying, copying, renaming, printing, etc., but specifically for the various types of "objects" of an IDEAL application, such as screen definitions, report specifications, procedures, data declarations, and so on.

To illustrate the menus, Figure 19 is an example of the "main level" menu that the user sees upon signing on to the system. An inexperienced user might select alternative #1, "program maintenance," which results in a second level menu such as the one in Figure 20. To illustrate a simple example, the user might select #6, "rename," which would result in the fill-in form shown in Figure 21. This form should be self-explanatory and the user fills in the old and new name. At the same time, the order of the words in the form (with the keywords pre-displayed) remind the user of the syntax "RENAME PROGRAM oldname TO newname" that could be used in the future as a command to bypass the three levels of menus.

3.2 Help Facilities

Even with the menus and fill-in forms, more involved forms may arise which also must be filled in. In these instances, such as the report detail definition form, the inexperienced user may need further help. The approach which was adopted is that a user in this situation should be able to issue a "HELP" command or in our case, a program function key that means "HELP", which can be depressed at any time, and which results in an explanation of the options displayed. Each fill-in form has a corresponding set of "help" screens that instruct the user on the particular situation. This should reduce the need for using manuals.

3.3 Screen Orientation

All the screens in the system, some of which were illustrated in this paper, are displayable upon a command or menu selection. These screens are processed interactively with immediate highlighted feedback on errors for the user to correct. They can be scrolled to designated positions and are edited via special-purpose editors.

```
IDEAL       MAIN   MENU                        MENU

ENTER DESIRED OPTION NUMBER ==>

1. PROGRAM MAINTENANCE
2. DATA-VIEW DISPLAY
3. SCREEN MAINTENANCE
4. REPORT DEFINITION
5. DATA DICTIONARY MAINTENANCE
6. PROCESS PROGRAM
7. DISPLAY
8. PRINT
9. END IDEAL SESSION
```

Figure 19: Main Menu

```
IDEAL         PROGRAM MAINTENANCE            MENU

ENTER DESIRED OPTION NUMBER ==>

1. EDIT/DISPLAY
2. DISPLAY NAMES/STATUS
3. PRINT
4. CREATE
5. DELETE
6. RENAME
7. SET STATUS
```

Figure 20: Program Maintenance Sub-menu

```
IDEAL         RENAME                       FILL-IN

RENAME  PROGRAM _____

        TO        _____
```

Figure 21: "RENAME" Fill-in Form

3.4   The Editors

The system has special-purpose editors for the various components
of the application definition.   The nature of the IDEAL/PDL
language editor is explained here.   In addition to the
capabilities of a traditional line-oriented text editor, this
editor is "language intelligent" in that it is sensitive to the
syntax of the language, helping the user with formatting,
structure, syntax checkout, and providing a shorthand.

For example, to delete a statement or a construct, a delete code
is placed in the margin of the edit screen on the line where the
statement or construct begins.   When the user enters this code,
the entire scope of the statement or construct is deleted.   If
this were a simple statement that spans two lines, the statement
would be deleted; if this were a multi-line structured construct
such as an IF, all statements up to and including the
corresponding ENDIF would be deleted.

Similarly, there is a capability to insert statements and
constructs.   For example, if the code "IF" is placed in the
margin area of the edit screen, a "skeleton"

    IF

    THEN
      statements
      ...

    ELSE
      statements
      ...

    ENDIF

is inserted, with automatic formatting and aligning by level.

Such editors provide not only for fewer keystrokes via a
shorthand, but also help in minimizing structure and nesting
errors, and aid in formatting and readability.

3.5   Importance of "Split Screens"

There are often occasions in application development where a user
would want to see or edit more than one portion of the
application at one time.   For example, a user may wish to display
a data-view definition from the dictionary in the upper part of
the screen and edit the procedure that uses the names of elements
of the data-view in the lower part of the screen.   Another
example is editing the procedure source statements in one part of
the screen, while displaying the errors from the compiler in

another part. For these and other reasons, a good development
support environment must provide split screen capability.   IDEAL
allows for up to four regions in one physical screen.

3.6 On-line Checkout, Compilation, and Execution

Another vital characteristic of a development environment such as
this is online checkout, compilation, and execution.
Productivity and morale benefits are enhanced when immediate
feedback is generated on errors rather than waiting for a
separate submission. The dictionary plays an important role
during this process as explained in the next section.

Immediate online execution of applications is also a vital
attribute of this environment. During development, for example,
a user may lay out a screen map, write a simple processing
procedure and immediately test it online and interactively.
Other methods which require the running of a utility to process
the screen definition, a batch compilation for the program, and
then online execution just do not provide for the degree of
productivity necessary in an interactive development environment.

Finally, a specialized symbolic debugging package, specifically
designed and oriented to the facilities and language in this
system, enhance the development and testing process.
Specialization towards the language means the capability to
request symbolically prior to a run, the dynamic formatted
display of values at user designated break points, such as upon
changing of an item's value, upon entry to an IDEAL "PROCEDURE",
upon execution of a particular FOR construct, etc. The requests
for breaks and displays for testing and debugging are themselves
entered on formatted screens for this purpose.

3.7 Use of a Data Dictionary and an On-Line Library

A trend that is observed is the increasing role and importance of
a centralized data dictionary. Beyond storing data definitions
that are shared across applications, our dictionary is used to
store information about the programs, projects or systems, users,
report definitions, screen definitions, and other entities -- and
their inter-relationships. As a result, the dictionary becomes a
cross-referenced directory on all the system resources.

For example, when a program is created on the online library, an
entry is made in the dictionary representing its name, date
created, location in the library, and other control information.
As was shown in the second example, the program creator is then
prompted for which data-views, reports, and screens the program
uses. These relationships are also represented in the
dictionary.

One result of storing all the entities and their inter-relationships in a central directory is a management and control facility to inquire about resource utilization. Commands exist in IDEAL to inquire about the status and names of the entities stored in the dictionary and their inter-relationships. Examples of some of these commands are as follows:

DISPLAY PROGRAM NAMES RELATED TO DATA-VIEW CUST

which displays the names of all the programs that use the data-view CUST. Or

DISPLAY PROGRAM NAMES RELATED TO SYSTEM ACCOUNTING

which will show the names of all the programs in the accounting system. The command

DISPLAY PERSON NAMES RELATED TO PROGRAM SALESANAL

will show the users who have access to the designated program. The levels of access authorized for each person, such as read-only, update, execute, or control, would also be displayed.

Another aspect of the integration of the dictionary with the library system is synchronization: the dictionary is guaranteed to reflect the actual status of source and object programs. For example, during online compilation of a program, the procedure portion of the program is checked to be sure that it only uses names authorized for use by that program and at the authorized level. For example, a statement such as

ADD CHARGE TO BALANCE

is checked not only syntactically, but also for the fact that CHARGE and BALANCE are valid dictionary names and that this program has authorization to be updating the BALANCE field, a fact that is also modelled in the dictionary. At execution time, the dictionary is again used to ensure that applications are always in synchronization with the data dictionary.

Another example of how the dictionary is used as a basis for authorization is the fact that each user's "profile" is stored in it. This includes both general privileges and particular authorizations to specific entity occurrences. Examples of general privileges are the authorization to create new data-view defintions, the authorization to update any program in a project or only those to which one is specifically authorized, the authorization to create programs, the authorization to set authorization levels, etc. In addition, a user may have specific authorizations to particular entity occurrences. For example, a person may be authorized to update or run a particular program. In short, we contend that a good data dictionary and directory system forms a solid basis for an authorization mechanism.

4.   Conclusions

In this paper, an overview of the main features of the IDEAL
applications development system and development support
environment have been demonstrated. The main thrust of such a
system is the provision of a specific set of tools and a language
that will ease the development and improve the productivity for
the production of a broad class of computer applications, in this
case online and database oriented commericial business
applications, and the provision of a companion set of
screen-oriented automated tools that provide an environment to
support the development of such applications. A user-friendly
support environment that is sensitive to the facilities,
language, and orientation of the system is vital for making the
development of the complex applications of the future
cost-effective. It is hoped that systems such as this will play
an increasing role in the development of applications in the
years to come.

5.   About the Author and Acknowledgements

The author is a staff consultant and product manager for the
IDEAL project at Applied Data Reasearch, Inc. He holds a Ph.D.
Degree in Computer and Information Science from the University of
Pennsylvania.

Acknowledgements are due to the many contributors for the success
of this project, including R. Kauffman, group product manager;
to the members of the design and development team: J.   Byrum, D.
Hoeschele, J. Metelitsa, W. Musselman, M. Shalgi, and S.
Wright for their many technical contributions; to the technical
documentation staff: M. Lyons, P. Runge, and K. Yaros; and to
the secretarial services of P. Cefaloni.

6. References

[1] Wirth, N. and Jensen, K., PASCAL User Manual Report, second ed., Springer-Verlag, New York, 1974.

[2] Weinberg, Wright, Kauffman, and Goetz, High Level COBOL Programming, Winthrop Publishers, 1977.

[3] "ADA Reference Manual," SIGPLAN Notices, Vol. 14, No. 6, June 1979.

[4] Myers, G.J., Reliable Software through Composite Design, Petrocelli-Charter, 1975.

[5] Yourdon, E., and Constantine, L., Structured Design, YOURDON inc., 1975.

[6] Warnier, L., Logical Construction of Programs, Van Nostrand Reinhold, 1974.

[7] Orr, K., Structured System Development, YOURDON inc., 1977.

[8] Wirth, N., Algorithms + Data Structures = Programs, Prentice-Hall, 1976.

[9] Codd, E.F., "A Relational Model of Data for Shared Data Banks," Comm. ACM, Vol. 13, No. 6 (June 1970), pp. 377-387.

[10] Date, C., Introduction to Databases, second ed., Addison-Wesley, 1979.

[11] Chamberlin and Boyce, "SEQUEL: A Structured English Query Language," ACM-SIGFIDET, May 1974.

[12] Wasserman, Sheretz, Kersten, van de Riet, Dippe, "Revised Report on the Programming Language PLAIN," SIGPLAN Notices, Vol. 16, No. 5 (May 1981), pp. 59-80.

[13] Kernigham, B. W. and Mashey, J. R., "The UNIX Programming Environment," COMPUTER, Vol. 14, No. 4 (April 1981), pp. 12-22.

Automated Tools for Information Systems Design
H.-J. Schneider and A.I. Wasserman (eds.)
North-Holland Publishing Company
© IFIP, 1982

A TOOL FOR DEVELOPING INFORMATION SYSTEMS

Bruce T. Blum

The Johns Hopkins University*
Baltimore, Maryland 21205
U.S.A.

This paper describes a tool designed for the life cycle of a
moderate sized information management system, i.e., a data base
application requiring up to 20 man-years to implement. The tool
includes a design methodology, a program generator, and a very
high level application language. Output of the tool is a set of
programs in a target language which can be transported to an
arbitrary computer system. A tool which generates MUMPS code is
in production use. The paper contains an overview of the system
philosophy, a description of the structure, and a preliminary
evaluation of the effectiveness of the MUMPS version of the tool.

1. INTRODUCTION

The problems associated with software development are widely recognized and
require lttle further substantiation. It is clear, for example, that the
reduction in costs for hardware are not being matched by a comparable decrease in
costs for system implementation. Various studies project the growing number of
programmers who will be required to service the ever increasing number of
computers to be manufactured. At the present time there is an alarming backlog
of software projects. Examples of incomplete implementations, unacceptable
performance, cost overruns, and delayed deliveries abound.

The use of tools to improve productivity in software development has gained wide
acceptance. Many tools such as preprocessors, link loaders, and compilers are
standard components in modern operating systems.

Beyond this mandatory set, however, overviews of available automated tools
(Houghton (1980); Software Research Associates (1980)) indicate that most
tools (1) are limited in scope with respect to the total system life cycle, and
(2) tend to be most effective for very large system applications. This paper
reports on an integrated set of tools designed to provide full life cycle
automated support for a specific class of applications: moderate sized
Information Management Systems (IMS).

The IMS is characterized by: a reliance upon a data base; user interaction
designed for an operational setting; limited computation beyond that which can be
expressed in the form of branching trees (decision tables) and closed algorithms;
and the frequent use of formatted printed and displayed outputs. These systems
are developed to satisfy an organization's information needs; they are subject to
constant modification; and--because of their reliance upon a permanent data
base--have a very long projected useful life. A moderate sized IMS is defined as
one which requires from one half to twenty man-years to develop using available

*Department of Biomedical Engineering and the Oncology Center, School of Medicine;
also the Applied Physics Laboratory. This work was supported by Mr. Blum with
the cooperation of the above organizations within the School of Medicine.

off-the-shelf hardware and software systems.

Some of the problems common to these applications are: documentation which is
incomplete and does not reflect recent modifications; the need to spend an
excessive portion of programmer time on the maintenance of existing systems; the
generation of many lines of code which serve only housekeeping functions; and the
absence of validity checks to assure a correct and consistent data base.

The prevalence of these problems can be illustrated anecdotally. For example,
a Datamation survey in 1980 found that IBM users had their applications so back-
logged that 37% would not be implemented in 12 to 24 months, 42% would not be
implemented in the next 2 years, and there was no estimate for when another 8%
would be available for use. Only 13% of the planned applications were scheduled
for completion in less than one year from the date of the survey (Schatz (1980)).
Clearly, a backlog of two years will impact the kinds of requests submitted;
further, the final utility of an application which is over two years in the
making is questionable. The same survey also indicated that only 46% of the
software staff was available for new application development; the remainder of
the staff was devoted to maintenance of old applications, system control
programs, documentation, etc.

In an experiment conducted by Barry Boehm (1980), first year graduate students
were divided into two groups to develop two different versions of an interactive
cost modeling system--one in PASCAL and one in FORTRAN. Five hypotheses were
tested. Among the results were that no difference in the choice of programming
languages could be detected, programming was not the dominant activity in this
small project, and large project software engineering procedures can be effective. Most significant, however, was that only 2% and 3% of the total code
had to do with the model; the remainder was "housekeeping." Moreover, a review
of the acceptance test results indicated that graduate students in computer
science produce systems with unacceptable user interfaces.

A final illustration considers the quality of data recorded (Basden (1980)). A
data base was established on 8,000 patients seen in a health center since 1975.
Data were recorded by encounter (visit). It was decided to test the data for
accuracy, and six tests were made. Among the tests were checks for a valid
registration identifier, consistency between sequential encounters, and the
use of valid problem codes. Four thousand five hundred and sixty-three encounter
records were examined; 1,137 violated at least one context test and 7% of the
total had major errors. Over half of all errors were either an invalid patient
identifier or problem code--inconsistencies which are trivial to avoid at data
entry time.

2.   REQUIREMENTS FOR AN INFORMATION DEVELOPMENT TOOL

There are a variety of tools available to support the implementation of information management systems. For example, each equipment vendor has a set of
proprietary tools which "enhance productivity" and/or "allow system development
in an Englishlike language." New proprietary systems are continuously being
announced, for example, C/SCRIPT by Commerical Systems (Data Base Monthly (1981)).
Unfortunately, few such tools provide a comprehensive environment for the
development and maintenance of small information management systems.

If one treated the development and maintenance of a small information management
system as an application, then the following represents one set of requirements
for a comprehensive tool.

   ●   Maintain all system definition in a data base which facilitates cross-
       referencing and coordination of changes throughout the system life cycle.

- Establish a user interface which allows different modes of use based upon user experience and application complexity.

- Define a specification language which eliminates the need for non-functional, housekeeping processes; provides direct access to data base elements; and which can be translated into compliable code written in an arbitrary target language (e.g., COBOL).

- Manage the system definition to facilitate top-down implementation, rapid prototyping, configuration management, and the preservation of multiple generations of the system and/or data base.

- Package the system in the form of a multistation word processor tied to a host computer. The system maintains the definition data base and transmits code in the target language to the host for compilation and execution.

The Environment for Developing Information and Utility Machines (TEDIUM^{TM}) is a prototype tool designed to satisfy the above requirements. A first generation system was partially implemented on an IBM Series/1 to generate COBOL programs. The present system, in production use on a PDP-11, generates MUMPS code. Portions of the system also have been written in FORTRAN and run on a LSI-11 and Series/1 (Bakalar (1980)). The remainder of this paper is devoted to a discussion of TEDIUM. The next section begins with a description of the IMS life cycle and shows how TEDIUM has been designed to support each phase. This is followed by an overview of how TEDIUM has been implemented. A final section provides a preliminary evaluation of the current MUMPS prototype.

3. OVERVIEW OF TEDIUM

TEDIUM provides an integrated support environment to implement and maintain an IMS. Figure 1 provides a model of this process. The Application Environment is that of the sponsor and user; this is where the delivered IMS will be used. The Descriptive Environment is the realm of the analyst. The media are documents which communicate among the sponsors, users, designers, and implementors throughout the life cycle. The next two environments support (1) the translation of the description (requirements) into a design (specifications) which details how the system will work and (2) the translation of this design into an executable and correct set of programs (coding and testing). System maintenance is shown as a feedback loop involving each step. Iterations and phases are not shown.

3.1 THE DESCRIPTIVE ENVIRONMENT

When considering the Descriptive Environment, several key points should be recognized. First, the greatest risk with an IMS is that the system will not do what the sponsor needed. This is a failure in the transfer of information between the application and descriptive environments. Next, about half (and as much as 70%) of the total life cycle effort is maintenance (Zelkowitz (1978)). Thus, there is a need to integrate documentation maintenance with system change. Finally, the Descriptive Environment provides the only interface between the user and implementor. Therefore, there is a requirement to link each user function with its associated implemented components.

TEDIUM provides support in this environment through the management of text. Because the primary process involves communication among sponsors, users, and designers, text and diagrams are the most effective media. (The current TEDIUM hardware has no graphics capability, and only text can be processed.)

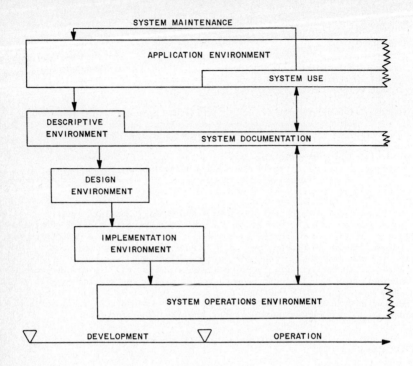

Figure 1
A Model of the System Life Cycle

All text is organized into discreet sections which can be (1) combined to produce
a document or (2) searched to establish a relationship. (A data model for the
text components is presented in the next section.) Material is generally used in
several documents. For example, sections of the top-level description are used
(1) for the initial design document which is accepted by the sponsor, (2) an
introduction to the software documents, and (3) as the introduction for Users'
Manuals. When changes in the systems are documented and approved, all document
sources are automatically updated. The primary reason for maintaining the
documentation in the data base, however, is to support the design process. An
example of how this is done has already been discussed in some detail with
respect to an appointment system (Blum and Brunn (1981));this section provides
only a simple overview.

Figure 2 illustrates the associations among three sets of text information. The
requirements describe what is to be done. The design of how this is to be done
is broken into processes and data groups. Because all text data is retained in
logical blocks, the text within each category is structured as trees. For
example, the requirements for an appointment system might be:

        Process Appointments
            Add an Appointment
                New Patient
                Established Patient
            Cancel or Reschedule
        List Appointments

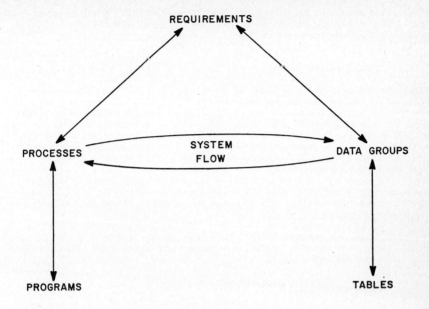

Figure 2
TEDIUM System Definition Tree

During the initial design phase, the analyst would complete the outline and
describe each node in sufficient detail to establish an agreement with the
sponsor.

After a preliminary version of the requirements is completed, structured analysis
(Yourdin (1979); Gane (1979)) is used to decompose the requirements into processes
and data groups. These are documented in similar, hierarchical structures.
Processes (data groups) and the requirements which spawned them are linked
together. A single requirement may initiate several processes (require several
data groups); a single process (data group) may be derived from many requirements.
These links and the system flow (links between processes and data groups) are
managed by TEDIUM. The analyst may interactively trace the design across a
category or within a category. There is also the ability to link the text to the
implementation entities: the programs and relations (called tables in TEDIUM).

3.2 DESIGN ENVIRONMENT

As shown in the previous two figures, all components of the design are linked
to and derived from some node in the descriptive network. The process of design
involves the definition of the identified entities for the creation of the
application system. TEDIUM provides an interactive environment for the analyst
to translate the written description into a very precise specification.

The specification is divided into two classes of information. The first is a
description of the data, the second is the specification of the program. These
specifications are free of data declarations; all programs are generated using

both the data model and the specifications. A discussion of the data model
(Blum (1981a)) and examples of the specifications (Blum (1981b)) are available
elsewhere. This section provides an overview of each.

3.2.1 TEDIUM Tables

TEDIUM uses a relational data model in which the relations are called tables.
The model allows variable length records with variable length indices composed
of more than one index element. In each table, an element is either an index
element or a data element. All tables are stored in alphabetical order by index
key. (Although the relational model is independent of sort order, any interactive system requires that data be accessible in some preestablished order).
The data elements have the following data types: fixed length character, variable
length character, integer, numeric (i.e., floating point), date (i.e., MM/DD/YY),
time (i.e., HH:MM XM), and text. The text data type calls in the TEDIUM text
processor. The value of a text data element may be arbitrarily long and may
include formatting commands. All requirement descriptions use data elements of
the text data type.

The notation used to describe a table differs slightly from that generally used
for relations. For example, assume that there is an application with a patient
data base. The following two tables may be required:

> PATID(<u>PATID</u>)=NAME,AGE,RACE,SEX
> PATNM(NAME,PATID)

The table PATID, indexed by the unique patient identifier PATID, provides the
name and demographic data. Note that the index element PATID is underlined.
This indicates that it has the attribute "defined" which means that the table
PATID will serve as a dictionary for all valid values for the element PATID. That
is, all error tests will reject any value for PATID unless an entry is already in
the table with that value for PATID. Of course, an element can only have the
defined attribute in one table, and a table can have only one defined index
element.

The second table, PATNM, is an alphabetical name index. It has two index
elements which provide uniqueness in the event of two patients with the same
name. TEDIUM allows the designer to relate these two tables by declaring PATNM
to be a secondary table to PATID. When this is done, all changes to PATID are
automatically reflected in PATNM, and PATNM becomes a read only table.

The declaration of these tables is done interactively. The analyst enters an
id (PATID) and name (Patient Identification) for the table. He is next allowed
to document the table using text. Once the table is defined, the system prompts
for index elements. If the element is not yet in the data dictionary, he is
asked if it is to be added. If yes, the user is prompted for the element id, its
name, format and validation criteria (e.g., range of values, pattern match, list
of valid codes, logical expression, etc.). There is also an opportunity to
describe the element. Finally, once the element is known, the system prompts for
the defined attribute (if appropriate) and the role of the element in the table.
The roles include declaring that the element must be supplied, is defaulted to
a given value if not supplied, is computed to be the current value of a given
variable, etc.

The entire process of entering the above tables with their element definitions
takes about 10 minutes. Figure 3 contains the table definition for PATID. All
fields, of course, can be edited interactively.

```
PATID       PATIENT IDENTIFICATION              +UD2001

RELATED TABLE PATNM    PATIENT NAME INDEX                 +UD2002


      This contains the standard patient identification

   INDEX TERMS :
PATID       PATIENT IDENTIFIER              INTEGER   (7)
            ***  ELEMENT IS DEFINED IN THIS TABLE  ***


            This is the standard patient identifier. It is a
            sequentially assigned number with the first two digits
            containg the year of initial assignment.


   DATA TERMS  :
NAME        PATIENT NAME                  VARIABLE LENGTH  (31)
            ROLE IN TABLE IS MANDATORY


            This is the patient name in the form last,first
            truncated to the first 31 characters.

AGE         AGE                           INTEGER  (3)
            ROLE IN TABLE IS MANDATORY


            Patient's age in years.

SEX         SEX                           CHARACTER  (1)
            F         FEMALE
            M         MALE
            U         UNKNOWN
            ROLE IN TABLE IS DEFAULTED TO "U"

RACE        RACE                          CHARACTER  (1)
            B         BLACK
            O         OTHER
            W         WHITE
            ROLE IN TABLE IS MANDATORY



                        Figure 3
                  Sample Table Description
```

3.2.2   TEDIUM PROGRAMS

The executable units in a TEDIUM generated system are programs. To describe how
they are specified, one must present several key TEDIUM concepts.

The first of these is the idea of system style. This defines the general program
structure, user interaction conventions and target language and operating system
to be used. The system style used for ENTRY programs in the current TEDIUM
prototype is partially described in Figure 4. Other system styles might generate
programs in different target languages, allow data entry using a full screen
fill-in-the-blanks methodology, accept inputs from function keys, have a reserved
space in the input screen for error or help messages, etc. The style selected
is typically facility dependent; the need for a consistent unified style is,
of course, obvious.

    1.   Target Language Considerations

- Standard MUMPS using 5K byte partitions for
  both program and data.

    2.   User Interface

- Prompt and scroll. First prompt for index elements.
  When all index terms are supplied, if the entry does not
  exist, prompt for each data element. If the entry
  exists, display the current value and allow user
  modification.

- Provide special functions for editing text and long
  character strings.

- Prompt the user to accept, reject or ignore each
  completed action before database update.
  .
  .
  .

    3.   Functionality

- Create new entries in the file (ADD)
- Edit data in the file (EDIT)
- Delete entries in the file (DELETE)
- List any entry in the file (LIST)
- Produce a tabular display of the contents of the
  file (SCAN)
- Perform all error checking by data type and
  specified range
- Respond to ! and ? and other system-wide operators.
  .
  .
  .

Figure 4
Johns Hopkins Oncology Center MUMPS Style, Entry Program

Once the system style has been defined, it can be used to create generic programs which perform a limited (but frequently used) set of functions. The functions of an ENTRY program in the MUMPS style (E_M) also are given in Figure 4. Other generic programs have been defined for menus (M_M) and prompting (P_M). In general, a generic program $\overline{P}$ may be created in the style S denoted $\overline{P}_S$.

The next concept of TEDIUM is that of the minimal specification. This is the least amount of information required to fully define a generic program. One may consider the minimal specification to be that information which, when given to a programmer together with a style manual, allows the complete and correct coding of the program without further communication. A minimal specification for an ENTRY program in the MUMPS style for the PATID table would be the name of the table. All required information is either in the generic program definition (Figure 4) or the table schema (Figure 3).

Stated from another perspective, the generic ENTRY program can be viewed as a macro which generates a sequence of instructions from its minimal specification. In this sense, it is little more than a very complex READ or WRITE statement. This expanded program follows all the conventions of the style; performs complete edit checks on all data elements; prohibits the generation of invalid entries in the data base; and provides the user with the style defined functions of listing, editing, deleting, etc.

Yet, as one works in an application domain, it is obvious that there are very few problems which can be implemented using a single flat file. Thus, it is necessary to allow for the specification of programs which (1) process more than one table and/or (2) modify the generic program by the insertion of special code. That is, TEDIUM must allow for more complex instructions to be included in the minimal specification.

This leads to the next concept: the TEDIUM language used to create the minimal specifications. This language is decomposed into definition elements (e.g., the table name for a generic program) and instructions (or statements). The definition elements (D) are nonprocedural and the instructions (I) are procedural. Each minimal specification requires that certain definition elements be supplied. Instructions are optionally used to modify the generic processing. For example, the user may insert TEDIUM statements in an ENTRY program before a new entry is to be processed, before an existing entry is to be edited, after the data base has been updated, etc. One type of generic program, the COMPUTATION program, consists exclusively of TEDIUM statements with optional definition elements.

The next concept to be presented is that of the frame (F). TEDIUM separates the functions of a program into those which deal with the logic (the generic specification) and those which deal with the output environment. The frame is used to define the mode of printing (e.g., scroll, full page, random positioning of characters), the output format (head lines, foot lines), and the device format (lines per page, columns per line, interactive or not). By isolating these general attributes, it is possible to use the same frame with many programs. The result is both greater consistency among outputs and ease of specification.

The final TEDIUM concept to be discussed in this section is that of program generation. We say that a program P is defined as a function of the frame F and the generic specification G, i.e., $P(F,G)$. The generic specification, in turn, is a function of the program type for a given style $G(\overline{P}_S,D,I)$. Program generation, therefore, is a transformation of $P(F,\overline{P}_S,D,I)$ as defined in the

TEDIUM data base into a string of instructions in the language specified by the
style S.   Figure 5 illustrates this flow.

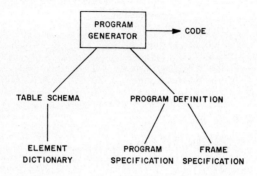

Figure 5
TEDIUM Specifications for Code Generation

The advantages of program generation are:

- The design machine and the execution machine need not be
  the same. Thus programs can be generated for an arbitrary
  computer and/or language; the design tool need not run under
  the same operating system as the target program and vice versa.
  This facilitates transportability and integration of the tool.

- The target language and system are independent of the generator.
  Thus the output programs can be designed to use a DBMS, compiler
  optimization, recovery procedures, or hardware features
  (e.g., light pen) not available to the generator. New
  functions and technology readily can be incorporated into the
  generated programs.

- Because the output programs are independent of the generator,
  they may be integrated with existing programs and systems.
  Generated and hand coded programs also are easily combined to
  support gradual transfer from a manually coded to a TEDIUM
  generated application.

- Generic programs can be modified to meet local style standards.
  In this way generic applications can be designed (e.g., an
  appointment system) and used to generate systems for a range of
  languages and equipment.

3.3 APPLICATION AND OPERATIONS ENVIRONMENTS

The Application Environment has needs which must be met. These needs are
independent of the kind of computer or programming language to be used.   The
hardware/software system, on the other hand, has a capability which is

independent of the application. While there are potentially some mismatches
between applications and computer systems, virtually all IMS applications can
be supported by virtually any off-the-shelf system with the proper capacity.
There are accounts receivable systems in COBOL, FORTRAN, PL/I, BASIC, MUMPS,
APL, and (perhaps someday) ADA. The limiting factor for these systems is not
the language and environment which they use; rather it is their design.

TEDIUM provides a comprehensive environment for translating a user's needs into
a system and assisting him in its use and maintenance. In the IMS application
environment there are users who understand their operation but know little
about computers. TEDIUM attempts to provide a friendly and comprehensible tool
to bridge the gap between user and implementor. For example, the term "table"
is used to facilitate understanding; the table schema (Figure 3) is readable
by both the user and designer.

4.   IMPLEMENTATION OF TEDIUM

TEDIUM transforms data. Starting with the minimal specification, it reads data
in one form and converts it to data in another form. The process continues until
the output is code in the target language. In the case of the present prototype,
the host and target languages are the same. Therefore, the generated program is
available for immediate testing. For configurations in which the host and target
differ, TEDIUM may be supported by an interpreter. In what follows, the TEDIUM
data model is described and then the process of program generation is explained.

4.1   THE DATA MODEL FOR TEDIUM

To illustrate the operation of TEDIUM, we first describe some of the basic tables.
The requirements, for example, are specified in

> REQ(REQID)=REQNM,REQTX

where REQID is a defined identifier, REQNM is the descriptive name (a variable
length character string not to exceed 60 characters) and REQTX is the text
description. (As previously stated, TEDIUM supports a text data type which
causes all inputs and edits for elements of that type to be managed by a text
processor.)

The requirements tree is then defined by

> REQT(REQID,REQN)=LREQID

where REQN is a number to sequence this node among all the nodes linked to REQID.
LREQID is a variable defined to have the same attributes as REQID. For all but
the lowest nodes, there will exist another entry in REQT with the index element
REQID containing the same value as LREQID.

Finally, an inverted table

> REQI(LREQID,REQN,REQID)

may be required to guarantee a hierarchical structure. Note that these tables
produce a hierarchical structure independent of the implementation. In the case
of the MUMPS prototype, a tree is defined in a relational model to be implemented
using a MUMPS hierarchical access method. The primary advantage of this definition, however, is that it provides rapid access to any individual node or branch
in the tree.

Similar tables are available for processes (PRO) and data groups (DAT). The

link illustrated in Figure 2 between requirements and processes is implemented
by

                    REQPRO(REQID,PROID)
                    PROREQ(PROID,REQID)

where PROREQ is a secondary table to REQPRO. Other links in the documentation
data base are constructed in a parallel manner. The system flow links are
somewhat more complicated because they represent the triple

                    process to data to process

The data model is implemented as a set of four tables. The first defines the
table identifiers

                    TID(TID)=TNAME,TTX

where TID is a 6 character identifier (a MUMPS restriction), TNAME is its
short descriptive name, and TTX is a text description. The contents of the table
are defined in

                    TEID(TID,TTYP,TNO)=EID,TDEF,TROLE

where TTYP is either "index" or "data", TNO is a sequence number to specify order,
EID is the element identifier, TDEF is the defined attribute flag, and TROLE is
the element's role in the table (e.g., mandatory, default, etc.).

The elements are defined in

                    EID(EID)=ENAME,ETX,EFMT,EVAL

where the data elements are the name, text description, format and validation
criteria. A secondary table to TEID provides a cross-index of element use with

                    ETID(EID,TDEF,TID)=TTYP,TNO

Note that this table provides facilities for rapid identification of all defined
elements and their associated dictionary tables.

The definition of the programs is slightly more complex. The program, frame,
and generic specification identifiers are each defined in the tables

                    PID(PID)=PNAME,PTX
                    FID(FID)=FNAME,FTX
                    SID(SID)=SNAME,STX

The program definition is given in

                    PSID(PID)=FID,SID

The definitions of both the frames and generic program specifications combine
defined elements and instructions in order to produce the minimal specifications.
Only the generic program specification will be discussed here.

Each defined specification element is identified in a special table. The
minimal specification for an ENTRY program contains the table to be processed.
This might be stored in the table

                    SDTID(SID)=TID

If one were to allow more than one table to be used by an ENTRY program, the table would be modified to

SDTID(SID,STNO)=TID

The specification of instructions is slightly more complex. In this case, the table must identify both the specification and the place in the generic specification where the instructions are to be inserted. To place instructions in an ENTRY program in the location which follows the code in which the data are written to the data base, the following table entries would be used

SDINS(SID,"AFTER WRITE",SINO)=command

where SINO determines the sequence of commands. All TEDIUM commands are composed of five data elements as is described below. Therefore, the general instruction table is

SDINS(SID,SLOC,SINO)=LABEL,GUARD,OP,INSTR,CONTR

From this brief discussion it can be seen how the data model implements the definition of a program as $P(F,G)$ and of a generic specification as $G(\overline{P}_S,D,I)$.
The table schema is not used in the definition; it is accessed only during the process of program generation.

4.2 PROGRAM GENERATION

All program generation uses the TEDIUM language. Each statement in the language is composed of five fields:

> LABEL   A statement label, generally optional.
>
> GUARD   A logical predicate which must be true if the command is to be executed. This is always optional.
>
> OP   The required command operator.
>
> INSTR   The instructions for the operator.
>
> CONTR   One or two statement labels which indicate where control should be sent following the execution of this command. If two labels are given, the second is used in the event of an abnormal action.

The language commands are IMS oriented, housekeeping-free and quite powerful.

To illustrate, the statement[1] "Input SID" performs the following operation

> 1. Prompt with the value of ENAME for EID="SID" in EID.
>
> 2. Read the input.
>
> 3. If the input is "?" print the EID definition of "SID". Go to 1.
>
> 4. Test input against EFMT and EVAL for "SID". If invalid, print "ERROR" and return to 1.
>
> 5. Test input for an entry in SID with the input value. If none, print "ERROR" and return to 1.
>
> 6. Store result in "SID".

Statement modifiers are available to accept undefined input values, allow or
disallow null inputs, change the prompt command, support editing, etc.

From this example, two facts are clear. First the language is very concise and
reduces the effort required to specify and implement the application. Secondly,
the implementation language is independent of the TEDIUM language; the flow for
Input can be coded in COBOL, MUMPS, PL/I, or any other target language. The
present prototype does this translation using custom coded routines. There are
extensions to the TEDIUM language, however, which allow all generation to be
bootstrapped from a set of TEDIUM primitives.

Given this set of TEDIUM commands, one may now build programs. A data entry
program for the table SID might look like the command set shown in Figure 6.

Label	Guard	Operator	Instruction	Control
INDEX		Input	SID	
	SID null	-		$QUIT
		Get	all data from SID	/NEW
		PRompt	(E)DIT (D)ELETE (Q)UIT	
	Return = Q	-		$QUIT
	Return = D	DELete	SID	INDEX
RETRY		Input	SNAME in EDIT mode	
		Input	STX in EDIT mode	
		PRompt	(A)CCEPT (R)ETRY (I)GNORE	
	Return = R	-		RETRY
	Return = I	-		INDEX
		Put	all data into SID	INDEX
NEW		PRompt	ADD AN ENTRY (Y/N)	
	Return = N	-		INDEX
		Undefine	SNAME and STX	RETRY

Figure 6
Sample Entry Program

The Get unpacks the data elements from the SID table entry with the preset index
element value of SID. If no such entry exists, the abnormal return is made to
NEW. PRompt prints the given string, reads an input, and accepts no values not
set off by parenthesis in the string. Input with the EDIT option echoes the
current value and allows the user to either alter or accept the value. If the
value is undefined, then there is no echo. Put writes the values of the data
elements to the table entry specified by the current value of SID. This is an
example of a COMPUTATION program which is composed entriely of TEDIUM commands.

To create a generic ENTRY program, three things are required:

 ● Fixed blocks of code (e.g., the PRompt command in Figure 6).

 ● Commands which are a function of the minimal specification (e.g., Put and
   Input).

● User supplied instructions.

In the case of the MUMPS prototype, each of these inputs is managed by custom code. The next generation of TEDIUM will allow each generic program to be defined with an extended set of the TEDIUM language (denoted by a period before the operator and processing values). Using this set, the first part of Figure 6 would be created by processing the input set:

```
(SID is preset to the specification identifier)
Get           TID from SDTID
For Each      TNO in TEID with TTYP = index
Get           EID from TEID
.Input        .EID
END
.Get          all data from .TID      /NEW
.PRompt       ...
```

The identifier of the table, TID, is established by getting it from the table SDTID for the present value of SID. For Each is a looping instruction which reads through the table TEID using the preset value of TID and the value of TTYP set to "index". It returns each unique value of TNO with those constraints. Get sets the value of EID from the TEID entry with the current values of TID, TTYP, and TNO. The .Input statements first sets .EID to the current value of EID and then writes to the processing output set the string

    Input   (Contents of EID)

The END indicates the end of the For Each loop.

When all index terms have been processed, the .Get command writes to the processing output set

    Get all data from (Contents of TID) /NEW

The processing continues in this manner. This flow creates n index prompts for each of the n index elements in the selected table. The insertion of user supplied instructions is processed by a special TEDIUM command to copy from the specification (SDINS) for a given location (SLOC) in the minimal specification to the output set. The final output set is composed of executable TEDIUM commands which then can be translated into strings of target language code.

This concludes the overview of TEDIUM implementation. Clearly, many details have been omitted. For example, in the case of MUMPS programs it is necessary to decompose the total program into logically complete routines which operate in 5K partitions. Also there is a requirement to alter the prompts in an ENTRY program beyond the facility provided by the Input command. Nevertheless, this brief overview indicates the general flow for program generation.

5. PRELIMINARY EVALUATION

TEDIUM is now in production use at the Johns Hopkins Medical Institutions. It is being used to:

● Generate all user TEDIUM programs.

● Convert a sophisticated clinical information system (Blum and Lenhard (1979)) which includes heuristic decision making tools (Blum (1980)).

● Generate an online ambulatory care information system with medical, registration and financial information (McColligan (1981)).

● Implement a resource management system which schedules
  operating rooms and associated resources.

● Produce smaller systems for social work management-by-objective,
  equipment inventory, etc.

Because the system is not yet complete or fully documented, it is premature to
evaluate its utility and impact. In what follows, the current experience with
TEDIUM is discussed in three broad areas: productivity, quality, and
acceptance.

5.1 PRODUCTIVITY

Figure 7 illustrates three models of the implementation cycle. Model A is the
historic early coding method. Model B shows that there is a reduction in testing
and the overall time frame when there is greater emphasis on design. The third
model represents the use of TEDIUM. If one accepts that TEDIUM performs as
described in the previous sections, the relative time frames for models B and
C can be justified as follows:

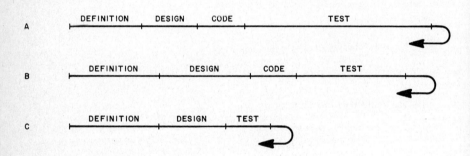

A. EARLY CODING MODEL

B. CAREFUL DESIGN MODEL

C. TEDIUM MODEL

Figure 7
Three Implementation Model Timelines

● Definition. TEDIUM provides some automated tools to assist in the
  definition phase. There is no evidence, however, that the
  availability of these tools reduces the time required for system
  definition.

● Design. Through the use of minimal specifications, TEDIUM
  reduces the quantity of information which must be included

in the full specification. By eliminating most of the
housekeeping, the specifications are more dense (concise)
and should, therefore, require less time to produce.

● Code. Since TEDIUM generates all code from the specifications,
there is no coding process.

● Test. The traditional testing phase includes unit and
integrated testing. Because of a heavy reliance upon
housekeeping-free specifications, little unit testing
is required. The result is the equivalent of rapid
prototyping in which the user interacts with the system
to refine the man-machine interface.

● Maintenance. Maintenance of software is a combination of
defect correction and design modification. A benefit
of program generation is that all specifications and
system documentation always accurately describe the
implemented programs. TEDIUM also provides tools which
access the design network to facilitate maintenance.

If one accepts this rationale, then TEDIUM clearly offers a potential for
significant enhancement in productivity. Is there evidence to support the
claim?

In order to begin an evaluation of TEDIUM productivity and its use in a rapid
prototype environment, a blind study was initiated on a new project. This
multi-year activity entails the development of a resource management system for
the Johns Hopkins Department of Anesthesiology and Critical Care. The first
application to be implemented is an operating room (OR) scheduling system which
will allow department secretaries to interactively schedule the OR's based upon
the surgeon's schedule and system constraints, e.g., certain services (surgery,
orthopedics, gynecology, etc.) have access to given rooms for fixed times,
allowances must be made for preparation and cleanup, etc.

A faculty member chose this task as her first TEDIUM assignment.[2] In approximately two manweeks, an interactive system which posted and reassigned schedules,
maintained a model of OR assignment by service, and produced a semigraphic
display of OR utilization was produced. It was accepted by the sponsor and
installed on his computer for prototype evaluation. The system consisted of
25 programs and a data base with 6 relations (tables) and 18 elements.

Figure 8 summarizes the number of program generations, lines of specification
written and resulting characters of MUMPS code produced. The program generations
are divided into two categories. Those called "new" are the generations which
occur during the first week of creation. These represent the elimination of
defects based upon compliance with the initial design concept. The program
generations after this period, "mods," represent changes which are brought about
as the result of integration, a user response, or a better understanding of the
problem. It is interesting to note that the preinstallation effort is roughly
equally divided between these two categories.

The specifications are counted in both "lines" and characters (including system
generated housekeeping). Since the MUMPS target language is dense and allows
many commands on a single line, only a character count is retained for MUMPS.
In general, MUMPS programs with one command per line will average less than 30
characters per line. Defining a MUMPS line to be 30 characters, a summary of the
average number of lines by program type follows:

Pgm Type	Pgm ID	Program Function	No. Gens New	No. Gens Mods.	Specification Lines	Specification Chars	Programs Gen	Program Size (Chars)
Menu	MANES	Main Menu	6	2	18	526	6	6,931
Comp	RSVOR	Reserve an OR	8	1	10	187	1	1,471
Entry	ADPOST	Post a new scheduled case	5	5	20	138	7	9,493
Entry	EDPOST	Edit a posted case	2	6	17	61	7	8,953
Comp	CHGSCH	Change a posted case	3	0	12	348	1	1,391
Comp	CHGRSV	Change a reservation	3	0	10	185	1	2,679
Comp	DELRSV	Delete a reservation	2	1	13	217	1	3,223
Comp	EDRESV	Edit a resveration	2	0	11	163	1	2,771
Comp	DSPSCH	Display OR schedule by service	18	7	27	604	2	3,263
Comp	DSPALL	Display OR schedule by room	5	9	15	348	1	2,463
Comp	DSPIND	Display schedule for an OR	6	8	17	427	1	2,859
Comp	DSPOR	Utility display routine	19	23	22	588	1	2,351
Entry	EDMODL	Edit schedule module	2	1	2	8	6	6,554
Comp	EDSHMD	EDMODL continued	2	8	18	357	1	1,994
Comp	MODSCH	Modify general schedule	6	10	31	690	1	2,499
Comp	MODLST	MODSCH continued	1	0	10	187	1	469
Comp	EDPAT	Edit patient identification	2	2	13	238	1	3,275
Comp	SELOR	Select valid OR	4	3	19	410	1	1,545
Comp	SELSRV	Select valid service	5	3	8	124	1	1,155
Comp	SELTIM	Select valid time	7	4	16	557	1	2,887
Comp	SELPAT	Select patient by name or identifier	3	7	17	364	1	1,349
Prompt	PRPAT	Patient name look-up	2	3	5	23	1	1,243
Entry	ADPAT	Add a patient to the data base	3	3	6	11	3	2,215
Comp	CHGHNO	Change a patient identifier (HNO)	1	3	11	295	1	3,360
Comp	CHGHN1	CHGHNO continued	1	1	5	61	1	419
TOTALS			118	110	353	7,117	50	74,349
AVERAGES			4.72	4.4	14.12	284.68	2	2973.96

Figure 8
Program Characteristics, OR Scheduling Project

		Specification Lines	MUMPS Lines
1	Menu Program	18	231
1	Prompt program	5	41
4	Entry programs	11	226
19	Computation programs	15	68
	All Programs	14	99
	Total Number of Lines	353	2,478

From this preliminary study, it can be seen that 35 lines of specification were created each day. While this is high, it is a reasonable target for a single programmer working on a relatively small project. The fact that over two thousand lines of code were required to convert these minimal specifications into executable code illustrates how much of a programmer's time generally is spent on housekeeping functions. In a traditional coding environment, this housekeeping is costly, prone to error, and can obscure one's understanding of the system objectives.

5.2 QUALITY

Program Quality can be measured in two ways:

- Number of defects in the final product

- Efficiency of the generated code

Defects are introduced into TEDIUM programs as the result of TEDIUM errors and application design errors. The number of TEDIUM errors is relatively low. This is primarily the result of 4-6 man-years of production use in which most errors were identified. Once a TEDIUM error is found and corrected, all affected programs are regenerated and the correction is propagated.

As long as a user may write DO WHILE 1=0 there is always the potential for design errors. Because the TEDIUM specifications are short, housekeeping-free, and easy to read, the number of errors tends to be small. Many syntax free errors such as invalid use of a table or data element are found by the program generator. Most other errors can be rapidly identified during the interactive testing phase.

The effectiveness of the programs has not been measured. Because the output is an independent program as opposed to a set of parameters used in calls to existing programs, there is little reduction in efficiency between generated and hand-crafted programs.

The TEDIUM generated programs tend to be a little larger than custom designed programs. This difference may be as much as 20% larger, but this has not been examined. Reasons for the increased size are (1) the completeness of TEDIUM programs (they always do the error testing and look for "?" inputs even where this may not be necessary), (2) the use of larger variable names and labels (generally eight characters), and (3) the difficulty in maximizing efficiency for special operations.

All generated programs follow a clearly defined structure, but the use of internally generated symbols makes the MUMPS code difficult to read. Thus, while the generated code is transportable and modifiable, the standard generated product is not readily suitable for general distribution.

5.3 USER ACCEPTANCE

There are two users--programmer/analysts and sponsors/end users. The latter are not aware of the use of TEDIUM beyond its ability to rapidly prototype and accommodate changes. Reaction of the first class of users is mixed but positive. The primary reason for the limited acceptance is that, unlike Paul Mason, we released our system before it was time. The justification for this was the desire to use TEDIUM for two major development activities. This premature utilization led to system use with incomplete or unavailable documentation, having users work with the system when it was incomplete and still being debugged, and not offering formal training on the use of the system. Further, the target language of MUMPS (1) has some very useful online features which are not available in TEDIUM and (2) is more fun to write programs in. The author believes that the availability of formal training, reference documentation and a complete system will improve user acceptance. It is assumed, moreover, that acceptance (and productivity) will be considerably higher with persons working in a less friendly environment (e.g., batch COBOL programming).

6. CONCLUSION

Recent conferences on software productivity and management have suggested that major gains can be achieved through the reuse of programs (NBS Workshop (1981)). It has also been postulated that defect free levels of 99% can be achieved only through reuse combined with program generation (Jones (1981)). TEDIUM provides a means to specify generic programs which can be modified for specific applications. These generic programs solve a general problem in a way which allows others to "reuse" the solution. The challenge of implementing generic programs provides the justification to invest in the proper and complete validation of these programs. In this way, only a few complex programs are written; the bulk of the application is derived from variations of the generic programs. Finally, this division of tasks into application design and special-ized programming may allow us to direct the limited number of computer pro-fessionals to those assignments which best suit their interests and talents.

Still, it must be recognized that the scope of TEDIUM is restricted to a single application area: the IMS. Moreover, even though the tool is in daily production use by ten persons, it is neither complete nor exportable. Nevertheless, the prototype demonstrates what can be done in an integrated program generation environment. The present version of the tool can be available in a multiuser system operating on hardware which sells in the $30,000 range. Thus, it is reasonable to project that later generations will be available as a "code generator/analyst work station" networked to computers, word processors, and communication devices.

FOOTNOTES

1 Lower case letters are included to enhance readability. They are not stored.

2 I wish to thank Elizabeth McColligan for her assistance with this preliminary evaluation. Since the study is no longer blind, we are collecting information about the system's implementation and expect to perform a more comprehensive evaluation once the OR scheduling system has been in operational use.

REFERENCES

1. Houghton, R.C. and Oakley, K.A. (eds.) NBS Software Tools Database, NBSIR 80-2159, National Bureau of Standards, Washington, October 1980.

2. Automated Tools for Software Engineering Seminar, (Software Research Associates, San Francisco, California, October 1980).

3. Schatz, W., FOCUS, Mainframe Industry Survey, Datamation, (June 1980), 45.

4. Boehm, B.W., Developing Small-Scale Application Software Products: Some Experimental Results, in: Lavington, S.H. (ed.), Information Processing 80, (North-Holland, Amsterdam, 1980), 321-326.

5. Basden, A. and Clark, E.M., Data Integrity in a General Practice Computer System (CLINICS), Int. Jrnl. Bio-Medical Computing 11 (1980) 519-521, (Elsevier/North-Holland).

6. C/SCRIPT Eases Programmer Burden, Data Base Monthly 1:4 (May 1981) 2.

7. Bakalar, K.M., Trocki, M., Blum, B. and Grossman, R., Internal Report, An Overview of the WHIM Database Manager for the IBM Series/1 (July 1980).

8. Zelkowitz, M.V., Perspective on Software Engineering, Computing Surveys 10:2 (1978) 197-216.

9. Blum, B.I. and Brunn, C.W., Implementing An Appointment System with TEDIUM, Fifth Annual Symposium on Computer Applications in Medical Care, (Nov. 1981).

10. Yourdon, E. and Constantine, L.L., Structured Design (Prentice-Hall, Englewood Cliffs, New Jersey, 1979).

11. Gane, C. and Sarson, T., Structured Systems: Tools and Techniques (Prentice-Hall, Englewood Cliffs, New Jersey, 1979).

12. Blum, B., A MUMPS Program Generator with a Relational Data Base Manager, MUMPS Users' Group (Niagara Falls, N.Y., June 1981).

13. Blum, B., Program Generation with TEDIUM, An Illustration, Trends and Applications 1981 (National Bureau of Standards, Gaithersburg, Maryland, May 1981).

14. Blum, B.I., Lenhard, Jr.,R.E., An Oncology Clinical Information System, Computer Magazine (November 1979) 42-50.

15. Blum, B.I., Lenhard, Jr.,R.E. and McColligan, E.E., Protocol Directed Patient Care Using a Computer, Fourth Annual Symposium on Computer Applications in Medical Care (November 1980).

16. McColligan, E.E., Blum, B.I. and Brunn, C.W., An Automated Core Medical Record System for Ambulatory Care, SAMS/SCM Conference on Computers in Ambulatory Medicine (Oct/Nov 1981).

17. NBS Workshop on Programming Environments, reported in ACM Software Engineering Notes, 6:4 (August 1981) and Fall Compcon 81, IEEE 81CH17023-0. Also in Fall Compcon 81, see note by Munson (p. 310), paper by Boehm (p. 2-16).

18. Jones, C., The State of the Art of Software Development, ACM Professional Development Seminar Vugraphs (April 1981).

Automated Tools for Information Systems Design
H.-J. Schneider and A.I. Wasserman (eds.)
North-Holland Publishing Company

AN INTEGRATED ENVIRONMENT FOR PROGRAM VISUALIZATION*

Christopher F. Herot, Gretchen P. Brown
Richard T. Carling, Mark Friedell
David Kramlich, Ronald M. Baecker**

Computer Corporation of America
575 Technology Square
Cambridge, Massachusetts, USA

This paper reports on the design of a program visualization (PV) environment, intended to provide lifecycle support for software development. The PV environment will capitalize on recent progress in the graphical representation of information and low-cost color graphics, to provide designers and programmers with both static and dynamic (animated) views of systems. The aim is to support maintainers of large (10**6 lines of code), complex software systems. The PV system will, in effect, "open the side of the machine" to permit users to look inside and watch their programs run. In this paper, we survey categories of program illustrations and then present and motivate the design philosophy that we are pursuing for the PV environment.

1. INTRODUCTION

Graphical representations have demonstrated their utility in a wide variety of design and implementation activities as a means of illustrating complex relationships among components of systems. It would be inconceivable to build a ship, airplane, factory, or piece of electronic equipment without the use of diagrams. These illustrations can capture essential features while suppressing extraneous detail, and they can often be understood more readily than ordinary text. While such illustrations find widespread use in computer programming, they are almost always manually generated, making production and revision laborious.

---

* This research was supported by the Defense Advanced Research Project Agency of the Department of Defense and was monitored by the Office of Naval Research under Contract No. N00014-80-C-0683. The views and conclusions contained in this document are those of the authors and should not be interpreted as necessarily representing the official policies, either expressed or implied, of the Defense Department, the Office of Naval Research, or the U.S. Government.

** R.M. Baecker also with Human Computing Resources Corp., Toronto.

237

One result of manual graphics generation is that diagrams have a tendency to become obsolete as the software they describe is implemented and changed. A second result is that the full variety and utility of graphical images remains unexploited. Third, the lack of tools for creating animated images restricts the ability to illustrate an essentially dynamic process such as a computer program. This is not to say that automated graphical representations have been totally neglected. There has been some success in automating production of static representations of programs (e.g., [8,16,18]). The idea of using computer-generated images to visualize the dynamic behavior of programs was developed in the earliest days of computer graphics ([10,20,34]), and dynamic visualizations have received continued attention (e.g., [3,4,6,9,15,21,22,40]). Only recently, however, have hardware and software advances been made which would allow automated production of both static and dynamic illustrations to become cost-effective for a broad range of applications. In addition, significant research remains to be done before diverse graphical representations can be successfully integrated within a single environment.

The Computer Corporation of America is in the first year of a three year effort to design and implement a program visualization (PV) system. The verb visualize means "to see or form a mental image of". We want to aid programmers in the formation of clear and correct mental images of the structure and function of programs. Program visualization has great promise for all stages of the software lifecycle. Our research will focus on illustrating the dynamic behavior of programs, which we expect to be of most use in testing, debugging, maintenance, and training. We want the PV system to, in effect, "open the side of the machine" so that the user can form an accurate model of the program.

The PV system will provide an integrated graphics environment, capitalizing on recent progress in the graphical representation of information and low-cost color graphics. The aim is to support builders and maintainers of large (10**6 lines of code), complex software systems. (We are excluding, however, real time systems.) This tool is targeted primarily for use with programs written in Ada [1], the proposed standard DoD language.

The system which is envisioned will provide individuals who must build and maintain a complex software system with access to a variety of graphical representations. These will include static descriptions, such as module hierarchies and requirements specifications, and dynamic illustrations, such as procedure activations and storage allocations. It will be possible to display several different representations of the same portion of a system (or the same representation of several different portions) simultaneously through the use of multiple screens or multiple viewports on one screen. Since we are focusing on the dynamic behavior of programs, we will make extensive use of computer animation.

This paper is intended to initiate a debate concerning the characteristics of a good graphics environment for software production. Section 2 surveys a number of categories of information that merit graphical presentation. The number and variety of these categories suggests that fuller exploitation of graphics can profoundly influence software production, just as text editing facilities have changed the way that papers are written. The challenge that we see is to encompass the volume and diversity of this information within a coherent conceptual framework. Section 3 expounds a design philosophy for PV. We address there three significant problems: integrating the categories of illustrations identified in Section 2, enhancing graphical facilities, and instrumenting the program. Implementation plans for the PV system are discussed in Section 4, with a summary in Section 5.

2. CATEGORIES OF VISUALIZATIONS

It is our claim that although graphics has long been a tool in program development and documentation, the full power of graphics has yet to be acknowledged or exploited. This section lists ten categories of program illustrations that, together, can be of use throughout the software lifecycle. These categories were one result of a six month study conducted to provide a conceptual framework for program visualization. Some categories of illustrations have already been well explored with respect to programs, and the PV environment will draw on this work directly. Other categories have been less thoroughly explored, and suggestions for new directions are included here. The ten categories are:

1. System requirements diagrams
2. Program function diagrams
3. Program structure diagrams
4. Communication protocol diagrams
5. Composed and typeset program text
6. Program comments and commentaries
7. Diagrams of flow of control
8. Diagrams of structured data
9. Diagrams of persistent data
10. Diagrams of the program in the host environment

Many of these categories can apply to either the program or its specific activations. Moreover, illustrations can be either static or dynamic. Static illustrations portray the program at some instant of execution time, or they portray those aspects of a program which are invariant over some interval. Dynamic illustrations portray the progress of an executing program.

We shall now look at each of the ten categories of illustration in more detail.

2.1 System Requirements Diagrams

A computer program always exists as part of some larger system (not necessarily a fully automated one). Therefore, PV tools must assist in the portrayal of the function and structure of that system. The tools should also aid in the specification of the constraints imposed by the system on the program.

One very powerful method of describing system structure is the IDEF or SADT technique, developed by SofTech [29]. An IDEF model is a graphical representation of a system in terms of its subsystems and in terms of the data and control flow that links them together. The method deals with the hierarchic nature of most systems quite naturally, and it provides a methodology for organizing the bookkeeping associated with large complex system descriptions.

A complete requirements specification also contains constraints on the program's design, constraints such as execution speed, program size, user interface style, implementation vehicle, implementation cost, and the like. We are investigating whether there is any significant role for graphics in describing these latter specifications.

2.2 Program Function Diagrams

"What does the program do?" is usually the first question that one asks about a program. For many types of programs, program function can be viewed as a mapping from program input to program output.

We can talk about the relationship of program input to output in two very different ways: a statement of the program's function in general terms or an enumeration of a number of input-output pairs. The former is a more powerful and useful description, but, because it is an abstraction, it poses difficult problems for graphical representation.

Graphical portrayal of sample behaviors is a much more straightforward proposition. Thus one approach to the visualization of program function is to provide a "casebook" through which the user can browse, inducing a model of what the program is supposed to do by seeing what it actually does on a carefully selected set of sample inputs. The choice of these sample inputs can have a significant effect on the utility of this technique. For example, in understanding a factorial function, important values and classes are 0, 1, positive integers, negative integers, reals, and non-numerics.

2.3 Program Structure Diagrams

"How is the program organized?" is often the second question that one asks about a program. Program structure has a well-developed history of graphical notation. Relatively recent examples are the HIPO (Hierarchy plus Input-Process-Output) technique [14,33], which integrates structure diagrams and function diagrams, and the composite design structural notation [23].

2.4 Communication Protocol Diagrams

Once it is known how a program is divided into its component parts, it is useful to know how those parts communicate. This is especially important when the program consists of many processes running on one or more processors. An illustration of the potential paths for data flow between modules can be displayed as part of another diagram. For instance, the program structure diagram can be overlaid with lines showing the data paths between modules. By using this technique dynamically, the actual flow of data can be monitored during execution. For example, the SDD-1 distributed data base system [30] at CCA employs a color graphics terminal to show data transfers between sites on the Arpanet as they occur. This monitoring technique has proven useful both as a demonstration and a debugging aid. Figure 1 is a reproduction of a typical SDD-1 illustration, streamlined for the purposes of this paper. Except where otherwise noted, the figures in this paper are all handdrawn mockups.

2.5 Composed and Typeset Program Text

The central activity in the visualization of programs has always been the reading of program code. While alternative graphical techniques are proposed here, there will still be cases where code must be examined. This task can be made significantly easier than it is at present. Some relevant typographic tools that can be applied to the display of programs are:

1. The use of _typographic hierarchies_ for distinguishing a program's constituent elements that belong to various syntactic or semantic categories. Typographic hierarchies are implemented by the consistent and controlled use of a variety of type fonts, type styles within a font (bold, condensed, italic, etc.), and point sizes.

2. The use of a _rich symbol repertoire_ employing a wider range of symbols and colors than are currently used. (Gutenberg had more than 300 symbols in his type case.)

3. The use of _composition and layout_ to facilitate the structured perusal of a program's constituent substructures. Layout conventions include the use of indentation, horizontal paragraphing, vertical paragraphing, pagination, footnotes, marginal notes, and page headers. The use of computer graphics also permits dynamic techniques such as colored highlighting over selected or active portions of program text.

These techniques can be applied both to produce displays on high resolution terminals and to produce hard copy on a demand basis. Figure 2 shows the application of some of these techniques to a subroutine written in C.

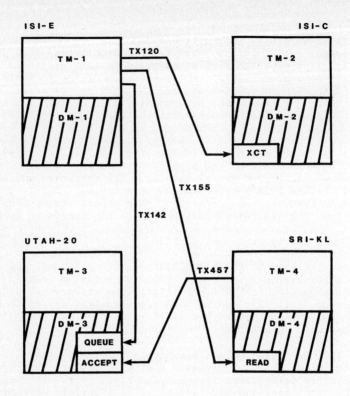

Figure 1. A snapshot of a dynamic illustration of communication in SDD-1, a distributed data base system. Four sites are shown. Transaction modules (TMs) send transactions (arrows) to data modules (DMs).

sdms_copy (afilm)	copy film from core buffer to local buffer
```struct node *afilm;{int curmap[], tvfilt[];int x1, y1, x2, y2; film = (struct filmdata *) afilm - > id; if (film = = NULL) return FAIL; framelink = film - > frame; frame = (struct framedata *) framelink - > id; if (frame = = NULL) return FAIL;```	
```x1 = film - > xfilm + frame - > dx;y1 = film - > yfilm + frame - > dy;if (frame - >len = = 0 I I frame - >ht = = 0) { x2 = x1 + film - > frame_len - 1; y2 = y1 + film - > frame_ht - 1; }else { x2 = x1 + frame - > len - 1; y2 = y1 + frame - > ht - 1; }```	compute coordinates of frame window (x1,y1) (x2,y2)
feedout **(curmap, tvfilt, x1, y1, x2, y2);** **show_frame (afilm);** **return SUCCESS;** }	call feedout to copy

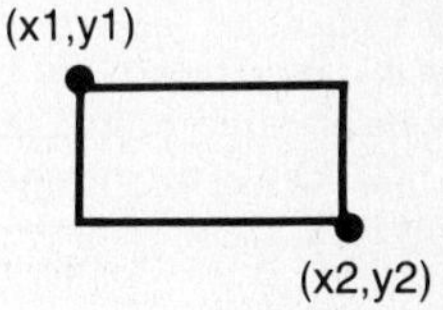

Figure 2. Use of layout and typography for code and comments. The subroutine sdms_copy is written in C. Typography is used to emphasize important lines of the subroutine, and comments appear on the right in blocks to indicate their scope.

2.6 Program Comments and Commentaries

Program comments, often known as internal documentation, are analogous to the footnotes and marginal notes of conventional literary expression. Program commentaries, often known as external documentation, are analogous to prefaces, introductions, postscripts, and critical expository analyses. Both comments and commentaries are an important part of conventional programming discipline, yet they fall far short of attaining their ultimate potential. How can they be improved?

The greatest potential for improvement comes from an area for which there is no technological fix, that is, the ability of programmers and documentation specialists to write in English with clarity and consistency. An integrated graphics system can, however, provide significant aid to the programmer in other respects. If a PV system supplies a variety of graphical representations to illustrate different facets of a program, then there will be much less need for pure text comments and commentary. Comments and commentary will tend to be limited to very general remarks on the one hand, and to very particular observations (e.g., noting exceptions and special cases), on the other. Comments and commentary, in their reduced role, can also benefit from the typesetting and composition techniques discussed above for program text. (See Figure 2, for the use of lines and spacing to delineate the scope of comments.) Finally, completeness and consistency of comments and commentary can be supported (although never, of course, assured) by the programming environment.

2.7 Diagrams of Flow of Control

"What happens when the program executes?" is another important question about a program. "In what order do things happen?" is one subquestion, with diagrams of flow of control as a relatively familiar means of conveying the answer. (Another subquestion, apropos of the effect of program execution on underlying data, is discussed in Section 2.8.)

Flow charts, Nassi-Shneiderman Diagrams [8,24], Software Diagram Descriptions [18], GREENPRINTS [5], and others are a beginning, but they portray only the static structure, not the actual flow of control during program execution. Some formalisms already provide a means to indicate flow of control (e.g., the tokens in Petri nets [26]). It is only a short distance to computer animations of flow of control, with tokens, highlighting, and/or color changes used to denote the current state of the execution.

2.8 Diagrams of Structured Data

"What happens when the program executes?" can also be answered in terms of the data base upon which the program is operating. This data base includes the program input at the initiation of execution and the program output at the termination of execution. The data base also includes the variables that are the raison d'etre of a program, such as the data being sorted by a quicksort, and the variables that are incidental to the program's function, that is, the artifacts of a particular piece of code or programming technique. The major difficulty in representing this information results from the size and complexity of the data bases of most interesting programs. It is for this reason that we have spoken of "diagrams of structured data." It is only through structuring the complexity (either at the design stage or under interactive programmer control) that we are able to comprehend it and master it.

An appropriate illustration of a program's data, updated dynamically during program execution, gives us the feeling of looking into the machine and seeing the program running. Baecker's pilot film on sorting algorithms [3], and the work of Knowlton [20], Hopgood [15], Myers [22], and others, have vividly demonstrated the power of this technique. Figure 3 shows one possible layout for displaying a two dimensional array. The visualization of structured data appears to be one of the most tractable and powerful of the approaches we have presented.

2.9 Diagrams of Persistent Data

An important category of structured data is that which remains in the computer system after the program has ceased execution, as occurs in a data base management system. Since this data is often several orders of magnitude larger than the memory capacity of the computer, different techniques are required to visualize it. Fortunately, the data base community has developed a rich set of symbols which can serve as a starting point in visualizing persistent data (e.g., [2,32]). In addition, the Spatial Data Management System (SDMS) [11] developed at CCA has demonstrated the feasibility of using graphics to access persistent data. Figure 4 shows layouts taken from an actual SDMS interface to a data base of information about ships.

2.10 Diagrams of the Program in the Host Environment

There is a collection of information about programs that is typically available in various forms from operating systems, but, just as typically, the information is presented in a rather dense and detailed tabular form. This information includes the files in which program parts are stored, their size, age, and ownership. For a program activation, performance and timing information is important. The type and percentage of resources currently in use, priority under which the program is running, and the average response time for interactions are all commonly of interest.

Much can be done to enhance the presentation of this information. Percentages can be displayed as pies, histograms, etc. Color coding can be used to point up similarities among pieces of information or to highlight particular properties of interest. Finally, the typographic hierarchies discussed for program text, comments, and commentaries can play a role here as well.

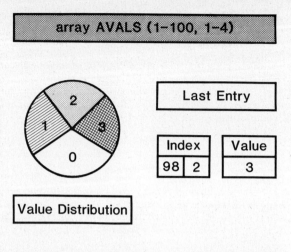

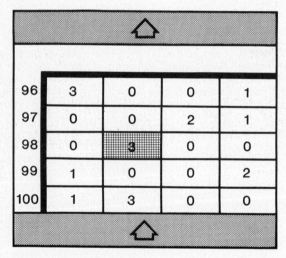

Figure 3. Display of the contents of an array called AVALS. Array is set in a window and values can be examined by pressing arrows to scroll up or down.

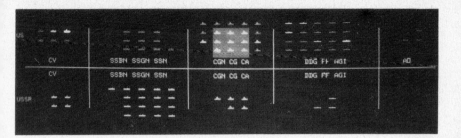

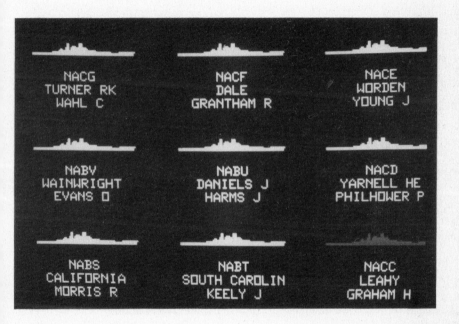

Figure 4. Photos from SDMS showing categorization of ship information by country (horizontal) and by ship type (vertical). Detail photo corresponds to highlighted portion of photo at top. Shape of the ship indicates ship type, and text is identification and command information taken from the data base. Additional information conveyed by color coding is visible as grey scale in these pictures.

3. A PV DESIGN PHILOSOPHY

The previous section enumerated a "shopping list" of ten categories
of graphical, and often dynamic, information about a program. It
should be clear from this list that graphics already plays a significant role in the software lifecycle; it should also be clear that
the possibilities of graphics have only begun to be exploited. Much
work has been done in developing techniques for describing programs
at various levels, but comparatively little has been done to automate these techniques to give programmers a clear concept of the
dynamics of the program. This latter goal is the focus of our work.
The PV system will "open the side of the machine" and give the user
the feeling of looking in and seeing the program run. The primary
impact of such a focus is on the testing, debugging, maintenance,
and training phases of a program's lifecycle. We expect good
dynamic program illustrations to greatly enhance the programmer's
effectiveness in each of these areas.

Before we can "open the side of the machine", there are a number of
problems that must be solved. We have chosen three of them to
explore in depth. These are:

    -- Integrating information:
       How can the ten categories of illustrations and text be com-
       bined meaningfully?

    -- Enhancing graphics facilities:
       How can we provide the PV user with very high level graphics
       facilities?

    -- Instrumenting programs:
       How can programs be instrumented to permit access to the
       relevant dynamic information without requiring extensive
       programmer intervention?

Other research problems exist, but we feel that, given the current
state of knowledge, these three are the most immediate. In particular, a whole series of research problems can be classified under the
heading of program soundness: how can the correctness of the design
and the code be guaranteed? While this is an important research
area, it is one that is already receiving a significant amount of
attention in a variety of contexts. Program verification is one
relatively well developed area, and promising work is also being
done in program understanding (e.g., [27,39]) and in the use of program templates to avoid errors (e.g., [37]). The treatment of
information about a program as a data base has been coupled with
enforcement of standards (e.g., in CADES [25]) and decision support
(e.g., in the DREAM System [28]). This treatment also opens the way
for application of more general work on the semantic integrity of
data bases. While the PV system will include some checking, cross-
referencing, and decision support, insuring the soundness of the
information is not a current research focus.

In this section, we present and motivate a PV design approach that addresses the three problems of integration of information, enhancement of graphics facilities, and program instrumentation.

3.1 Integrating Information

We expect a large volume of diverse information to be involved in the visualization of a program. This is true first because the PV environment will support the production of large programs and, second, because it will provide a variety of graphical representations. The challenge is to integrate the various techniques identified in Section 2 into a coherent whole.

The organization of program information ("program space") that we are currently exploring is the placement of visualizations in a hierarchy of two-dimensional surfaces. The levels in this hierarchy would match the structure of the program under investigation. As one descended in the spatial hierarchy, one would view successively more detailed representations, for instance viewing increasingly lower-level modules. For each node in the hierarchy, the surface would contain examples of some or all of the illustration categories described in Section 2. (This includes dynamic illustrations, which can be thought of as movies embedded in surfaces, runable under user control.) A mechanism would also be available, most likely on a separate screen, to provide a workspace for the PV user to accumulate views that are currently of interest.

Movement through the program space is illustrated in Figure 5, which shows three displays related to the SDD-1 communication visualization from Figure 1. The first two displays were formed by selecting transaction modules (TMs) and data modules (DMs), as a PV user might do in localizing a bug. The third display is formed by zooming to another level of detail, to access a table of information about transactions running at a particular TM.

While we are emphasizing the hierarchic organization of illustrations because it is the dominant organization, there will actually be a network of links between the illustrations from different categories. The complexity of this subordinate organization poses two types of challenges: the implementation problem of handling multiple connections, and the knowledge representation problem of keeping the information manageable for the user. For the first, a surface must permit an arbitrary number of ports, i.e. links to locations on other surfaces. For the second, clean organization is important, and navigational aids must be provided for the PV user.

Our approach to these problems draws on experience with SDMS [11], the Spatial Data Management System. SDMS was motivated by the needs of a growing community of people who need access to information in a data base management system but who are not trained in the use of such systems. We briefly describe some of the aspects of SDMS that are relevant to PV.

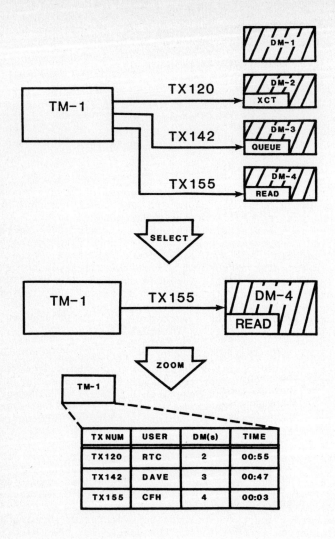

Figure 5. Three successive views of SDD-1. Top, the same
snapshot as Figure 1, Section 2.4, but this time only TM-1 and
the four DMs are shown. Middle, further selection yields
display of a single TM/DM pair. Bottom, zooming in on TM-1
results in a display of the transactions originating from that
site.

In SDMS, information is expressed through color graphics, with different categories of structured data having associated icons, i.e., prototypical pictograms. Icons are generated semi-automatically from the data base, according to a predefined set of rules. Information retrieved from the data base is presented in SDMS in a multidimensional framework, so that the user can "zoom" through ports on the data surface to see more detail or to see alternative views of the data. The SDMS workstation includes three screens, a joystick for panning and zooming, touch sensitive screens to permit the user to select icons by pointing at them, and a data tablet for the creation of new pictograms. As a navigational aid, one screen displays a <u>world-view map</u> which shows an entire data surface. A highlighted rectangle on the world-view map indicates the portion of the data that is being presented in detail on another screen. The rectangle moves as the user manipulates the joy stick to move over the data surface. One world-view map was shown in Figure 4, Section 2.9.

The program space that we have described for PV fits well into the multidimensional paradigm of SDMS, and we expect much of the SDMS experience to be applicable to PV. The multilayered PV program space is analogous to the SDMS data surfaces, and the further connections needed between illustration categories can be implemented with multiple ports. The combined use of joy stick, touch sensitive screens, and data tablet can enable the PV user to move through and augment the program space easily. The world-view map is of proven utility; we do, however, have more to say on this count.

It is possible that the complexity of the PV environment will require other navigational aids in addition to the world-view map. We are investigating several different approaches to helping the PV user navigate within the system, and to helping him/her maintain a sense of context. One such approach is the use of a list of miniaturizations of past displays, both to provide context and, when a miniaturization is selected, to provide a means to "pop" the stack back to a past view.

We have, then, a dominant hierarchical organization with a subordinate network organization, realized in a hierarchy of surfaces containing multiple ports. We next take a closer look at the specification of illustrations, both in program space and in the user's workspace.

3.2 Enhancing Graphical Facilities

As a comprehensive environment, it is crucial that the PV system be easy to use or, where it must be more demanding, that the system repay the investment. Graphics makes this imperative all the more challenging. Designers and programmers want access to information about a program without having to spend a great deal of time specifying how the information is to be displayed.

We have identified three ways in which graphics facilities can be enhanced:

1. Incorporation of domain-independent higher level constructs
2. Incorporation of graphical and text constructs specific to programming
3. Automated layout

Work in each of these areas has important implications both for getting information into the PV environment and getting it out. Each area is discussed briefly.

First on our list was the incorporation of domain-independent higher level of constructs. SKETCHPAD [35], PYGMALION [31], the SDMS PAINT program [12], and others, have permitted picture production without programming, by combination of shapes and free drawing. These techniques can be enhanced. The graphical vocabulary need not be restricted to geometric shapes but also can include higher level organizational devices, such as overlays and split screens. Production of animation can move away from frame by frame specification to specification by combining high level dynamic constructs. For example, a growing and then shrinking arrow used to represent communication between modules should be specifiable as a unit. (One approach to this problem is given in [17].) Throughout, defaults for graphical conventions can be more fully exploited.

As powerful as high level domain-independent graphical constructs can be, we believe that the PV environment will also have to provide graphical (and textual) constructs specific to programming. For those times when programmers must dynamically specify displays, we expect the predominant mode of interaction to be the instantiation of templates, not the creation of new pictures from scratch. Programmers will have both default representations for a wide range of data structures and the means to change these defaults to meet special needs. (See, e.g., [22].) Templates for standard programming utilties (e.g., stacks, memory maps) will also be provided. The templates need not be limited to single structures such as stacks; we are exploring the use of composite templates that combine information that is generally useful for particular types of programming. Finally, for those cases in which totally novel pictures are required, the user can turn to a graphics editor that will be included in the PV environment.

Once the PV user selects the components of a display, automated layout can arrange the diagrams on the display area. For layout, we intend to build upon work done as part of the SDMS project. Additional work will be needed to handle the more richly connected, and often heterogeneous, pictures that will be common for PV.

The three facilities listed -- high level domain-independent graphical language, graphical constructs specific to programming, and automated layout -- can permit the PV user to produce visualizations with a minimum of effort, and without being inundated in detail.

3.3 Instrumenting Programs

The central focus in the PV project is on providing an environment
that runs programs, not merely one that manipulates static information. Traditional debuggers give us some models and a set of
experiences to draw on, but there are ways that they can be improved
in terms of bringing the level of interaction with the debugger up
to the conceptual level of the user. We outline briefly our philosophy.

First, the user's goal is to see information about the running program. The use of two or more windows on the screen to display a
running program is one approach that has been used successfully
([36,38]). For programs designed to communicate with a terminal,
one window simulates the terminal screen. Characters typed by the
user appear there and output from the program is directed there.
Meanwhile, other windows can be used to examine the operation of the
system. Sets of windows can also be used to display multiple
processes or to display causes and effects.

We intend to experiment with the multiple window approach and other
modes of display as well. In setting up the display environment, we
are paying particular attention to displaying choices that have been
made by the user. This is in hopes of remedying one of the problems
with traditional debuggers -- the difficulty of keeping track of the
constraints that the user has set up as a filter for viewing the
behavior of the program.

Given a display environment, the user's problem is to specify what
is to be displayed. The use of high level graphics constructs,
including programming construct templates, was discussed in the previous subsection.   These templates must also be instantiated, i.e.
tied to the code or other representations of the program. For this,
debugging statements and code will be conceptually separate entities, so the user will not be thinking in terms of altering code
(and later having to remove debugging statements). Pointing (graphical cursors and/or touch sensitive screens) will be used exten-
sively to specify instantiations of the templates. Many slots in
the templates can be filled by pointing at variables in the code.
The programmer can point to locations in program structure diagrams
or typeset listings to specify areas of interest. When these areas
are active, the program is slowed down to a visible speed. At other
times it runs at normal speed, unobserved but much faster.   Similarly, breakpoint locations can be indicated by pointing.

The mechanics of coding the display specification and producing the
information desired from the running program have been left almost
entirely to the PV system. This is the area about which we have the
least to say right now, but about which we expect to have more to
say in the coming months. In brief, our philosophy is that whether
code is compiled or interpreted should be transparent to the programmer. Further, we hope to stay out of the compiler writing business. We intend to use existing compiler(s), perhaps augmented to
save information that might otherwise be thrown away (e.g., a full

symbol table). Unix facilities that allow one process to gain control of another process between statements will be exploited [19].
Finally, we are exploring the tradeoff between accumulating histories of program execution as opposed to facilitating rerunning of
programs, particularly as this tradeoff is affected by persistent
data.

***

We have outlined three areas of particular concern in the design of
a program visualization system: integration of information about the
program, design of high level graphical facilities, and instrumentation of the program. Readers interested in more background on the
PV framework are referred to [13].

4. IMPLEMENTATION

The current work is focused on the implementation of a tool usable
by Ada programmers by 1984, and is proceeding in three phases. The
various implementations will explore a variety of techniques on a
powerful high-resolution color display environment, with an eye
toward identifying a useful subset of techniques which can be implemented on a low-cost terminal costing in 1985 what an ordinary
alphanumeric terminal costs today. The three implementation phases
are:

1. The design of a visual language for describing programs,
   together with the processing, translation, and display routines
   necessary to create a visualization of a program. This language
   and its concomitant machinery is being developed through
   interactions with programmers responsible for large-scale working systems and with information-oriented graphic designers.
   Static and dynamic mock-ups of program illustrations are being
   created and evaluated.

2. The implementation of a breadboard system which incorporates the
   results of the first phase and allows integration with the
   results of other research efforts, for use with a selected
   language on Unix. It will be evaluated through use by people
   maintaining and developing software on Unix.

3. The implementation of a production program visualization system
   for Ada, incorporating improvements identified in the breadboard
   version.

One early result of the Phase One exploration of illustrations is a
five minute videotape of dynamic illustration mock-ups for SDD-1
(from which Figures 1 and 5 were taken). The feedback on this
effort has led us to conclude that if the operation of a program is
not intuitively obvious, the graphics used must bridge the gap. We
are therefore developing (and videotaping) another set of dynamic
illustrations with graphical symbols that are more perceptual than

symbolic ([7]) i.e., that portray the semantics more immediately.

5. SUMMARY

This paper, and the project itself, started from the premise that graphical illustrations can make a significant contribution to the process of program visualization. In support of this premise, we first surveyed a variety of existing graphical representations and discussed possibilities for extended uses of graphics, especially animation. We then outlined a design philosophy for an integrated graphical programming environment to support the development of large systems. Our focus was, and is, on the dynamic aspects of programs, to permit the PV user to "open the side of the machine" and watch programs run. Work is underway to provide such an environment, with the goal of making the advantages of graphical representations available without placing an excessive burden on the people responsible for implementing and maintaining the programs. We believe that a comprehensive and integrated approach to program visualization can have great impact on the entire process of software engineering, and on the cost-effective production and maintenance of reliable software.

ACKNOWLEDGEMENTS

The authors wish to thank Jane Barnett, Diane Smith, and Gerald Wilson for helpful comments on drafts of this paper. We are also grateful to Jane Hathaway for the artwork.

6. REFERENCES

[1] Preliminary ADA reference manual, SIGPLAN Notices, 14, 6, Part A, (June 1979).

[2] Bachman, C.W., The evolution of storage structures, Communications of the ACM, 15, 7 (July 1972) 628-636.

[3] Baecker, R.M., Sorting Out Sorting, 16mm color, sound, 25 minutes (Dynamic Graphics Project, Computer Systems Research Group, Univ. of Toronto, 1981).

[4] Baecker, R.M., Two systems which produce animated representations of the execution of computer programs, ACM SIGCSE Bulletin, 7, 1 (Feb. 1975) 158-167.

[5]   Belady, L.A., Cavanagh, J.A., and Evangelisti, C.J., GREEN-
      PRINT: a graphical representation for structured programs, IBM
      Research Report RC 7763, T.J.Watson Research Center (1979).

[6]   Dionne, M.S. and Mackworth, A.K., ANTICS: a system for animat-
      ing LISP programs, Computer Graphics and Image Processing, 7
      (1978) 105-119.

[7]   Fitter, M. and Green, T.R.G., When do diagrams make good com-
      puter languages?, Int. J. Man-Machine Studies, 11 (1979) 235-
      261.

[8]   Frei, H.P., Weller, D.C., and Williams, R.A., Graphics-based
      programming-support system, Computer Graphics, 12, 3 (August
      1978) 43-49.

[9]   Galley, S.W. and Goldberg, R.P., Software debugging: the vir-
      tual machine approach, Proceedings: ACM Annual Conference
      (1974) 395-401.

[10] Haibt, L.M., A program to draw multilever flow charts, Western
      Joint Computer Conference (1959).

[11] Herot, C.F., Carling, R.T., Friedell, M., Kramlich, D., A pro-
      totype spatial data management system, SIGGRAPH '80 Proceed-
      ings: ACM/SIGGRAPH Conference (1980) 63-70.

[12] Herot, C.F., Carling, R.T., Friedell, M., Kramlich, D., and
      Thompson, J., Spatial data management system: semi-annual
      technical report, Technical Report CCA-79-25, Computer Corpora-
      tion of America (1979).

[13] Herot, C.F., Carling, R.T., Friedell, M., and Kramlich, D.,
      Design for a program visualization system, Technical Report
      CCA-81-04, Computer Corporation of America (1981).

[14] HIPO -- A Design Aid and Documentation Technique (IBM Corpora-
      tion, Data Processing Division, White Plains, New York).

[15] Hopgood, F.R.A., Computer animation used as a tool in teaching
      computer science, Proceedings of the 1974 IFIP Congress, Appli-
      cations Volume, (1974) 889-892.

[16] Presentation on AISIM at the Software Tools Fair, Fifth International Conference on Software Engineering (Hughes Aircraft Company, Ground Systems Group, Fullerton, California, 1981).

[17] Kahn, K.M., Creation of computer animation from story descriptions, AI TR-540, Artificial Intelligence Laboratory, Massachusetts Institute of Technology (1979).

[18] Kanda, Y. and Sugimoto, M., Software diagram description: SDD and its application, Proceedings: Computer Software and Applications Conference (1980) 300-305.

[19] Kernighan, B.W. and McIlroy, M.D., Unix programmer's manual (Bell Laboratories, Murray Hill, New Jersey).

[20] Knowlton, K.C., L6: Bell Telephone Laboratories Low-Level Linked List Language, two black and white films, sound (Bell Telephone Laboratories, Murray Hill, New Jersey, 1966).

[21] Model, M.L., Monitoring system behavior in a complex computational environment, CSL-79-1, XEROX Corp., Palo Alto Research Center (1979).

[22] Myers, B.A., Displaying data structures for interactive debugging, CSL-80-7, XEROX Corp., Palo Alto Research Center (1980).

[23] Myers, G.J., Composite/structured design (Van Nostrand Reinhold Company, New York, 1978).

[24] Nassi, I. and Shneiderman, B., Flowchart techniques for structured programming, SIGPLAN Notices of the ACM, 8, 8 (1973) 12-26.

[25] Pearson, D.J., The use and abuse of a software engineering system, Proceedings: 1979 National Computer Conference (1979) 1029-1035.

[26] Peterson, J.L., Petri nets, ACM Computing Surveys, 9 (1977) 223-252.

[27] Rich, C. and Shrobe, H., Initial report on a Lisp programmer's apprentice, IEEE Trans. on Software Eng., 4, 5 (1978).

[28] Riddle, W.E., An assessment of DREAM, in: Huencke, H. (ed.), Software Engineering Environments (North-Holland Publishing Co., 1981).

[29] Ross, D.T., Structured Analysis (SA): A Language for Communicating Ideas, Software Engineering, SE-3, 1 (1977) 34.

[30] Rothnie, J.B., Jr., Bernstein, P.A., Fox, S., Goodman, N., Hammer, M., Landers, T.A., Reeve, C., Shipman, D., and Wong, E., Introduction to a system for distibuted databases (SDD-1), ACM Trans. Database Syst. 5, 1 (1980) 1-17.

[31] Smith, D.C., PYGMALION: a creative programming environment, AIM-260, Stanford Artificial Intelligence Laboratory, Stanford Univ. (1975).

[32] Smith, J.M. and Smith, D.C.P., A data base approach to software specification, in: Riddle and Fairley (eds.), Software Development Tools (Springer Verlag, New York, 176-201).

[33] Stay, J.F., HIPO and integrated program design, IBM Systems Journal, 15, 2 (1978) 143-154.

[34] Stockham, T.G., Some methods of graphical debugging, Proceedings of the IBM Scientific Computing Symposium on Man-Machine Communication (1965) 57-71.

[35] Sutherland, I.E., SKETCHPAD: a man-machine graphical communication system, Proceedings of the Spring Joint Computer Conference (1963) 329-346.

[36] Swinehart, D., COPILOT: A multiple process approach to interactive programming, AIM-230, Stanford Artificial Intelligence Laboratory, Stanford Univ. (1974).

[37] Teitelbaum, R.T., The Cornell program synthesizer: a microcomputer implementation of PL/CS, TR 79-370, Department of Computer Science, Cornell Univ. (1979).

[38] Teitelman, W., A display oriented programmer's assistant, Fifth International Joint Conference on Artificial Intelligence (1977) 905-915.

[39] Waters R.C., A method for analyzing loop programs, IEEE Trans. on Software Eng., SE-5, 3 (1979) 237-247.

[40] Yarwood, E., Toward program illustration, Tech. Report CSRG-84, Computer Systems Research Group, Univ. of Toronto (1977).

LIST OF AUTHORS